GREAT WALKS
IRELAND

DAVID HERMAN
Photography by Michael J. Stead

BROCKHAMPTON PRESS
LONDON

Author's Acknowledgements

I would like to thank the following most sincerely for their generous help in researching and editing this book. Any remaining errors in content are of course my own responsibility.

To Catherine Coxon and Mark Hennessy for checking my facts on the *clachan* system and early settlement patterns; to Dawson Stelfox for information on Cecil Newman and the hydro-electric scheme at Lough Belshade; to Graham Seymour and James McEvoy of the Northern Ireland Department of the Environment for details of right-of-way legislation in Northern Ireland; to Jimmy Murphy of Cospoir for information on Long Distance Routes; to Paddy Prendergast of the Ordnance Survey and Maurice Sheehy of Ventry for information on the tracks of Mount Eagle; to Sylvia and Victor Morrow who calmed my rising panic when faced with the Beenkeragh Ridge (it didn't turn out to be so terrifying!); and to Mark Herman who edited the 'semi-final' manuscript.

Lastly (and primarily) to my wife Mairin Geraty who pondered nearly every word in the manuscript and who walked nearly every mile of the routes with me.

First published in Great Britain in 1991
by Ward Lock Limited, Villiers House, 41/47 Strand,
London WC2N 5JE, England
A Cassell Imprint
This edition published 1999 by Brockhampton Press,
a member of Hodder Headline PLC Group

ISBN 1-86019-958-5

Under Licence from Cassells

Text filmset by August Filmsetting, Haydock, St Helens

Printed at Oriental Press, Dubai, U.A.E.

British Library Cataloguing in Publication Data
is available upon application to the British Library

CONTENTS

INTRODUCTION

Though it is a matter of supreme indifference to the rest of mankind, I have to declare that I really enjoyed 1990. Late in the previous year I had taken early retirement and almost immediately, received the offer to write this book — an offer I not only *could* not, but one that I certainly *would* not refuse under nearly any conceivable circumstance.

I have been wandering Ireland's mountains for 25 years, starting with my home base of Wicklow and gradually extending to nearly all the mountains of Ireland — and yes, there are still a few minor ranges in Ireland that I have not yet climbed. My expeditions have taken me farther afield, to Britain, the Alps, Malawi and the Himalayas. While these trips have been memorable and have provided a context for my own country, I still return to Ireland happy in the chauvinistic and irrational belief that they are the best and most rewarding mountains in the world.

To return to the present: the offer to write this book gave me the opportunity to do what I enjoy most, and so it was that in the spring, early summer and autumn of 1990 (high summer was too hot and humid for walking) I and a small team consisting of my walking companion — a nurse, a manager of food and accommodation and a general factotum — in a word my wife Mairin, set out to explore Ireland's mountains. It was an instructive project. Walking the mountains in a haphazard manner over a number of years and usually on someone else's route is one thing; a programme over six months with the necessity to record, compare, contrast and evaluate quite another. It brought formerly vague impressions into sharp focus and, like the supposed effect of the imminence of execution, it concentrated the mind wonderfully.

You may be interested in how I went about choosing routes in an area as large and diverse as Ireland. The first constraint was of course the limited number of routes I was allowed. I have already written guide books containing 60 or so different routes in *one* Irish mountain range so I quickly realized that to achieve 30 routes for the entire country, a ruthless, nay brutal, discarding of potentially attractive routes would be the order of the day. After that I decided that variety, a very easy objective in Ireland, would be my watchword.

I applied the rule of variety *within* each region so that the walker would explore a wide range of terrains, and also *within* the walks so that he would not be invited to walk a route of unchanging scenery. Even walking in superb country can eventually become a trudge along a conveyor belt running in reverse if the views are unvarying.

I also decided to limit the number of routes entailing a second car or a well-disposed, non-walking driver willing to pick up the walkers at the end. Where I have chosen such A to B routes, I have made the starting and finishing points either so close together that they are within walking distance for those who cannot organize a car at the finish, or so far apart that the walkers will have a sense of having made a long, hopefully satisfying traverse at the end of the day.

I am acutely aware that my 30 routes are unlikely to be those favoured by everyone or, worse still, *anyone* familiar with Ireland. The end result is a mixture: some easy strolls, some tough walks, some well-known classics, some virtually unknown territory. I have also omitted a few popular routes, omissions which I explain at appropriate points in the text. In spite of what may be considered a slightly idiosyncratic choice I hope that you, the reader and potential walker, will get more than a few good walks from my selection. As has been said before in another context: if only one person gets only one enjoyable walk from this book — I shall be bitterly disappointed!

One problem that I expected to come up against was the daunting task of attempting to describe the beauty and atmosphere of Ireland's mountain ranges. I need not have worried. Michael J. Stead in the magnificent photographs which embellish this book has done the job far, far better than my mere words. If these photographs don't entice you to don your walking boots and set off forthwith, nothing will.

'Warts and all' tends to be my approach, even though my conclusion after the intense programme of walking is that Ireland's mountains are as lovely as I ever thought they were and even more varied. With this in mind, I hope that readers will take the occasional criticism as a counterbalance to the considerable praise and appreciation which these pages contain. At a basic level, criticism has the virtue of making praise credible. I also feel it is important for visitors to realize that Ireland is 'different', and that these differences may express themselves in ways which they might occasionally find infuriating rather than engaging. If you know beforehand about the few problems that may occur, you will be far better prepared to take them in your stride. Please don't be put off by them.

I began by saying how much I enjoyed 1990. It is my sincere wish that when you come to Ireland you too will get at least as much pleasure and enjoyment in walking our mountains as I did in the happy year I spent exploring them.

D.H.

The Face of Ireland

INTRODUCTION

In extending a cordial invitation not only to peruse this book, but also to come to Ireland and explore the mountains, it is necessary to face honestly the fundamental question: why come to Ireland; and, if you do come, why make the additional effort of climbing the mountains?

Perhaps the most evident quality of Irish mountains is their small scale. They lack the soaring and overpowering majesty and vast panoramas of Alpine peaks — but are no whit inferior on that account. What they have is a human scale, a landscape in which a changing scene unfolds round every corner, a terrain in which only modest efforts are needed to achieve worthy peaks. It is not a country for the hardened and super-fit only: anyone who is moderately fit can experience and enjoy it. This is not to claim that Irish mountains are the only ones in the world to have a human scale. Of course, this is not true. Visitors from Britain, to cite the nearest example, can validly make exactly the same claim. So what are the qualities that make Irish mountains unique, and that will attract hillwalkers to this somewhat remote island?

Perhaps Ireland's unique attraction for the hillwalker lies in two characteristics that at first glance appear to be incompatible. These are remoteness and accessibility, and since they appear to be mutually exclusive it is necessary to consider them in conjunction.

Let us take remoteness first. Primarily and obviously, Ireland's mountains are by and large unfrequented. It is quite possible to walk for hours in many Irish ranges without encountering a single soul. In the Alps the hillwalker of average ability can slog upwards for hours to be greeted at his highest goal by a restaurant whose coffee-sipping patrons feel entitled to cast disparaging glances at his honorably dishevelled figure. In the Lake District and parts of Wales there are usually other hillwalkers around, many in large groups. Of course you cannot grudge their presence, any more than they can afford to grudge yours. Nevertheless, large numbers do significantly detract from the remoteness of mountain areas. How refreshing, therefore, to roam hills where the only human contact in a day of walking may be a solitary farmer checking his flock.

Remoteness also manifests itself in an absence of trails and paths through the mountains. Trails and paths are at once facilitating and restricting — facilitating because they allow walkers to enter territory into which they might not otherwise safely venture, restricting because they do not encourage exploration. The lifeline of a path is difficult to forsake once it is grasped. Ireland — and there are of course exceptions to this statement — has mountains that are without paths, without trails, without cairns except on the summits. This is not to say that there are *no* paths anywhere: an excellent system of Long Distance Routes girdles, but in general does not encroach upon, the mountains.

There is, however, a down-side to remoteness; it puts greater responsibility on the individual walker. With the knowledge that he is likely to have no ready help and be far from a mountain rescue service in the case of an accident, the ability to use a map and compass becomes a necessity rather than a luxury. A walker might think twice before venturing into remote mountains. It is not justifiable to make too much of this; after all, every hill-walker worth his salt should be able to use a map and compass. In Ireland, quite simply, there will be more occasions when it will be necessary, in spite of the accurate and detailed route descriptions in this book!

The other quality which, when taken together with remoteness, constitutes the unique attraction of Irish mountains is accessibility. No point in Ireland is more than 5 miles (8 km) from a motorable road. This bland statement needs a slight qualification: what with potholes, bumps, bends and rough surfaces, some overseas motorists might ruefully conclude that some are *not* motorable. (This comment emphatically does not apply to Northern Ireland's excellent road network.) Providentially the layout of Ireland's small discrete mountain ranges means that even if the road is diabolical, the motorist does not have to endure it for a long distance. Any peak can be climbed in a single day from a comfortable base; many fine circuits, some described in the course of these pages, can be walked without recourse to rough camping. No need, therefore, for long, hard expeditions or bruising backpacking trips (although there are many opportunities for these). To summarize: in Ireland there are mountains that are easy to reach and explore, but which are nevertheless unfrequented and possess a remote and wild atmosphere. Where else does such a fortuitous combination occur?

Lastly, perhaps mention should be made of one unique though blindingly evident characteristic of Ireland: it is the only country inhabited mainly by Irish people! Like them or loathe them, the Irish and particularly Irish country people, are a race of individuals, of characters in a western world that is becoming as bland and uniform as sliced bread. Praise their religious devotion or deride their religious formalism, admire their strong patriotism or deplore their unthinking nationalism, the Irish, North and South, are a race of individuals, not ciphers. Yet, whatever their differences, most Irish people — and especially Irish country people — share this much: they are kind, inquisitive in a friendly, non-threatening way, polite, generous and warmhearted. This is something worth bearing in mind given the tragic events on this island in the last two decades.

AN OVERVIEW OF THE MOUNTAINS

That omniscient entity, 'every schoolboy' of Victorian fame, was undoubtedly aware that Ireland is shaped like a saucer, the higher land round the coast, the lowlands in the centre. Though it is a very rough saucer, there is more than an element of truth in the old cliché. The main mountain ranges *are*, broadly speaking, grouped near the coast, particularly the Atlantic coast, and the central area is an undulating plain which reaches the sea only in the 50-mile (80 km) stretch from Dublin to Dundalk.

In a purely statistical sense Ireland is not mountainous: only 5 per cent of the total area is over 1000 ft (305 m), and a mere 0.25 per cent over 2000 ft (610 m). Nor are the mountains high; there is only a handful of Munros (strictly, mountains in Scotland over 3000 ft (914 m), but a term used for those in other areas), and of these but two peaks reach the 1000 m contour. But statistics can be misleading. Over large areas of the country mountain ranges rear up impressively to belie their modest heights, dominating the plains in soft purple and blue hues in summer, gleaming with snowcaps in winter, disappearing in murky gloom and dull grey clouds at any time of year.

To some extent the mountains of Atlantic Ireland from Donegal in the north, through Mayo, Galway and Clare and reaching down to Kerry in the south have, whatever their many individual differences, two major features in common. Firstly, the sea. The sea, whether it is the wild Atlantic, the long, straight, drowned river valleys of the south-west, or the inlets, bays and fiords further north, is never far away. It is often within sight from the hills, and sometimes even from lower ground.

Secondly, and even more apparent than the sea is the setting of the mountains of Atlantic Ireland, a rugged environment in which human habitation clings precariously to the narrow strip between ocean on one side and mountain and bog on the other. Drive west from Oughterard in Galway or from Tralee in Kerry, and the ambience changes swiftly and perceptibly. The ruins of a wayside cottage, the whiff of turf fires and the donkeys grazing by the road — all hackneyed tourist clichés — clearly betoken a land in which man struggles to retain a precarious foothold in an unpromising terrain dominated by nature. In this terrain the mountains are a major and pervasive element.

The mountains of the rest of the country consist mainly of a group of ranges in the south and south-east and the Mournes in Northern Ireland. The typical east-west folds of the mountains of Munster in the south, of which the Galtees and the Comeraghs are the chief, give way further north to the granitic north-east to south-west trend of the Mournes and the Wicklow Mountains. The latter comprise the largest stretch of upland in Ireland with the highest peak outside Kerry.

The Mournes, Co. Down

These mountains are nearly as high as the mountains of the Atlantic coast and many are just as rugged. What these mountains have in common is that they rise, not from a bleak environment like that to the west, but from rich agricultural land, from pastoral fields and arable land or even from the outskirts of towns and villages. Similarly, though all except the Galtees are considered to be coastal ranges, they rise not from the wild Atlantic but from the narrow Irish Sea, the North Channel and St George's Channel. Though the mountains of the east lack only a little of the grandeur and ruggedness of the mountains of Atlantic Ireland, they do lack much of its harsh and splendid ambience.

Cummeengeera, Co. Kerry

MOUNTAIN BUILDING: A CLASH OF PLATES

Mountain building occurs when tectonic plates, which are enormous segments of the earth's crust, collide. Two such collisions had repercussions in the area which is now Ireland, and between them they account for the general orientation and to some extent the type of rock that is exposed on the hills today. These two periods are termed the Caledonian and the Armorican.

The Caledonian episode of mountain building occurred over a long period which ended about 450 million years ago. This episode was not confined to Ireland; most of the mountains of Scotland were formed in the same period, and indeed give their name to the whole phenomenon. The collision of the plates resulted in compression wrinkles running in a north-east to south-west line over most of the country, with the significant exception of the south-west corner. Not only were mountain folds raised; the existing rock was metamorphozed by the intense heat and pressure of the collision into hard quartzites, schists and marbles.

The mountains of the south-west — that is, the mountains of Kerry, the Galtees and other ranges along or south of this line — were oriented into their now characteristic east-west line much later, about 340 to 280 million years ago in a collision of two plates to the south of Ireland. This, the Armorican mountain building episode, also affected the hills of South Wales and Devon. Once again, the existing rocks were metamorphozed.

In the many millions of years since these two mountain building episodes, the areas of the present hills have been submerged under the sea and subsequently uplifted. They have since been greatly weathered, the extent of which depends on what rock is exposed to the elements. Thus limestone, a soft rock, eroded away from the mountains of Kerry, leaving the hard underlying sandstone exposed; and the granite, which is a hard rock but one susceptible to chemical attack, weathered into the characteristic, gentle domes of the Wicklow Mountains.

By contrast, the Ice Age began in Ireland only a few hundred thousand years ago and ended a mere 10,000 years ago, an eyeblink in geological terms. Although a comparatively minor event, the Ice Age, because it is so recent, has left a lasting imprint on the mountain landscape, transforming what might otherwise be dull upland plateaux into sharp cliff-bound peaks. Glaciers, which at one stage or another affected the entire island except the highest peaks of the south, gouged out the corries from the sides of mountains and deepened shallow V-shaped valleys into deep U-shaped ones. These and other effects are discussed in more detail where glacial features are encountered on the routes themselves.

MAN AND THE UPLANDS

The 4500 years that elapsed between the end of the Ice Age and the first arrival of man are a period of conjecture, and more conjectural still for the mountain areas. We can, however, say with some certainty that the retreat of the ice left a tundra-like landscape, particularly on the uplands. However, as a milder climate developed, great forests — both deciduous and coniferous — advanced over the lowlands and spread less surely onto the uplands where the conifers, which are less demanding, tended to predominate.

This was the terrain into which the first settlers ventured about 5500 years ago, at a time when the climatic optimum for the forests was already over, with the coming of a wetter, colder climate more akin to our own. Assisted by the tentative clearances for agriculture made by succeeding generations of settlers, this deterioration in climate caused the beginnings of the demise of the great forests.

From about 2000 BC the upland forests — and they grew at altitudes of 2000 ft (610 m), maybe higher — began to succumb to blanket bog (so called because it 'blankets' the existing terrain) just as the trees of the lowlands were yielding to raised bog. However, bogs — blanket and raised — have one useful characteristic which enables scientists to find out about this remote period of pre-history. By sinking tubes into the bog and removing cores from different depths, and analyzing the pollen count found in them, scientists can establish the vegetational history of the area. The bog is almost literally a history book. This technique together with carbon-dating, by which the age of a specimen can be determined, tells us much of what we now know about pre-history.

Today, in many places in the uplands the walker will come across evidence of these ancient forests in the form of tree stumps in the lower layers of the now-decaying bog. This so-called 'bog oak' (it is more likely to be pine) had been smothered by the encroaching bog and preserved in its anaerobic (oxygen-free) environment. As we shall see, the bogland is now in turn coming under attack and so the tree stumps are being exposed.

The demise of the great forests, discontinuous though inexorable, went on throughout the Christian era, though climate changes caused retreats as well as advances in the extent of blanket bog on the uplands. However, humans, in increasing numbers and with increasingly sophisticated techniques, became the final arbiters of vegetational history on both upland and lowland.

To examine the effects of human habitation it is interesting to go back in time to look at the settlement pattern that developed all over the country, but especially in the less fertile west and north. The original Celtic settlements seemed to have been ring-forts, rough circular enclosures of earth surrounding huts belonging to a group of related families. From this tradition the *clachan* and the related farming system, *rundale*, developed in the Middle Ages. The *clachan* was a cluster of small farm-houses owned by a group of blood-related families. It was surrounded by an arable open-field. The field was divided into narrow strips, each strip held by a family. In some areas the strips were not held permanently, but by each family in turn. Further out were pastures, meadows, mountain land and bog, all held in common. At the beginning of summer cattle were moved with their herders into the mountain pastures to allow crops to grow untrampled; this was the booley tradition that survived vestigially on Achill Island as late as the 1950s. Traces of old booley dwellings are frequently encountered in the mountains, as well as ringforts and the occasional *clachan* lower down, the latter rarely easily recognizable especially since not all clusters of ruined houses are *clachans*.

The old, sad story of the Norman invasion of Ireland in the twelfth century and the Tudor plantations in the seventeenth, the latter resulting in the ebb and flow of war and destruction which Ireland suffered for so long thereafter, is sufficiently known in broad outline that we need not dwell on it. Suffice to say that most of the native Irish landowners were eventually driven to the poorer lands of the west and into the uplands. Indeed, the mountains provided the last refuge for rebels even as late as the end of the eighteenth century.

The *rundale* system existed into the time of a great population explosion that began about 1750 and ended in disaster less than 100 years later, a disaster which destroyed the system, the remaining remnants of forest and much else besides. The population rise was facilitated by the potato, a vegetable peculiarly suited to Ireland, even in the ill-drained mountainous west. It provided a deadeningly monotonous but nourishing diet to an increasing, and increasingly impoverished population. As numbers rose, more and more marginal land (even booley land) was turned over to potato growing, thus putting severe pressure on the traditional *rundale* system, which depended on the rotation of crops. The increasing numbers also meant that *rundale* became an encumbrance because of endless sub-division. Contemporary literature quotes a story of a holding of 4 acres (1.6 hectares) spread over 1 mile (1.6 km); and one of a horse shared by three men, each of whom claimed a leg so leaving the fourth hoof unshod. In circumstances as bizarre as these it is little wonder that many landlords encouraged the re-organization of their land.

The effect of land pressure was also felt in the forests. The remaining forests, already depleted over preceding centuries for fuel and to deprive rebels of shelter, were doomed. Except for the remnants behind the high walls of the landlords' demesnes, all that was left was ruthlessly stripped to provide additional land for potatoes and for fuel. But even such panic measures could not stave off disaster. The Great Famine struck in 1844 and was caused by the complete failure of the potato crop. It lasted five terrible years. Out of a population of $8\frac{1}{2}$ millions, the Famine left 1 million dead and caused another million to flee the country. The de-population was particularly acute in the mountain areas of the south and west. Today, though again uncertainly increasing, the total population of the whole island is still only 5 million.

The results of the Famine linger on today or have only recently abated: socially in continuing emigration and in late marriages or celibacy, physically in ruined houses and cottages and in the traces of former tillage ridges climbing up the hillsides, now being invaded by bracken. You will find many tragic reminders of this sea-change in the environmental (and social) history as you walk the mountains.

The Famine also resulted in a change in the settlement pattern and eventually the ownership of both uplands and lowlands. The *rundale* system, already seriously weakened before the Famine, gave way to tenant-occupiers and later to owner-farmers. Houses are now strung out along roads with individually owned, enclosed fields running up towards the hills. Above these fields is mountain land held in common, with each of a group of farmers entitled to run a fixed number of sheep on it. The state has planted new forests, but these can hardly be said to replace the old deciduous woods, being all too often monotonous swathes of conifers planted on marginal land far into the hills. The remnants of the old woods can be seen in Killarney (County Kerry) and Glendalough (County Wicklow), though even these may not be primeval forests but secondary woodland of a later age.

THE HILL LANDS TODAY — AND TOMORROW?

Let us now look at the present picture in more detail, and in doing so examine how the changes are affecting, and probably will increasingly in the future affect, the hillwalker. Unless otherwise indicated the conditions described are relevant to the Republic of Ireland, not Northern Ireland, though conditions there do not differ all that radically.

First, let us examine the effect that a comparatively recent decision taken in faraway Brussels has had on the Irish mountains.

16

A peat stack

European Commission grants for sheep have greatly contributed to at least the impairment of the blanket bog in many areas, particularly in the west. This was perhaps initiated by climatic changes, but over-grazing by too many grant-aided sheep has certainly accelerated it. With the vegetation cover depleted, fissures occur in the bog, particularly in the more level stretches, eventually leaving peat hags (mounds of vegetated bogland). The penultimate stage in the destruction of the bog is the collapse of the hags into a thin layer of black mud. And finally, when even this is washed away, all that is left is bare rock.

To meet the threat of over-grazing, some commonages are being divided up into individual plots complete with the fencing in of each plot and an 'agricultural' road, the former an all-too-effective barrier to access, the latter an eyesore visible for miles around. For the hillwalker, and this is in the context of the Republic's antiquated laws on rights-of-way, commonage land has the great advantage that once gained, the walker is most unlikely to be challenged. Though a minor threat at present, the division of commonage might close off more and more areas to the walker.

Some of the divided plots might be given over to impenetrable forestry, also EC-aided, thus extending access difficulties for hillwalkers into private lands — difficulties that up to now have been almost exclusively confined to publicly-owned forested lands.

The encouragement of state forestry (now to be augmented by private) has been the policy of successive governments for 50 years. Though the first forests were planted with scant regard for the terrain, later ones are more sympathetic to it and have included amenity planting of deciduous trees, especially at their margins. In addition, as forests have grown to maturity they have been progressively opened to the public and provided with picnic sites, paths and trails. Whether this enlightened approach will survive under new 'hard-nosed' semi-state management (as opposed to the previous state control) remains to be seen.

Because of the poor right-of-way legislation in the Republic, forest tracks have served another useful purpose: Long Distance Routes, especially the first ones, have tended to be routed along them, thus avoiding private property. Appropriately, because of its more up-to-date legislation, Northern Ireland developed the first Long Distance Route in the island, the ambitious Ulster Way, which encircles the entire area. Northern Ireland also has a modest system of shorter right-of-way paths which the Republic as yet lacks.

The Republic, however, has no fewer than 20 Long Distance Routes, totalling 590 miles (950 km), ranging in length from a few miles to 135 miles (217 km). Some are waymarked, some not yet. The walks traverse all varieties of country — lots of forest, but also agricultural countryside, bogs, hills, river and canal banks. In general they do not venture over the tops, but instead skirt the mountains. An exception to this is the Wicklow Way, which rises to over 2000 ft (610 m), an aberration made before policy was finally decided. The Long Distance Routes of the Republic are not well depicted on the maps (except for part of the Western Way), mainly because maps on which they can be satisfactorily depicted do not yet exist. Details of all Long Distance Routes can be obtained from the addresses given in the Appendix.

Lastly, National Parks. These can hardly be considered a recent development since the first National Park was established as long ago as 1932. Fortunately the area under National Park control continues to expand, though at present it still constitutes less than a half of 1 per cent of the Republic's area. A pitiably small proportion indeed, but it does encompass some of the prime mountain landscapes. Six of the walks in this book are through or close to National Parks and the reason for this is not simply because of their presence, but more importantly because of their inherent beauty and attractiveness.

National Parks in Ireland differ fundamentally from those in England and Wales in that they are wholly state-owned (this is, incidentally, the internationally recognized norm). This means that they are devoted to the needs of visitors where this does not clash with conservation. Each National Park is well and sensitively managed with an interpretative centre, trails and informational material. Individual National Parks are described in more detail under the appropriate route description. Northern Ireland has no National Parks, but it does have Areas of Outstanding Natural Beauty (AONBs), which have the same standing as in the rest of the United Kingdom. One, which covers the entire area of the Mournes, Northern Ireland's most attractive mountain range, is of particular interest to walkers. While an AONB cannot provide as high a degree of protection as the Republic's National Parks, it does provide adequate protection at the same cost for a greater area.

THE TWILIGHT OF THE GAELIC LANGUAGE

The Gaelic language (generally called 'Irish' in Ireland) was a major victim of the Famine of the 1840s, though already on the decline before that. Widely spoken in the western half of the country before the Famine, the cycle of emigration, exclusively to English-speaking countries, which that disaster set in train, resulted in English being seen as the language of economic advancement. The new state set up in 1921 has tried to reverse that trend, with a conspicuous lack of success in all but externals. It has been a costly policy with little of real value to show for it. What we have now are much of the outward paraphernalia of a Gaelic-speaking country (such as in signposting, names of government and semi-government agencies, etc.). What we don't have, except in some western seaboard areas, are living communities which actually speak Gaelic.

One of the Celtic group of languages, Gaelic is closely related to Scots-Gaelic and Manx, and less closely related to the other Celtic branch comprising Welsh, Breton and Cornish. The script was modernized in the 1950s and the artistic but technically troublesome old Gaelic script was dropped in favour of the present one, which is the same as English and other modern European scripts. This explains the ugly proliferation of the letter 'h' in the present standard script; it is a circumflex, not a letter, and cannot be neatly accommodated. Generally it softens the preceding consonant, though it sometimes has the effect of a literary black hole, swallowing it and leaving nothing to pronounce.

Irish shopfront

One field in which Gaelic has a direct impact on the visitor is in place-names, even if this impact is nothing more than the difficulty they present in pronunciation, a subject on which this book can offer only a little help where difficult words occur in the text. Nearly all place-names in Ireland are of Gaelic origin, particularly those of natural features, which are of special concern to the walker. Each name was once appropriate and meaningful to the Gaelic-speaking local people. When the English-speaking Ordnance Survey officials of the nineteenth century tried to give official place names for the new maps they were preparing, they had the obvious difficulty of writing down the unfamiliar sounds of a strange language. The resulting official names, which are still on the OS maps, are in many cases far from felicitous.

The Gaelic-speaking areas ('Gaeltachts') have now shrunk to a few margins on the western seaboard covering perhaps 10–20,000 people who habitually speak Gaelic, areas which providentially coincide with some of the best hillwalking country. The walker will therefore have a good chance of hearing, in its cultural setting, a language which had a rich literature and was already a millenium old when English was a primitive, emergent *patois*.

INTRODUCTION TO THE ROUTE DESCRIPTIONS

1. ACCESS	See page 170. **NB** The representation in this book of a road, track or path is not evidence of the existence of a right-of-way.
2. ASCENT	The amount of climbing involved in each route has been estimated from the appropriate map and should be regarded as approximate only.
3. CAR-PARKS	Many routes start at a public car-park. For other routes places are indicated where a car can be parked by the wayside, but it must be done with care, as indiscriminate parking can be a great nuisance to local people.
4. INTERESTING FEATURES ON THE ROUTE	The best position for seeing these is indicated both in the route descriptions and on the maps by *(1)*, *(2)*, etc.
5. LENGTH	These are strictly 'map miles' estimated from the appropriate map; no attempt has been made to take into account any ascent or descent involved.
6. MAPS	The maps are drawn to a scale of approximately 1:25 000 or 1 : 50 000 and all names are as given on Ordnance Survey maps. Field boundaries in particular, which can be a mixture of hedge, fence and wall, should be taken as a 'best description'. The arrow on each map points to grid north. The scale of some small features has been slightly exaggerated for clarity. A discrepancy has arisen between the OS imperial and metric maps. Mathematically-inclined readers armed with a calculator and much idle curiosity will have noticed that the imperial heights given in this book do not always correspond to the metric. The reason is that the heights are taken from the relevant metric and imperial maps and these do not exactly correspond, either because they are recorded on slightly different points or because of the higher accuracy of the metric.

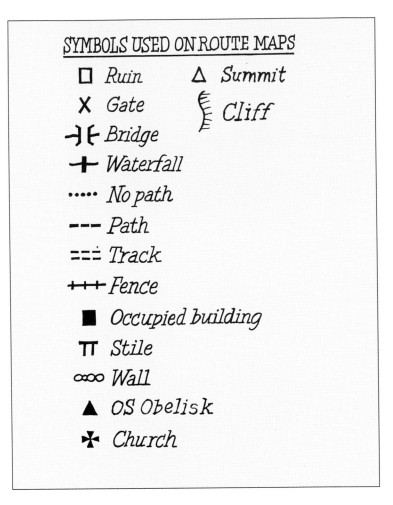

SYMBOLS USED ON ROUTE MAPS

- ☐ Ruin
- △ Summit
- ✗ Gate
- Cliff
- ⊣⊢ Bridge
- ┷ Waterfall
- ····· No path
- --- Path
- ===˙ Track
- +++ Fence
- ■ Occupied building
- ᴨ Stile
- ∞∞ Wall
- ▲ OS Obelisk
- ✚ Church

7. ROUTE DESCRIPTION

The letters 'ʟ' and 'ʀ' stand for left and right respectively. Where these are used for changes of direction they imply a turn of about 90° when facing in the direction of the walk. 'Half ʟ' and 'half ʀ' indicate a half-turn, i.e. approximately 45°.

8. STANDARD OF THE ROUTES

The briefest examination of the route descriptions that follow will show that the routes described cover an enormous range of both length and difficulty; the easiest can probably be undertaken by a family party at almost any time of the year whilst the hardest are only really suitable for experienced walkers who are both fit and well-equipped. Any walker therefore who is contemplating following a route should make sure before starting that it is within his or her ability.

It is not easy in practice, however, to give an accurate picture of the difficulty of any route, because it is dependent upon a number of factors and will in any case vary considerably from day to day with the weather. Any consideration of weather conditions must, of course, be left to the walker himself (but read the section on safety first). Apart from that, it is probably best to attempt an overall assessment of difficulty based upon the length, amount of ascent and descent, problems of route-finding and finally, upon the roughness of the terrain.

Each of the routes has therefore been given a grading based upon a consideration of these factors and represented by the bold numerals which precede each walk title. A general description of each grade follows:

Easy (1) Generally short walks (up to 5 miles, 8 km) usually over well-defined paths, with few problems of route-finding. Some climbing may be involved, but mostly over fairly gradual slopes with only short sections of more difficult ground.

Moderate (2) Rather longer walks (averaging about 8 miles, 13 km), but with sections where route-finding will be more difficult. Mountain summits may be reached with climbing over steeper and rougher ground.

More strenuous (3) Generally longer walks (averaging about 10 miles, 16 km), with prolonged spells of climbing. Some rough ground calling for good route-finding ability, perhaps with stretches of scrambling.

Very strenuous (4) Only for the few, involving long distances (up to 15 miles, 24 km), with a considerable amount of climbing, and perhaps stretches of scrambling.

The walks are arranged in order of increasing difficulty within each region.

A summary of each walk is given at the beginning of each route description with information on length, amount of climbing and any special difficulties, such as scrambling, that will be met along the way.

9. STARTING AND FINISHING POINTS

The location of each starting and finishing point is described along with its six-figure grid reference (see page 172).

10. TIME FOR COMPLETION

The usual method of estimating the length of time needed for a walk is by Naismith's Rule: 'For ordinary walking allow one hour for every 3 miles (5 km) and add one hour for every 2000 feet (600 m) of ascent; for backpacking with a heavy load allow one hour for every $2\frac{1}{2}$ miles (4 km) and one hour for every 1500 feet (450 m) of ascent.' However, for many this tends to be over-optimistic and it is better for each walker to form an assessment of his or her own performance over one or two walks. Naismith's Rule also makes no allowance for rest or food stops or for the influence of weather conditions.

11. GETTING TO THE STARTING POINT BY CAR

In Northern Ireland there should be no difficulty with road designations. The system used is identical to that used in the rest of the United Kingdom; that is, A, B and C designations. In the Republic of Ireland, however, an older system — T (for trunk) and L (for link) — is gradually being replaced by N (for national) and R (for regional) not necessarily respectively. While the change-over of the main roads to N is virtually complete, many secondary roads still have the old T or L designation. Worse still, some signposts indicate T or L and others R. For this reason, both designations have been used in the text where appropriate.

Many minor side-roads have no designations and may even be too modest to demand signposts. Nevertheless, they must be negotiated to reach the start of some of the walks in this book. To minimize the chance of getting lost in this confusing network, *precise* distances (to tenths of a mile or km) have been given, rather than the usual rougher approximations, where necessary. In these instances, it would be prudent to measure distances using the car's odometer. It is rather a nuisance, but better than the frustration of getting lost in a maze of minor roads.

Route locations

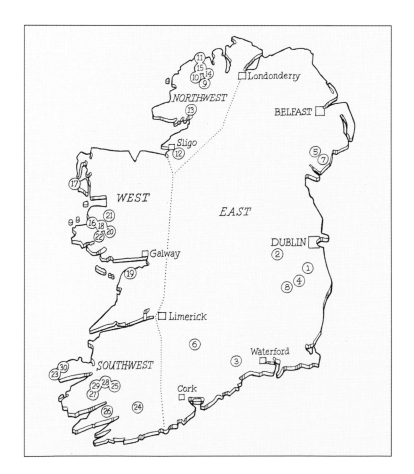

Introduction

Even a casual glance at the map of Ireland opposite will reveal that the East covers a large area, the whole island except the Atlantic seaboard, and that it contains a number of high mountain ranges, most of them in the south of the region. These ranges are not quite as wild and rugged as those further west, and they are surrounded by 'civilized' farmland, with towns and even cities close by, rather than by the inhospitable barren land of the west. Nor is the sea all that much in evidence; and when seen it is tame and placid. Access to these mountains by car, as might be expected, is comparatively easy though it is certainly not effortless, as some of the complicated access directions will testify.

In this large and diverse area, two routes, or rather two mountains, stand out: the two Munros. Galtymore in the Galtees can be reached by a very easy but dull route from the south or a somewhat longer and much more attractive route encircling high corries on the northern side — an easy choice. Lugnaquillia in Wicklow can be climbed by several good routes. The circuit of the Glen of Imaal, the route to Lugnaquillia finally chosen, is strenuous, but the long, lingering high-level descent from the summit offers fine panoramic views.

The Glen of Imaal is on the quieter, western side of Wicklow (quieter, that is, when the Artillery Range in Imaal is not in use). The two other routes in Wicklow are on the sharper eastern side, the side of steep glacial valleys and corries etched into otherwise rounded mountains. The Cloghoge Valley is the loveliest in Wicklow, a superb blend of woodland, valley and lake, and a good area for visitors who have only a short time to spend around Dublin. The Lugduffs give a high-level panorama of much of the best of the range and as a bonus take in Glendalough, a valley justly famous for its monastic associations as well as for its wooded beauty. This whole area is now safe in the arms of the new Wicklow National Park, a most welcome development.

One cautionary and sad word on Wicklow before moving on. Do not leave valuables visible in your car; better, do not take valuables with you at all into any area of the Wicklow Mountains, remote or not. There have been too many cases of robbery in this region to risk it.

Glendalough, the mine workings

Between the Galtees and Wicklow lie the Comeraghs, probably the finest mountains in the area between these two major ranges. They are noted for their dramatic corries (and are notorious for their dull bleak uplands), one of which is probably rightly reputed to be the most dramatic corrie in Ireland. This has not been included in a route, because the route chosen, with three fine corries, gives better overall variety.

Far to the north in County Down are the Mournes, a small but rugged range of uneroded granite mountains, and with Connemara by far the best-mapped area in the entire island. Two routes are included here: a short but steep ascent to castellated Slieve Bearnagh; and a comparatively short traverse of the range (much longer traverses are possible). This traverse runs from the south at Slieve Binnian, where the Mournes really do 'sweep down to the sea', to the north at Newcastle, bypassing Slieve Donard, the highest peak in the range. *Bypassing* Slieve Donard? If you are keen on peak-bagging by all means climb it, but it is a smooth-sloped, dull, inverted pudding-bowl.

Lastly there is Robertstown, an area where the nearest hills are but a faint blue smudge on the eastern horizon. Its quiet backwaters, under-used canals and out-of-the-way villages are just the place to recuperate after the rigours of the mountains.

1·1

THE CLOGHOGE VALLEY

STARTING AND FINISHING POINT

On the L of the R759/L161 heading towards Sally Gap (172064). Take the R755/T61 and turn west (R coming from Dublin) onto the R759. Drive uphill for 2 miles (3.2 km) and park carefully on the side of the road near the set of large pillars on the L.

MAPS

OS 1:50 000 Sheet 56 and OS Wicklow District 1 inch to the mile are equally satisfactory.

LENGTH

4 miles (6.5 km) for the easy route; 6 miles (9.5 km) for the harder.

ASCENT

700 ft (210 m) for the easy route; 1700 ft (520 m) for the harder.

NOTE FOR DOG-OWNERS

Please do not take your pet on the longer route. It runs through a deer-rearing area and the land is poisoned.

Wicklow at its most scenic, a complex interplay of woodland and valley, lake and mountain, which is reminiscent of the less rugged, more scenic parts of England's Lake District. Two routes are described and both give marvellous views of Lough Tay, the rocky cliffs of Luggala which end in great boulders at its lakeshore and the partly wooded Cloghoge Valley (pronounced 'Clock-oge') which connects Tay to Lough Dan, the large secluded lake to the south. The *easy* route works its way diagonally down to the floor of the Cloghoge Valley and returns on a short but sharp ascent from near the shores of Lough Dan to attain a higher level than on the outward stretch. The *harder* route diverges from the easy one near Lough Dan, continues along the north shore of the lake, climbs rocky Knocknacloghoge and returns through a side valley to the road.

ROUTE DESCRIPTION (Map 1.1)

Go through the gates labelled 'Ballinrush' 70 yards (65 m) downhill from the large pillars and on the same side *(1)*. The walk from here to Lough Dan is as navigationally simple as it is scenically delightful: a straightforward stroll along a track downhill or level almost all the way *(2)*. (You will realize that there is an unpleasant snag to a looped walk which starts innocently with a lot of downhill.) When private property in the form of a large forbidding gate blocks the way ahead turn R down a narrow path through an ancient wood to the bank of the Cloghoge River directly opposite a two-storey house — a lovely place for a bite to eat and a rest, the latter hard to justify. The two routes part ways here.

Easy route Return along the path to the main track. Turn L onto it and branch first R steeply uphill onto a green track just before the first holiday home. At the first ruin on the L, turn R again steeply uphill with forest on the R. Turn L at the first track (it plunges on the R into forest) and follow it across open country, which gives marvellous views L across to the high peaks of the range.

When forest blocks the way ahead, turn R uphill on another track thus heading for a prominent gate on the skyline. Pass

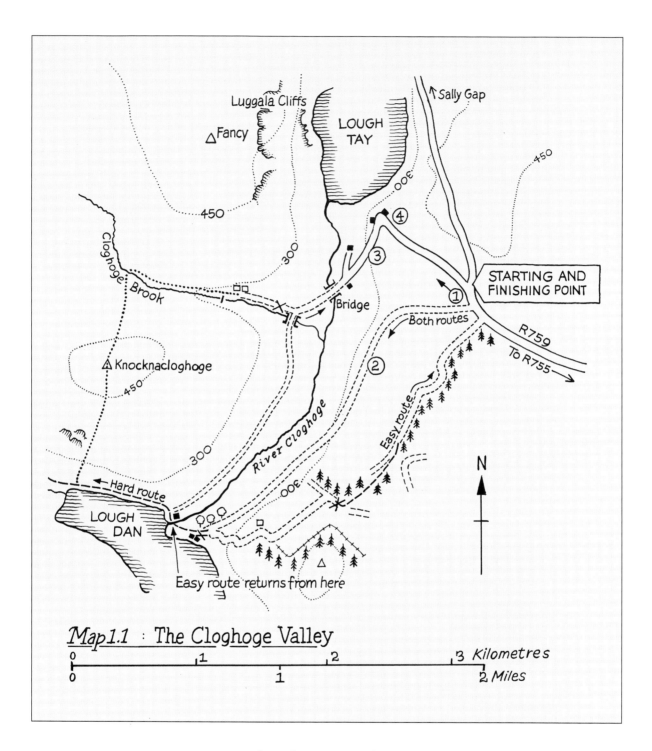

Map 1.1 : The Cloghoge Valley

through it, turn L and with forest on the L continue straight ahead through forest. Where a forest road sweeps in — and away — on the R, cross the fence L and follow the track all the way back to the road. Turn L and walk the few yards back to the starting point.

Harder route Wade across the river using a rough weir a little way down-stream of the two-storey house. Turn L and pick up a path which hugs the northern shore of Lough Dan. At the spit of silver sand, which marks the western end of the lough turn R steeply uphill avoiding the crags L on the climb. At the sudden easing of the slope, head for the L of the two rocky hillocks ahead, picking up a path that improves as it nears the summit of Knockacloghoge (1754 ft/534 m).

From the summit walk directly north over rough, heathery ground to cross the Cloghoge Brook, then turn R down-stream following the L-hand bank closely. At a delightful pool below a tiny waterfall, join a green track and follow it through a gate and thence down to a main track. Turn L here, cross a wide bridge and walk to tarmac at a farmhouse on the R. Continue uphill (3) to a hairpin bend (4) and beyond it take the steep incline to the road and the starting point.

Lough Tay and Luggala cliffs

29

1   *The Peregrine Falcon*

The peregrine falcon nests on the Luggala cliffs which can be seen from the start, but better from the end of the walk. A fast and strong flyer, it has fast wing-beats interrupted by occasional gliding. Its wing span is about 3 ft (0.9 m). The bird is rare in Ireland (and elsewhere) but its range is slowly spreading.

2   *Heather*

The heather moorlands here are a blaze of purple in August, when walking across them produces a cloud of pollen. This area is generally reputed to be the best-managed heather moorland in Wicklow.

3   *Luggala House*

The elegant house which is built on the northern shore of Lough Tay, but only whose grounds are visible on this steep ascent, is owned by a member of the Guinness family (of brewing fame). Many famous people have visited the house, including the philosopher Bertrand Russell, who was captivated by the scenery. He returned years later and could not find the spots from which he had previously so enjoyed the view. He concluded philosophically that one should not re-visit places which one enjoyed the first time round.

4   *Two Irish Miles*

A notice on the house on the L encouragingly (and a trifle whimsically) announces in archaic Irish lettering and in plain English that it is 2 Irish miles to Lough Dan. It does not say that an Irish mile is considerably longer than an English one. The distance is actually 2 *standard* miles because the notice exaggerates the Irish mileage — so we are back to square one! At this juncture you will probably be less concerned about that and more about the climb to the road and the car. For the record, the climb is 300 (English) ft (90 m).

The Cloghoge Valley and Lough Dan

HOW
SEX
WORKS

A clear, comprehensive guide for
teenagers to emotional, physical, and
sexual maturity

Elizabeth Fenwick
& Richard Walker

DORLING KINDERSLEY
LONDON ■ NEW YORK ■ STUTTGART

DK

A DORLING KINDERSLEY BOOK

Project editor Charyn Jones
U.S. editor Mary Ann Lynch
Art editor Ursula Dawson
Deputy editorial director Daphne Razazan
Managing art editor Derek Coombes

First American Edition, 1994
2 4 6 8 10 9 7 5 3 1
Published in the United States by Dorling Kindersley Publishing Inc.,
95 Madison Avenue, New York, New York 10016

Library of Congress Cataloging-in-Publication Data

Fenwick, Elizabeth.
How sex works: a clear, comprehensive guide for teenagers to emotional, physical, and
sexual maturity / by Elizabeth Fenwick and Richard Walker. -- 1st American ed.
p.   cm.
Includes index.
ISBN 1-56458-505-0
1. Sex. 2. Sex instruction for teenagers -- United States.
3. Teenagers -- United States -- Sexual behavior. 4. Hygiene, Sexual.
I. Walker, Richard.
II. Title.
HQ35.F39   1994
613.9'0835--dc20   93-37638   CIP
Reproduced by J. Film Process Pte., Thailand
Printed and bound in Great Britain by Butler and Tanner Ltd.

CONTENTS

BECOMING AN ADULT
Preparing yourself for relationships is crucial.
Relationships don't just happen; making and sustaining
them is a skill that everyone needs to learn.

INTRODUCTION

There is probably no more sensitive or controversial topic involving
teenagers today than their sexual lives. In the discussion of whether
teenagers "should" or "should not" be sexually active, other
important aspects of growing up are often overlooked. Becoming
sexually active is just one aspect of becoming an adult. *How Sex
Works* is a guide for teens to all aspects of growing up – emotional,
physical, and sexual. Our aim throughout has been to provide straight
answers to all the kinds of questions a young person naturally has.
Every section is clearly illustrated, so that the reader can see, as well
as read about, the body in different stages.

Each person develops at such different rates that "Am I normal?" is
probably one of the most common questions teens want to ask. The
introductory section, "Understanding the Body," addresses this
question, covering the major physical changes a teen can expect, and
including illustrations of both the male and female reproductive
systems. "Relationships and Emotions" focuses on feelings, social life,
and friends, acknowledging that various cultural and religious
backgrounds also influence young people's developing values. "What
Happens During Sex" explains what sex is actually like, providing
clear, illustrated answers to the sorts of questions the average teen has.
"Contraception" covers the various methods of contraception
available and how to use them properly. How pregnancy starts,
childbirth, and unplanned pregnancy are included in the section
"Pregnancy and Being a Parent." "Sex and Health" features a
comprehensive list of sexually transmitted diseases as well as a section
on HIV/AIDS, and general information on taking care of one's body.
Sex and the law, sexual harassment, child abuse, and rape are included
in "Problem Areas," followed by a list of useful addresses.

We hope that every reader, male and female, will read the entire
book. The best decisions are those based upon the most complete
information possible. And where sexual health is concerned, it is just
as important to know and understand one's partner as it is to know

and understand oneself. Knowing about sex doesn't mean you have to have sex; rather, it should give you the confidence to proceed at your own rate, and not be rushed into having a sexual relationship just because someone else wants you to.

Whether the decision is to postpone sexual activity until marriage or the post-teen years, or to become sexually active at an earlier time, every teen needs to take responsibility for his or her own sexual activity and sexual health. Every sexual action carries with it consequences. No one can afford to assume that the other person will be the one to make sure sex is handled in the "safest" possible way. In covering the many aspects of growing to adulthood, *How Sex Works* provides information for teenagers trying not only to understand themselves and their friends, but to chart their way through problems never dreamed of in earlier generations.

UNDERSTANDING THE BODY

Becoming a woman

Between the ages of 10 and 18, the female body changes from that of a child to that of a woman. The shape becomes more rounded, the waist narrows, the breasts and hips develop, and the weight almost doubles.

The way a person looks is determined mainly by what they inherit from their parents. When the mother's egg and the father's sperm met during fertilization (*see page 70*), each was carrying a package of information consisting of thousands of genes. These packages fused to provide a complete set of pairs of genes. Each pair controls, or helps control, one of the body's features, such as skin color, breast size, and height. A gene inherited from the mother may be stronger than one from the father, or the other way around. For example, if a baby inherited a brown-eyed gene from the mother, and a blue-eyed gene from the father, that baby will probably have brown eyes because brown is a dominant color.

Bodies don't differ just because of inherited characteristics, however. Lifestyle can make a difference as well. Some people eat a lot, and their metabolism makes them put on weight; whereas others might eat the same amount and not gain weight. A well-balanced diet and exercise contribute to maintaining a weight appropriate to one's body type.

PERSONAL HYGIENE

At around 12 or 13, sweat glands in the armpits start to work. Everyone sweats when they exercise or are excited or nervous – some more than others. Fresh sweat doesn't smell; its characteristic odor develops after a few hours. A daily bath or shower is important, and so is a deodorant that covers the smell. For those who sweat heavily, there are deodorants combined with an antiperspirant to reduce sweating. Shaving the armpits and legs is a matter of personal choice. Shaving and hair-removal creams can inflame the skin for a few hours so it is best not to apply a deodorant immediately after removing hair. Shaving is an easy way to remove unwanted hair, though hair removal creams (depilatories) and waxing are also effective methods.

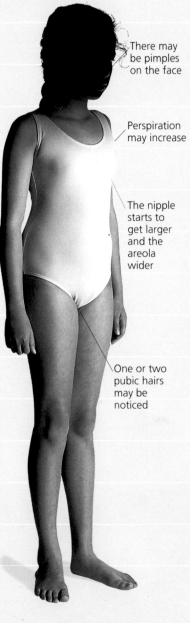

GROWING UP
Until the age of 10 or 11, children grow steadily and slowly. But as puberty begins, growth accelerates. This growth spurt usually starts two years earlier in girls than it does in boys (*see page 20*) and lasts about a year. Growth continues at a steady rate until, by the age of 18, adult height and shape have been reached.

There may be pimples on the face

Perspiration may increase

The nipple starts to get larger and the areola wider

One or two pubic hairs may be noticed

12 years
Height: 4 ft 6 in/137 cm
Weight: 70 lb/32 kg

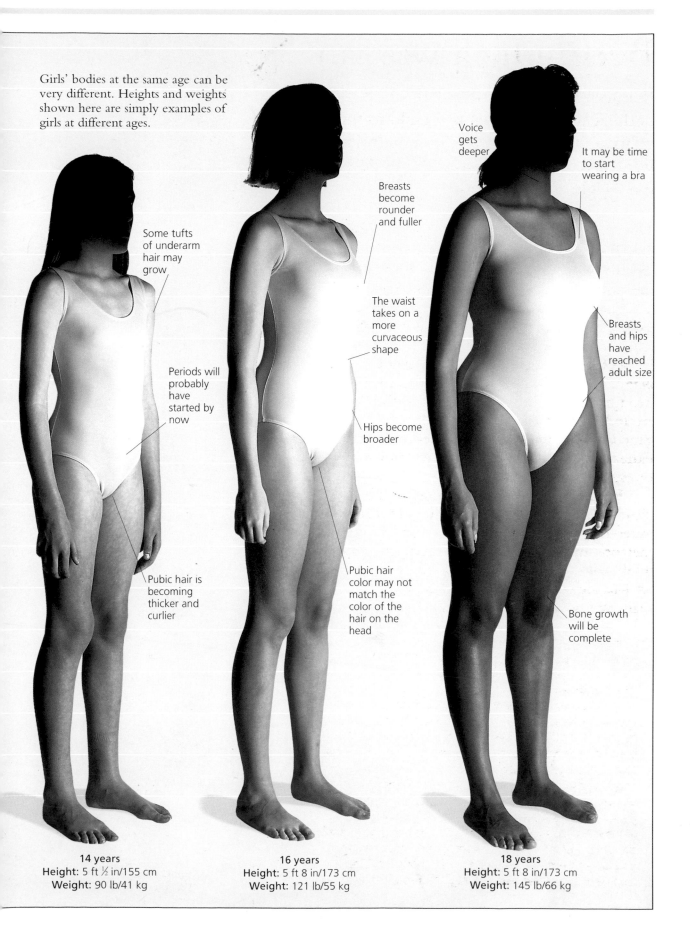

Girls' bodies at the same age can be very different. Heights and weights shown here are simply examples of girls at different ages.

Some tufts of underarm hair may grow

Periods will probably have started by now

Pubic hair is becoming thicker and curlier

Breasts become rounder and fuller

The waist takes on a more curvaceous shape

Hips become broader

Pubic hair color may not match the color of the hair on the head

Voice gets deeper

It may be time to start wearing a bra

Breasts and hips have reached adult size

Bone growth will be complete

14 years
Height: 5 ft ½ in/155 cm
Weight: 90 lb/41 kg

16 years
Height: 5 ft 8 in/173 cm
Weight: 121 lb/55 kg

18 years
Height: 5 ft 8 in/173 cm
Weight: 145 lb/66 kg

A girl at puberty

Puberty is the time during which the female body starts to change from a child's body to that of a woman. The changes do not begin at the same age for every girl, and the speed of change varies, too.

The changes that occur during puberty happen because of the increase in the levels of the female sex hormones estrogen and progesterone (*see page 16*). Puberty generally starts earlier in girls than in boys, usually around the age of 10 or 11, although it may begin before or after this age. Each person, male or female, has his or her biological time clock. As the body changes, so, too, will feelings and attitudes.

Some will notice that they are growing more rapidly – this is known as a growth spurt. Some girls find themselves taller than many of the boys in their class. Breasts start developing now; strands of hair may grow on the pubic area (*see page 14*) and under the armpits; hips, thighs, and breasts become more rounded. Periods may begin, too (*see page 17*).

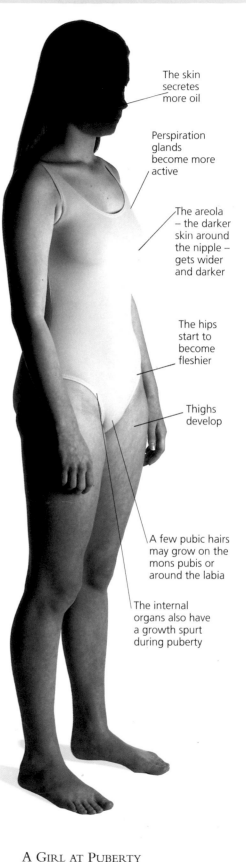

The skin secretes more oil

Perspiration glands become more active

The areola – the darker skin around the nipple – gets wider and darker

The hips start to become fleshier

Thighs develop

A few pubic hairs may grow on the mons pubis or around the labia

The internal organs also have a growth spurt during puberty

A GIRL AT PUBERTY

EATING WELL

The attitude that thin is beautiful is widespread in some cultures; in the western world, it has been found that almost every woman diets at some time in her life. There may be a real sense of achievement when weight is lost. However, it is obvious that not everyone grows up to look like a model in a magazine – thin and tall. For some girls, being thin becomes an obsession. Anorexia is an illness in which the sufferer sees herself as fat and continues to diet and perhaps exercise in an attempt to lose more weight. Even though she may be painfully thin, this will not be her perception of herself. Her weight may drop dramatically, and her periods may stop. Some anorexics starve themselves to death. Some develop bulimia, which is maintaining a normal weight by "binge eating" and then making themselves vomit the food up. People with these eating disorders need help, not just to get back to a healthier eating pattern, but because the disorder is usually a sign of underlying unhappiness. Those with anorexia or bulimia need medical attention but may also benefit from counseling.

DIFFERENCES IN GROWTH

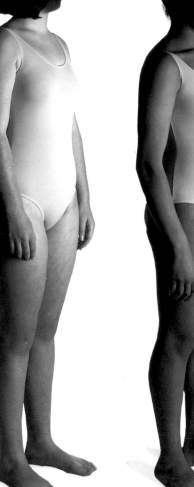

Height: 5 ft 9 in/175 cm
Weight: 125 lb/57 kg

Height: 5 ft ½ in/155 cm
Weight: 97 lb/44 kg

Height: 5 ft 8 in/173 cm
Weight: 147 lb/67 kg

Height: 5 ft 3 in/162 cm
Weight: 112 lb/51 kg

RATES OF GROWTH

Although changes to the body shape and size happen in a fairly orderly way, all girls develop at different rates. Some girls may experience a growth spurt at 11; others may not notice any difference in height until they are 13. It is also at the time of this growth spurt that the body changes become noticeable and the first period occurs. The girls pictured here are 13 and all aged within six months of one another.

QUESTIONS AND ANSWERS

I seem to get pimples just when I really want to look good. Would it help if I stopped eating chocolate?
Schula, 14 years

There is no conclusive evidence that diet impacts acne, although some may find certain foods aggravate skin eruptions. It is high levels of sex hormones that lead to acne during adolescence. Washing your face regularly may help. If the acne is bad, see a dermatologist, who may prescribe an oral medication or a gel.

My breasts are small, but my friend says I still ought to wear a bra, or the muscles will get weak. Do I have to?
Sally, 13 years

Breasts have no muscles. Large breasts may droop without a bra. The time to start wearing a bra is probably when you start to feel uncomfortable without one. Special sports bras are available for those needing extra support when involved in exercise or sports.

The female body

The reproductive system in the female body, including the eggs in the ovaries, is in place at birth. A signal in the brain at the onset of puberty starts the fertile stage of your life, causing one egg to be released every month until around the age of about 50.

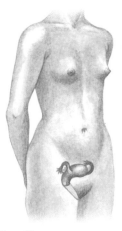

THE PELVIS
The reproductive organs lie in the pelvis (body cage) where they are protected. The uterus lies above and behind the bladder and in front of the rectum.

Each month, one egg matures and is released into one of the fallopian tubes. If sperm are there after recent sexual intercourse (*see pages 70-71*), the egg may be fertilized. The tubes lead to the uterus where the baby grows. The neck of the uterus is called the cervix. This has a mucous plug that thins at ovulation (when an egg is released), making it easier for sperm to swim through. The vagina is an elastic tube running to the opening at the vulva. It is quite separate from the urinary system, which has its own opening – the urethra.

The uterus is about the size and shape of a pear. It is the most muscular organ in the body and it is capable of huge expansion. It usually tilts forward, almost at a right angle to the vagina. Its lower part, the cervix, opens into the vagina, and the tip of the cervix can just be felt at the top of the vagina.

During puberty (*see page 12*), the external sexual organs develop and mature. The mons pubis – the pad of fat covering the pubic bone – becomes fleshier and more prominent. Pubic hair grows on the labia.

THE VULVA
Between two outer fleshy lips, or labia, on which the pubic hair grows, are two thinner and hairless inner labia. Between these are the clitoris, at the front; the opening of the urethra, in the middle; and the larger vaginal opening behind that.

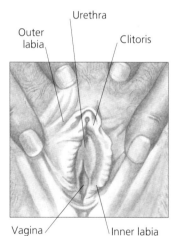

Urethra
Outer labia
Clitoris
Vagina
Inner labia

THE STRUCTURE OF THE BREASTS

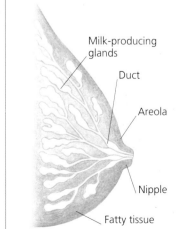

Milk-producing glands
Duct
Areola
Nipple
Fatty tissue

Breasts are made up of fatty tissue containing tiny milk-producing glands. All women have a similar number of glands, but some have more fatty tissue than others. This is why some breasts are larger than others. Ducts run from the glands to the surface of the nipple. The nipple is the most sensitive part of the breast. It is soft, but cold, and both touch and sexual arousal make it hard and erect. Around the nipple is the areola, an area of pink or brown skin, which darkens with age and during pregnancy. During pregnancy the milk-producing ducts increase in preparation for lactation. They replace much of the fat that is normally in the breast. Milk is produced inside the glands when a woman has had a baby. The milk travels through the ducts to the nipple as the baby sucks.

Fimbriae lie near the surface of the ovary and receive eggs

At birth, the ovaries contain about 400,000 eggs, or ova, in sacs called follicles. One egg is released each month. The empty follicle develops into the corpus luteum. Ovaries also produce the female sex hormones, estrogen and progesterone

The inside of a fallopian tube is no wider than the diameter of a human hair. Cells in the tubes sweep eggs to the uterus. If sperm are present, fertilization may take place in the tube

Bladder

Clitoris

Urethra

The vagina is about 3 in (8 cm) long, with ridged walls. These normally lie against each other, but because they are elastic, they can open during intercourse and stretch in childbirth. In childhood, the vaginal opening is partially covered by a membrane called the hymen

FROM OVARY TO UTERUS

At its upper end, the uterus opens out into the fallopian tubes, whose fringed ends lie near the surface of the ovaries. In this illustration, the fallopian tubes and ovaries are shown larger than life size; in reality, an ovary is about 1¼ in (3 cm) long, and the eggs in it are minute. The fallopian tube is about ⅟₂₅ in (1 mm) thick.

The uterus is a hollow, pear-shaped, muscular organ. It is capable of huge expansion to accommodate a baby

The cervix, the neck of the uterus, leads to the vagina. It is plugged with mucus, with only a small hole to allow blood to pass through during periods. However, at ovulation, the mucus thins, making it easier for sperm to enter the uterus

Rectum

QUESTIONS AND ANSWERS

If you're a virgin, is your vagina completely closed?
Rebecca, 14 years

No. A membrane called a hymen surrounds the vaginal opening, but only very rarely does it block the whole opening. There is normally a hole in it at least big enough to allow the menstrual blood to flow out. The hymen is eventually torn or stretched by vigorous exercise, using tampons, or sexual intercourse.

What happens to the eggs that don't get used?
Jan, 13 years

Out of the 400,000 eggs present in your ovaries at birth, probably only about 400 mature to be released at ovulation. The rest fail to mature and are reabsorbed into your body. When there are no more eggs to be released, menopause occurs.

Someone told me twins happen because of something in the

woman's system, and that they run in families. Is this true?
Adam, 14 years

Fraternal twins do tend to run in families. If a woman's ovaries shed two eggs at once and if they are both fertilized, she will have fraternal twins. These twins are not identical and may be different sexes. Identical twins develop when one egg is fertilized by a single sperm and the egg divides to form two babies. These twins are the same sex and look alike.

The menstrual cycle

If an egg is not fertilized by sperm on its voyage down the fallopian tube, the lining of the uterus, which has prepared itself for the egg, is shed through the vagina. This monthly shedding of the lining of the uterus is called menstruation, or a period.

Periods are the sign that hormones have stimulated the ovaries to begin releasing eggs. They also mean that the body is physically able to have a baby. First periods usually begin between the ages of 11 and 14, but some girls start as early as nine and others not until they are 16.

The blood that comes out through the vagina is often scant at first, and for the first six months it may not be bright red, but brownish. There may be just a trickle the first day, a heavier flow during the second and third day, then less and less until the discharge is back to normal on the fifth or sixth day. For the first two days, there may be some discomfort, with abdominal cramps. This is quite common.

The menstrual cycle may be irregular for a while – periods may be missed – but after a few months, there will be a regular pattern. The average length of the menstrual cycle (from the first day of one period to the first day of the next) is 28 days, but all women have slightly different cycles.

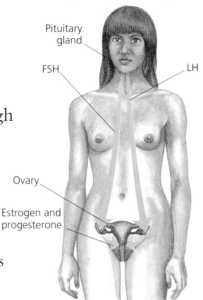

Pituitary gland
FSH
LH
Ovary
Estrogen and progesterone

HORMONAL CONTROL
The events of the menstrual cycle are controlled by hormones. Follicle-stimulating hormone (FSH) and luteinizing hormone (LH), released by the pituitary gland in the brain, are carried by the bloodstream to the ovary. Here they cause an egg to ripen and be released, and the ovary to release another two hormones, estrogen and progesterone, that thicken the lining of the uterus, or endometrium.

DYSMENORRHEA

This is the medical word for very painful periods. The lower abdominal pains are called cramps, and they feel as if something is pulling the body inside. Painkillers can help. Some girls become bloated, some depressed, some feel very ill, and some even vomit. If period symptoms are particularly severe, a doctor may prescribe a drug that will relieve the symptoms. Dysmenorrhea can be treated successfully. The pains usually get less as one gets older, or they may decrease if one is using contraceptive pills. Exercise or yoga can also help relieve the discomfort.

QUESTIONS AND ANSWERS

Is it true you can't get pregnant before your periods have started?
Simone, 13 years

No. In theory you could, because your period might be about to start. However, usually no egg is released during the first few menstrual cycles.

How do I know when I'm likely to start having my period?
Alison, 14 years

Your period won't start until your growth spurt has begun and your breasts and pubic hair are growing. Starting early or late runs in families: if your mother started her periods late, you may, too. You may notice some whitish discharge for about a year before the bleeding begins.

Some girls at school stay out of gym when they have their period. Will I need to do this?
Connie, 14 years

You can do anything during your period that you do at any other time. Depression, irritability, pimples, headaches, swollen or tender breasts, and stomach cramps are symptoms that some women get during their period. When these symptoms occur before your period, they are known as premenstrual syndrome (PMS). Whatever the symptom, you need to find a remedy that works for you. One of the best remedies for cramps, for example, is a hot water bottle. There are also painkillers, especially for menstrual or premenstrual pain.

THE MENSTRUAL CYCLE

Although the average length of the menstrual cycle is 28 days, the variation in the length of a cycle can be anything from 21 to 42 days. However long the menstrual cycle is in days, ovulation occurs 12 to 16 days *before* the beginning of the next period. If the egg is not fertilized, the uterine lining is shed through the vagina. During the cycle, the cervical mucus also changes. This can be used as an indication of ovulation (*see page 68*).

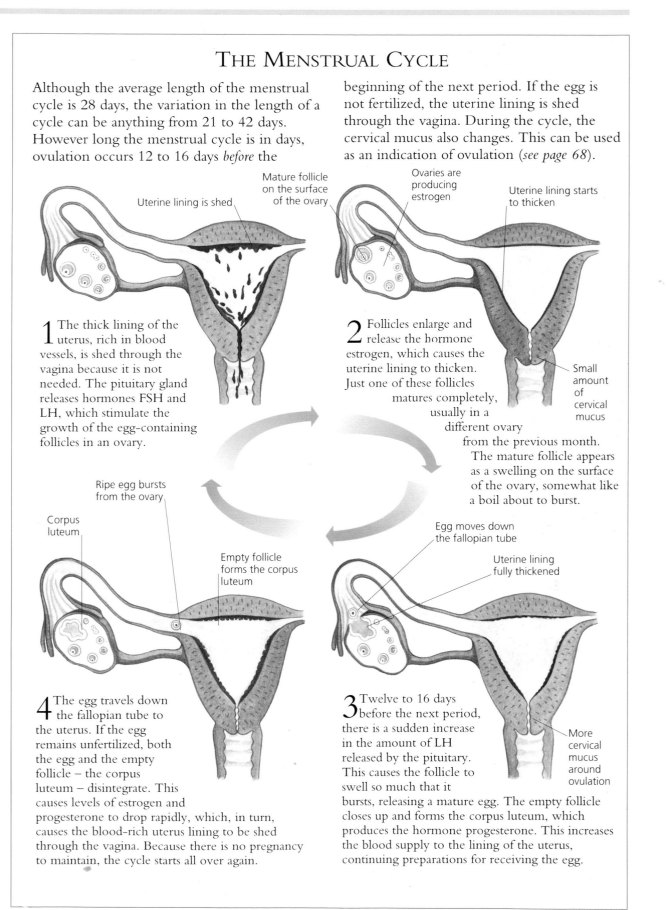

Uterine lining is shed

Mature follicle on the surface of the ovary

1 The thick lining of the uterus, rich in blood vessels, is shed through the vagina because it is not needed. The pituitary gland releases hormones FSH and LH, which stimulate the growth of the egg-containing follicles in an ovary.

Ovaries are producing estrogen

Uterine lining starts to thicken

2 Follicles enlarge and release the hormone estrogen, which causes the uterine lining to thicken. Just one of these follicles matures completely, usually in a different ovary from the previous month. The mature follicle appears as a swelling on the surface of the ovary, somewhat like a boil about to burst.

Small amount of cervical mucus

Corpus luteum

Ripe egg bursts from the ovary

Empty follicle forms the corpus luteum

4 The egg travels down the fallopian tube to the uterus. If the egg remains unfertilized, both the egg and the empty follicle – the corpus luteum – disintegrate. This causes levels of estrogen and progesterone to drop rapidly, which, in turn, causes the blood-rich uterus lining to be shed through the vagina. Because there is no pregnancy to maintain, the cycle starts all over again.

Egg moves down the fallopian tube

Uterine lining fully thickened

3 Twelve to 16 days before the next period, there is a sudden increase in the amount of LH released by the pituitary. This causes the follicle to swell so much that it bursts, releasing a mature egg. The empty follicle closes up and forms the corpus luteum, which produces the hormone progesterone. This increases the blood supply to the lining of the uterus, continuing preparations for receiving the egg.

More cervical mucus around ovulation

Monthly periods

No one knows quite why menstruation starts, but we do know that around 9 to 16 years a gland in the brain triggers the process by releasing hormones. These in turn stimulate the ovaries to produce the female sex hormones that encourage the body to change.

For past generations of women, menstruation was an unmentionable, and in some cultures a time when women were seen as unclean. Today, with more open attitudes toward sexuality, girls can feel proud realizing that menstruation signals their entry into womanhood. Even so, many girls still start their periods without ever having been told what to expect.

Having a period is a completely normal part of a woman's life, but it is understandable for girls to feel embarrassed and uncomfortable when they first begin. This may depend upon how helpful and supportive their parents are. Girls often worry that they may smell, or that blood will leak onto their clothes and everyone will know what is happening to them. Girlfriends will understand these feelings, but boys may be insensitive and make jokes. Knowing what to expect helps ease initial embarrassment.

Some find it a good idea to keep track of their periods so that they can see how their personal cycle develops. It is then possible to know what to expect.

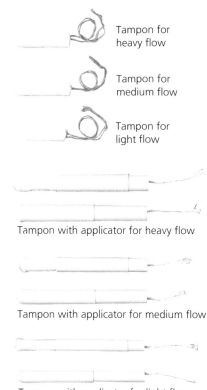

Tampon for heavy flow

Tampon for medium flow

Tampon for light flow

Tampon with applicator for heavy flow

Tampon with applicator for medium flow

Tampon with applicator for light flow

TAMPONS

A tampon is a tight roll of cotton fiber with a string at one end. Tampons are available in different thicknesses to suit the rate of flow. If there are leaks, then use either a higher absorbency tampon, change the tampon more often, or use a napkin during the heavier flow of your period. A tampon cannot get lost inside or be put in the wrong opening.

PERSONAL HYGIENE

Good personal hygiene is particularly important during a period. The area around the vagina should be washed, but not inside – the lining is sensitive. A daily bath or shower is the best approach to keeping clean and warding off odors. Scented bubble baths and oils may also cause irritation. It is important to change tampons frequently – at least four times a day – to prevent the growth of bacteria in the vagina. This can lead to a condition called toxic shock syndrome (*see page 64*).

SANITARY NAPKINS

Sanitary napkins are soft cotton pads with one waterproof side. They are used to absorb menstrual blood and are worn outside the body, unlike tampons. Napkins come in thicknesses suited to the rate of flow, which varies over the course of a period. They adhere to the lining of panties; some have wing shapes to hold them more firmly and provide for a heavier flow and prevent staining. Napkins should be changed several times a day. Some women prefer napkins when there is spotting rather than a steady flow and at night.

Panty liner with wings

Shaped panty liner

INSERTING A TAMPON

Tampons are worn inside the vagina, inserted with an applicator or with a finger. They are convenient for sports and can be worn during swimming. Low-absorbency tampons are useful when there is spotting rather than a steady flow.

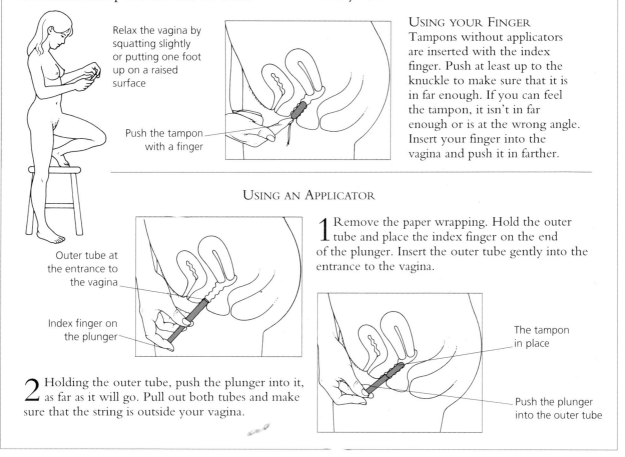

Relax the vagina by squatting slightly or putting one foot up on a raised surface

Push the tampon with a finger

USING YOUR FINGER

Tampons without applicators are inserted with the index finger. Push at least up to the knuckle to make sure that it is in far enough. If you can feel the tampon, it isn't in far enough or is at the wrong angle. Insert your finger into the vagina and push it in farther.

USING AN APPLICATOR

Outer tube at the entrance to the vagina

Index finger on the plunger

1 Remove the paper wrapping. Hold the outer tube and place the index finger on the end of the plunger. Insert the outer tube gently into the entrance to the vagina.

The tampon in place

Push the plunger into the outer tube

2 Holding the outer tube, push the plunger into it, as far as it will go. Pull out both tubes and make sure that the string is outside your vagina.

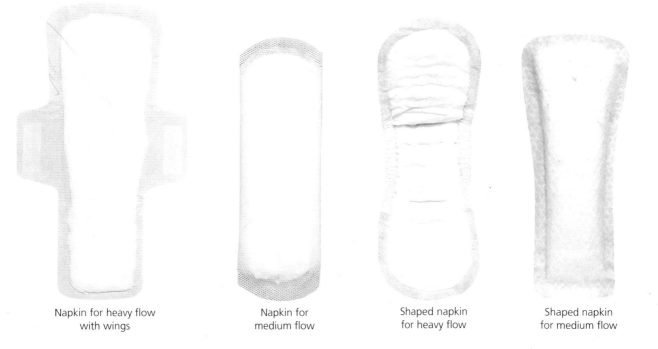

Napkin for heavy flow with wings

Napkin for medium flow

Shaped napkin for heavy flow

Shaped napkin for medium flow

Becoming a man

Between the ages of 13 and 18, the male body changes from that of a child to that of a man. The weight almost doubles, and the height increases. However, no two boys change in precisely the same way at the same age.

As a boy develops into a man, hair starts to grow and the voice becomes deeper. This changing voice can be embarrassing, because one minute it is a deep voice, and the next it is high and squeaky. What a person looks like depends a lot on what their parents look like and the genes they inherit from them (*see page 10*). Boys whose fathers have a lot of body hair will probably also have a lot. Body development also depends on factors such as exercise and diet.

Every boy is different, and physical changes in some boys may start at age 12, while other boys will develop even later. Many boys worry that they are developing too slowly or too quickly. It is easy to tease someone because they are bigger and hairier, or smaller and less hairy, than everyone else. However, everyone will eventually go through the same changes, although no two boys will look exactly alike.

QUESTIONS AND ANSWERS

My friends have started laughing about me and saying that I smell. What can I do?
William, 14 years

Many things about your body change as you grow up. One of these is that you start to sweat more and your sweat has a different smell. A bath or shower every day is the best safeguard against odor. Wear clean clothes and socks whenever possible. Use deodorant or an antiperspirant; you can buy these in supermarkets and drugstores.

What should I do about the fluffy hair on my face?
Ben, 15 years

The first facial hair is easily and safely removed using soap and water, or shaving foam, and a disposable razor. This first facial hair is not thick enough yet to be removed with an electric shaver.

My breasts have started to swell, and they are quite sore under the nipples. Am I going to change into a girl?
Adam, 15 years

No. This happens in quite a few boys of your age and is nothing to worry about. It is caused by a reaction to the sex hormones that are causing all the changes in your body, and it should not last more than a few months.

GROWING UP
Most boys will have reached their adult height by the age of 18. By the early twenties full height and breadth will have been reached. Those who have tall people in either parent's

Some pimples may appear on the face

A few underarm hairs may appear

Perspiration may increase

One or two pubic hairs may be noticed

12 years
Height: 5 ft 1 in/156 cm
Weight: 99 lb/45 kg

family may also be tall. Heights and weights shown here are simply examples of boys at different ages.

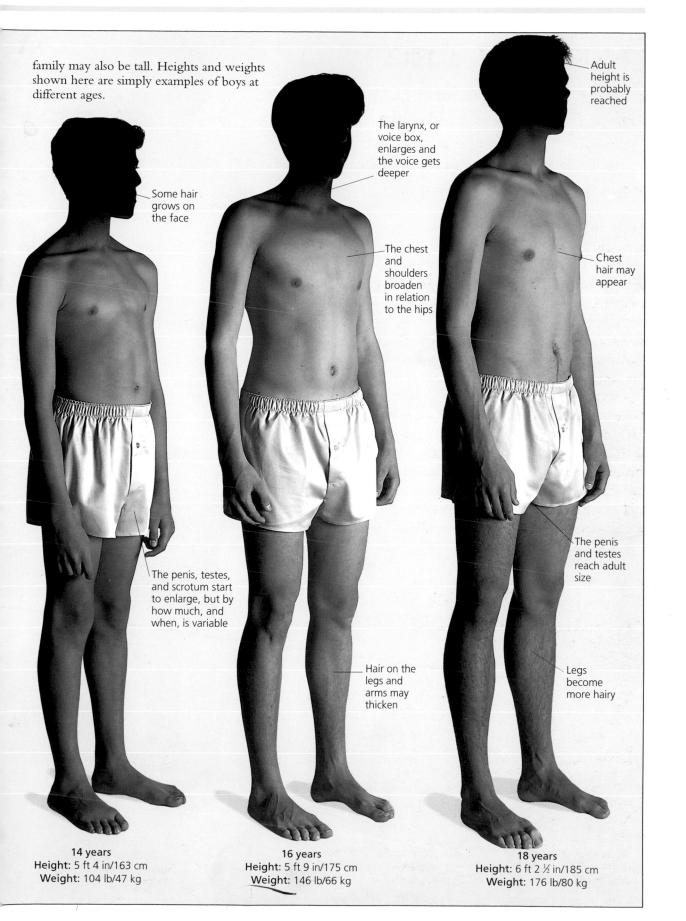

Some hair grows on the face

The larynx, or voice box, enlarges and the voice gets deeper

The chest and shoulders broaden in relation to the hips

Adult height is probably reached

Chest hair may appear

The penis, testes, and scrotum start to enlarge, but by how much, and when, is variable

Hair on the legs and arms may thicken

The penis and testes reach adult size

Legs become more hairy

14 years
Height: 5 ft 4 in/163 cm
Weight: 104 lb/47 kg

16 years
Height: 5 ft 9 in/175 cm
Weight: 146 lb/66 kg

18 years
Height: 6 ft 2 ½ in/185 cm
Weight: 176 lb/80 kg

A boy at puberty

Puberty is the time of life when a boy starts to become sexually mature. The reproductive organs develop, and the testes start producing sperm. The body begins a phase of growth and change in shape that will continue until the late teens.

Puberty is triggered by a hormone released by the pituitary gland in the brain. This stimulates the testes to release the male sex hormone, testosterone. This controls the changes happening to the body. Puberty starts later in boys than girls, usually around the age of 14, although it may begin before or after this age. Puberty does not happen overnight. It forms part of the transition from boy to man called adolescence. This is a time of overall growth: as the body matures, feelings and attitudes change as well (*see pages 30-31*).

THE MAJOR CHANGES

By the age of 13 or 14, some bodily changes will probably be noticeable. There may be differences in the age at which the different stages of change happen. First, the testes start to grow. As they do so, the scrotum (the bag containing the testes) expands, hangs low, and gets more wrinkly. The scrotum's skin gets redder in color in those who have fair skin, or darker in those who have dark skin; it also becomes thicker. A few pubic hairs grow around the place where the penis joins the body, and some hair may grow under the armpits.

The penis starts growing longer and thicker, and the skin color also darkens. The testes and scrotum continue enlarging, and one testis, usually the left, hangs lower. Tiny bumps appear on the skin of the scrotum and sometimes the penis, showing where hair may grow. Pubic hair will eventually spread upward and to the sides and become thicker and more curly. The body starts its growth spurt, getting larger and heavier, with broader shoulders and narrower hips.

The body sweats more, and it will be necessary to wash more often and use deodorants and antiperspirants to avoid body odors. Pimples might appear, usually on the chin or nose, which is the area on the face where the skin secretes the most oils.

The skin secretes more oil

Sweat glands become more active

Some hair growth under the arms

A few pubic hairs appear at the base of the penis

The body starts to grow taller

A BOY AT PUBERTY

DIFFERENCES IN GROWTH

Height: 6 ft ½ in/183 cm
Weight: 154 lb/70 kg

Height: 5 ft 6 in/167 cm
Weight: 128 lb/58 kg

Height: 5 ft 10 in/178 cm
Weight: 167 lb/76 kg

Height: 5 ft 9 in/175 cm
Weight: 139 lb/63 kg

LOOKING AT DIFFERENCES
Everyone is different, both in
the rate of the changes they
experience, and in the shape
and size they eventually reach
at adulthood. This is partly
inheritance from one's parents.
Some may feel gawky and
unattractive, or smaller and
less hairy than their friends –
everyone has some feature that
they are embarrassed about.
The boys pictured here
are all 15 or 16 years old and
aged within six months of
one another.

QUESTIONS AND ANSWERS

**I've started getting pimples. Why?
Jason, 14 years**

Testosterone also makes the skin
produce extra oils. Sometimes the
glands in the skin that produce these
oils get blocked, and pimples appear.
Keep your skin clean with an
antibacterial soap, and don't pick the
pimples; you may get scarring. If they
are really bad, you may have a
condition called acne, and your doctor
or dermatologist should be consulted.

**How big should a penis be? My
friends' all look much bigger than
mine. It makes me really depressed.
Bobby, 15 years**

Ask any male what part of his body he
feels most unhappy about, and he will
probably say the size of his penis,
whatever age he is. A fully grown
penis is usually between 3-4 in
(8-10 cm) long when soft, and
between 5-7 in (12-18 cm) long when
it is erect, or stiff.

Male reproductive system

The male reproductive system isn't just a penis and testes that lie outside the body. Inside the body there is a system of ducts and glands that play an essential part in sperm production and delivery. Sperm are the male sex cells needed to make a baby.

From puberty to old age, millions of sperm are formed every day in the testes. It takes about 70 days for a sperm to be produced. Sperm can't develop properly at normal body temperature, so the testes hang outside the body, in the cooler scrotum. From the testis, sperm pass into a tube at the back of each testis – the epididymis – where the sperm mature. When a man ejaculates, muscle contractions squeeze the sperm along the sperm duct and into the urethra, passing on the way, the openings of the seminal vesicles and the prostate gland. These produce seminal fluids, which mobilize the sperm and make up the bulk of the semen that is ejaculated from the penis.

The shaft of the penis contains spongy erectile tissue, which fills with blood during an erection. The head, or glans, is highly sensitive. Sperm are ejaculated from the penis along the urethra. This is normally a channel for urine, but muscles at the bladder entrance contract during erection, so that no urine enters the semen, and no semen enters the bladder. Any sperm that are not ejaculated are reabsorbed within a certain time into the man's body.

MALE HORMONE

Testosterone is the male sex hormone that is made in the testes, and is needed for sperm production. During puberty, it also:

- Enlarges the penis, testes, and scrotum, and increases their sensitivity.
- Promotes growth and increases muscle bulk in the body.
- Stimulates growth of facial and bodily hair.
- Deepens the voice.
- Increases skin thickness and oily skin secretions, causing pimples.
- Increases a boy's sex drive and interest in sexual activity.

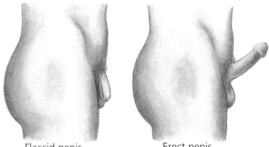

Flaccid penis   Erect penis

ERECTIONS AND SIZE DIFFERENCES
The penis hangs down, but during sexual arousal it becomes larger and points outward and upward, designed to deposit sperm in the vagina. Penises vary in size; size has nothing to do with masculinity, sexual performance, or pleasure.

CIRCUMCISION

Boys are born with a foreskin, a fold of skin that covers the glans of the penis. This foreskin is often cut away by a doctor soon after the baby's birth, in an operation called a circumcision. In the Jewish and Muslim religions, the operation is performed in a religious rite. Once practiced for supposed hygienic reasons, the necessity of circumcision is increasingly being questioned: whether one has a foreskin or not will not affect sexual health or performance.

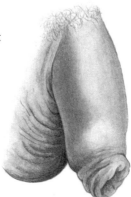

Uncircumcised penis   Circumcised penis

THE MALE REPRODUCTIVE ORGANS

The external organs are the penis and the testes. The testes hang in the scrotum, a pouch of skin behind the penis: the left usually hangs slightly lower than the right. During intercourse, semen is ejaculated from the penis into the woman's vagina to fertilize her eggs.

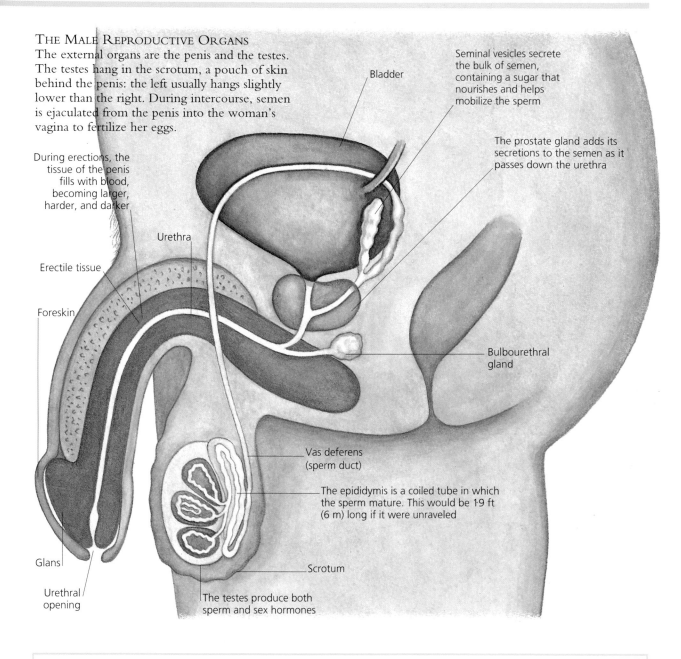

Seminal vesicles secrete the bulk of semen, containing a sugar that nourishes and helps mobilize the sperm

Bladder

The prostate gland adds its secretions to the semen as it passes down the urethra

During erections, the tissue of the penis fills with blood, becoming larger, harder, and darker

Urethra

Erectile tissue

Foreskin

Bulbourethral gland

Glans

Vas deferens (sperm duct)

The epididymis is a coiled tube in which the sperm mature. This would be 1·9 ft (6 m) long if it were unraveled

Urethral opening

Scrotum

The testes produce both sperm and sex hormones

QUESTIONS AND ANSWERS

Why do I seem to wake up with an erection every morning? Is this normal?
Paul, 14 years

This happens to many boys. Erections can occur in dreams, whether or not the dream is sexual, when it may result in a "wet dream" (*page 27*). Sometimes when you wake up with an erection it is just because your bladder is full.

Why do I keep having erections all the time, even when I'm not thinking about girls or anything?
Will, 14 years

Most boys have spontaneous erections, which are embarrassing if they happen at the wrong time or in the wrong place. They are caused by the raised levels of testosterone in the body and will stop as puberty passes. They do go away if you think about something else.

Is it true that wearing tight jeans can make a man infertile?
Joanna, 16 years

Anything that affects sperm production affects fertility. Tight jeans can raise the temperature of the scrotum, preventing sperm from developing properly. Sperm are produced all the time, however, so while wearing tight jeans may lower a man's fertility temporarily, it would not affect it in the future.

The body's sensuality

As the body matures, so does one's awareness of its sensitivity and sensuality. Discovering, exploring, and understanding its sensitivity can help one to enjoy sexual activity in the broadest sense: sexual enjoyment involves the whole body, not just the sex organs.

WHAT IS MASTURBATION?

Masturbation means touching or rubbing one's genitals or a partner's to give sexual pleasure, and usually to have an orgasm. Orgasm is a throbbing feeling that brings intense pleasure. For many people, masturbation is their first sexual experience. It is a harmless and natural way for people to enjoy their sexuality on their own. It relieves the tension that results from sexual urges and is a way to discover exciting sensations – knowledge that can be shared with a partner to show them how one likes to be aroused. Masturbation also helps the young appreciate that sexual pleasure is not the simple mechanical exercise so often represented in the media. Good sexual relations take time and consideration.

Some people find out about masturbation from brothers, sisters, or friends, while others discover it on their own. By the late teens, the majority of boys and girls will have masturbated. However, some people never feel a need to masturbate, and this is quite normal as well.

HOW PEOPLE MASTURBATE

There are no fixed ways to masturbate. Everyone does what pleases them. Many people daydream about a person they care about or pretend they are in a different place while they masturbate. Other people have sexual fantasies (*see page 28*). All of this is completely normal.

Stimulation of the clitoris is the main way that girls experience orgasm. Girls generally rub and stroke around and over the clitoris with their fingers, moving faster and faster until they have an orgasm. As sexual excitement rises, the vagina becomes moist. Girls can have several orgasms, one after the other. Boys masturbate by stimulating the penis. Most boys hold their penis and move their hand up and down to stimulate it; some boys just rub the penis, increasing speed until they reach orgasm and semen is released, or ejaculated. The penis becomes limp after ejaculation.

Boys commonly experience arousal without masturbation while sleeping. A "wet dream" is the result of dreaming about

WHO MASTURBATES?

Surveys show that by their late teens, about 90 percent of boys masturbate. The numbers for girls vary from as low as 60 percent to as high as 80 percent. Social attitudes and education may account for these differences: sexual double standards and the discredited idea that women shouldn't enjoy sex might make girls feel more guilty about masturbating than boys, and make some girls less likely than others to masturbate.

something sexually exciting. As a result, the penis is aroused and ejaculates sperm, even though the boy is sleeping. A boy then wakes up because the semen is cold on his skin or wets his clothes. He might even be shocked because his dream was about a girl or boy whom he would not normally think about in a sexual way. Wet dreams are quite normal and are one sign that a person is becoming sexually mature, although not all boys have them. Boys may also experience spontaneous erections at unexpected times and even in public places.

Many girls also have dreams that make them sexually aroused, and sometimes they will have orgasms in their sleep. These are not really "wet" dreams though, because girls don't ejaculate.

I had my first orgasm while I was in the shower. Soaping myself down there felt really good, so I just kept going.

Martha, 15 years

EROGENOUS ZONES

The body is covered with touch and pressure sensors that, when touched or stroked, can arouse a person sexually.

These are known as erogenous zones. The genitals are usually the most sensitive zones on the body.

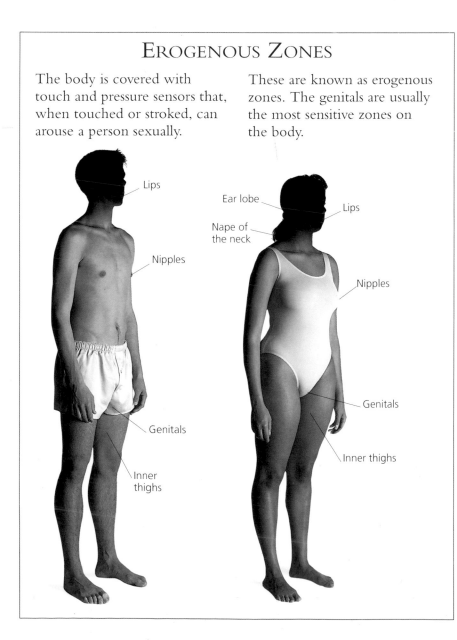

Lips

Ear lobe

Nape of the neck

Lips

Nipples

Nipples

Genitals

Genitals

Inner thighs

Inner thighs

I have really strange thoughts when I masturbate but I don't think I would ever do what I think about in real life.

Colin, 15 years

> The first time I had a wet dream, I thought there was something wrong with me. When it happened to my younger brother, he was really embarrassed because he thought he'd wet the bed, and I had to explain it all to him.
>
> Brian, 18 years

GUILT AND MYTHS ABOUT MASTURBATION

Many people feel guilty about masturbating. Small children find natural pleasure in touching their genitals, only to be reprimanded by adults. This can lead to confusion and leave feelings of guilt and shame about touching themselves. These guilt feelings can conflict with their sexual urges when they reach puberty and, later, when they become sexually active.

Many parents will not talk to their children about masturbation, and some will tell them that masturbation is wrong. This is probably because of what their parents told them when they were young. Masturbation was once believed to cause poor health, loss of sight, paralysis, and madness, and boys and girls were punished for touching their genitals. Even today, some repeat the same fears and myths, but they are completely untrue and ought to be ignored.

SEXUAL FANTASIES

Most people have fantasies – or daydreams – at some time. Some might imagine that they are great athletes or singers or dream about what they will achieve. No one will ever know these thoughts, unless the person having them, reveals them. Sexual fantasies are the same. It is normal to have sexual fantasies during masturbation or at any other time. Some people worry because they fantasize about things they would never do in real life: some might imagine that they are having sex in public or with someone unexpected, or watching others have sex. How one thinks during sexual activity is a private, personal matter.

QUESTIONS AND ANSWERS

I'm in a football team. We've been told not to masturbate for 24 hours before games because it'll spoil our performance. Is this true?
Jon, 15 years

No. This is one of many masturbation myths. People once thought that masturbation would weaken your body, and, although totally false, the story lives on. What you do with your body is your own business and nobody else's.

Do older people still masturbate if they're married or living together?
Terri, 15 years

Many people do. They may do it on their own, or with – or to – their partner.

If I don't have sex or anything, will all the sperm build up in my balls and make them burst?
Leroy, 14 years

No: unused sperm are stored for a while until they get old, and then they are reabsorbed into your body and replaced.

I heard that masturbation changes how the vulva looks. Will my doctor be able to tell that I do it?
Thea, 17 years

No. Masturbation does not change your genitals, so nobody can tell. But don't worry if you ever need to tell your doctor that you masturbate (if you have some sexual problem, for instance): they know that it is normal.

RELATIONSHIPS AND EMOTIONS

Changing feelings   Friends
Social life   Looking at others
Starting a relationship
Sexual preference   Emotional decisions

Changing feelings

In adolescence, feelings are often changing as fast as the body. The young person feels things more deeply and becomes more emotional. This is a time when a person may be happy one day, miserable or irritable the next. This is a tumultuous time and an exciting one.

FEELING SELF-CONSCIOUS

The body is changing so rapidly that it may seem that everything – hair, shape, and skin – is wrong. It is common for a young person to feel awkward and self-conscious, or worried about being attractive. Remember, everyone has their good points physically, whether a smile, freckles, shining eyes, or dimples in their cheeks. And we all know that it isn't just looks that makes people attractive; a sense of humor and friendliness, for example, are just as important.

CHANGING RELATIONSHIPS WITH FRIENDS

Relationships become more intense during adolescence. Friends in general become more important: friendships made in adolescence last longer than those made during childhood, and when a friendship does break up, as it probably will, it can be especially painful.

Some will develop a close, best friend now, or a group of friends they see all the time. It often feels more comfortable to form friendships as part of a group at first; a one-to-one relationship can then develop naturally.

INDEPENDENCE AND CONFLICT

Adolescents' relationships with their families will probably change dramatically during these years. Teens may find there are some topics they don't want to discuss with their parents or siblings – not because they are doing anything wrong, but simply because they are trying to develop their own independence. Often these feelings of independence lead to conflict.

Some may feel that their parents expect too much of them, or that they want them just like they are. Those who have been brought up with certain beliefs and attitudes may begin to question them and be interested in finding out about others. This can lead to conflict in families. It is not always easy for parents to accept their children's different views and attitudes. It is important to discuss such issues openly with parents as well as friends to avoid unnecessary, possibly painful, conflicts.

When I look at myself in the mirror, I hate myself. I'm too fat and my hair is all wrong. When I go out, I feel like everyone is looking at me.

Marisa, 16 years

UNDERSTANDING PARENTS' FEELINGS

Sex is often an uncomfortable subject between parents and children. Some parents find it difficult to accept that their child is growing up sexually. No matter what their own experience was when they were teens, they will probably feel differently when it comes to their child. Some teens find that their parents read sex and danger into every situation, or refuse to accept their child's sexuality, or change the subject whenever sex is mentioned. Some teens might find themselves educating their parents; there are free pamphlets available from various agencies and counseling centers that give advice to children and parents.

It's natural for a loving parent to worry, especially when their child starts to go out on his or her own. Discussing concerns openly and trying to see things from a parent's point of view can help keep the lines of communication open.

SEXUAL THOUGHTS AND FEELINGS

Sometimes sexual feelings may be so strong that they make it hard to think about anything else. These feelings need someone to focus on, and this can be almost anyone. It is very common for an adolescent to have a crush on a teacher or an unattainable rock star, even though realistically there is no hope of forming a real relationship. However strong such feelings are, that is all they are. They don't necessarily mean that one is emotionally ready to start a sexual relationship yet. Learning not to respond to every physical urge is just as important a part of growing up as learning how to save money or eating a well-balanced diet and not just sweets.

> *I know I ought not to worry and nag, but unless she's okay, I worry and I can't sleep. Now she telephones if she is coming home late, and then I can relax.*
>
> Derek, father

QUESTIONS AND ANSWERS

I'm writing to this girl I met on vacation. My parents are always asking me about her. They seem to think they have a right to know everything. Do they?
Mike, 15 years

It sounds as though your parents can't accept that your emotional life is private, perhaps because they are afraid you may be hurt and they want to protect you. However, your feelings are your own and very personal – you do not have to share them with anyone else unless you want to. Let your parents know gently that you want some privacy.

Sometimes I feel like bursting into tears – for no reason at all, really. My mother always says I'm just in one of my moods and tells me to snap out of it. But how am I supposed to do that?
Sarah, 14 years

You can't snap out of it just like that. But you will feel better if you tell someone how you feel: talking to a friend may help you see things differently. Activity helps these moods too, the more physical the better. Remember that when you are feeling low, everything looks bleak, and that this is just a passing mood.

Friends

Childhood friendships don't always last. It's during junior high and high school that many friendships that will last throughout life will be made. Friendships made during adolescence can include peers as well as teachers or other older role models.

My best friend and I always talk for hours every day, and we talk about everything. If anything's wrong, we can always cheer each other up.

Amy, 12 years

BEATING SHYNESS

It's hard to stop being shy, but you can learn to act as if you're not.

Practice playing the part of a nonshy person: it will eventually become natural.

Look at the person you are talking to. If you look past them or down at your feet, you will look bored.

Try to forget about yourself. Concentrate on other people and what's going on around you.

Pretend that the other person is shy, and try to put them at their ease.

If you get tongue-tied, at least ask a question or make a comment, even if "great" is all you say.

BEING A GOOD FRIEND

Being part of a group of friends gives one a sense of belonging as well as self-confidence. If your friends like you, you feel good about yourself. This can work both ways: if you feel good about yourself, people will be comfortable with you. Those who are unkind, too critical, or talk only about themselves won't be much in demand as friends.

Friends will probably come from among classmates at school, or be people with similar interests, or neighbors. The most popular people don't necessarily make the best friends. People who seem different from you in some way may pleasantly surprise you once you get to know one another.

A good friend is often the person with whom you share all the ups and downs of becoming an adult, exchanging the secrets you wouldn't dream of discussing with your parents.

RESISTING PRESSURE FROM FRIENDS

Most young people want to be like their friends, dress like them, look like them, go where they go, and do what they do. Most of all, they value the opinion of their friends, and being part of a group and all the strengths and security it offers. Sometimes it can be hard to resist when your friends try to persuade you to do something you don't feel like doing, such as smoking, drinking, trying drugs, or skipping school. Experimentation is part of growing up, but it's up to you to decide when and if you want to experiment. You may also be under pressure to have sex before you feel ready for it.

Whenever you are under this kind of pressure, the most important thing to remember is that you don't have to lose good friends over it. Friends who drop you if you don't do everything they do are not worth having in the long run: good friends will respect you if you are your own person, and not just a mirror of them. This can take real courage, though, because it isn't comfortable to be left out. You don't have to be critical, you can just say "That doesn't feel right for me." The more sure of yourself you sound, the less pressure there is likely to be.

STARTING TO DATE

Most of your closest friends will probably be of your own sex.
You might be interested in the opposite sex, think about them,
and talk about them with your friends, but you may not feel
quite as comfortable with them as you do with your own sex.

Going around in a mixed group of friends is often the
easiest way to get to know one another. Couples may pair off
within the group, but you might find yourself dating just to
prove that you can, rather than because you really enjoy
someone's company. These first relationships may not last very
long, but they do help you experience closer relationships
based on sexual attraction. By the time you're 17 or 18, you
may be much better able to make more serious relationships.

FEELING LEFT OUT

Making and keeping friends is not always easy. You may feel
as if you are the odd one out, that everyone else is having a
great time, and that you are the only one who is feeling
insecure and shy. But these are very common feelings, shared
by even apparently confident people.

If you find it hard to make friends, remember that they
don't just fall into your lap. Everyone has to work to make
friends, and if you always wait around for others to make the
first move, you may have to wait a long time. You could also
choose a more active route – join a youth club, take up a
hobby, or go out for a sport at school.

*There's a boy in our
class who has a really rough
time because his mother
buys him these awful
clothes. I feel sorry for him,
but I'm afraid that if I
talk to him, I'll get picked
on too.*

Kevin, 13 years

FRIENDSHIP
Shared interests provide
the basis for friendship –
these might include an
interest in music, movies,
fashion, art, or sports.

Social life

It is natural as you grow up that you'll want to spend more time with your own friends. Going places and doing things with friends who are interested in the same sorts of things is the start of an exciting new phase and time of discovery in your social life.

FREEDOM TO BE YOURSELF

Sometimes you may feel that you are quite a different person with your friends than you are at home. Parents may have a strong idea what their child is like and find it difficult to accept their child's increasing sense of self-sufficiency and desire for independence. Your friends, like you, are also growing, changing, and experimenting and so it is natural to feel more comfortable with them. Sometimes this can cause friction at home because your parents may not approve of the way they see you are changing.

PARENTS AND FRIENDS

If your parents dislike or disapprove of your friends, it is probably because they don't know them. They may have formed an impression based solely on the way your friends look or dress. It may help if you use your home as a base for your social life for a while; when your parents get to know your friends better they may understand why you like them. If they refuse to accept these friendships, and you truly value your friends, you are left with the difficult choice of giving up your friends, or confronting your parents and asking them to trust you.

SMOKING AND DRINKING

Alcohol, cigarettes, and drugs are substances teens are inevitably exposed to, and are all dangerous when abused. Alcohol and drugs both lower inhibitions and can lead people to behave less cautiously than

All my friends smoke, but I just coughed and felt horrible. It's too expensive anyway.
Clare, 16 years

YOUR CLOSEST FRIENDS
As adolescence progresses, groups of boys and girls mix more, even though your closest friends may still be your own sex.

usual or than they would choose to, if not under their influence. Many unprotected sexual experiences as well as traffic accidents happen as the result of being temporarily out of control.

The dangers of alcohol abuse as well as drug abuse among teens should not be underestimated. Teens are by nature risk takers, but it is important that they learn what their own bodies can safely tolerate and that they learn to set limits. Girls in particular need to know that in general their tolerance level for alcohol is lower than that of boys. Many boys and girls have, when drunk, done things sexually that they have later regretted.

Tobacco is another drug that carries significant health risks. Although it may seem like fun to experiment with smoking cigarettes, their connection to lung cancer and other health problems has been clearly established. Being fully informed about any substance one wants to try is always a good idea, and may help a young person decide what to try and how much.

My parents are so concerned about the furniture, I couldn't ask my friends home. Something would get broken. It's better to hang out at the mall or in the park.
Josh, 17 years

QUESTIONS AND ANSWERS

Why is it that I only have two or three drinks and I start feeling drunk very quickly?
Naomi, 16 years

Girls shouldn't try to keep pace with boys. With the same amount of alcohol in the bloodstream, girls become drunk much more quickly because their bodies contain less water than boy's. Have a meal or snack before you drink. You get drunk more quickly if your stomach is empty. Have some water or soft drinks first to quench your thirst. Learn to say no and switch to soft drinks when you've had enough. This way you will avoid doing something you will later regret.

What is sensible drinking?
Oliver, 17 years

It is sensible to limit your alcohol intake to two drinks on the weekend. Drinking beer or alcohol daily can be a sign of dependence. Binge drinking is especially dangerous, and can be fatal. Don't take lifts from anyone you know who has been drinking, and never drive yourself if you have been drinking.

Why is my boyfriend so aggressive when he drinks?
Anna, 16 years

Alcohol changes behavior. Often people don't realize how much until friends tell them the next day what they did while they were drunk. Tell your boyfriend that you don't like the side of his character that shows itself when he drinks too much.

It's really hard to avoid drugs at the parties I go to. What should I do about this?
Emily, 16 years

You should never be afraid to say no if you don't want to use drugs. If some of your friends are experimenting with drugs, you may be tempted to experiment yourself. You have to make up your mind if the risks are worth taking. If you do experiment, find out all you can about the drug first so that you know what the dangers are. Ecstasy, for example, can cause dangerous dehydration and other serious problems. Never experiment on your own; make sure you are with people you know and trust.

I got pregnant because I was drunk, and I didn't even ask if he used a condom. I really don't remember much.
Annette, 16 years

Looking at others

Everyone has expectations of themselves and of others, and these may not always be realistic or fair. Sometimes they are based on stereotypes that can affect the way we see the world. Real people, however, don't conform to such patterns.

WHAT IS A STEREOTYPE?

Stereotypes are generalizations about groups of people — perhaps a social class or ethnic group — and they are often the root cause of prejudice. Stereotypes are inaccurate and unfair. They encourage you to think of someone as a type because of their gender or color or appearance, for example, rather than as an individual.

REJECTING SOME OLD IDEAS

In the last 30 years social attitudes have changed in many ways. These changes have made it easier for both men and women to break out of many of their traditional roles if they want to — girls become doctors, women have successful careers, boys experiment with clothes and take on more domestic roles.

Old rules about sexual relationships need not apply today. There's no good reason, for example, why a girl shouldn't ask

The first thing dad said when I told him I didn't want to play football was "That's ridiculous, I was a great athlete and so are you." He just couldn't believe I wanted to study art.

Mark, 18 years

HAPPY FAMILIES

Today in the United States, two out of every three marriages end in divorce. Living with a stepparent or relating to divorced parents creates added pressures for an adolecsent. However, chances are there are many others who share your concerns and who can help you realize your family is actually normal by today's standards.

QUESTIONS AND ANSWERS

My parents have told me that they are separating and probably getting a divorce. What can I do?
Katrina, 14 years

If your parents are divorcing, try to understand that they have decided to be honest by separating instead of staying together and being unhappy. If the atmosphere at home has been very bad, the divorce may even be a relief to you. But if they are so preoccupied with their problems that they are unaware of your anxieties and possible guilt feelings, talk to your brothers and sisters or a close friend. You can give real comfort to each other in this difficult situation. If you are really distressed and have no one to turn to, there are telephone helplines with counselors who can give you advice (*see pages 92-93*).

My friend picks on me about not having a dad. I want to tell him to shut up. What should I say?
David, 15 years

The two-parent, married, heterosexual couple is widely regarded as "normal," although it is far from being the only model. Being a good parent need not have anything to do with being married or single, or straight or gay. Conventional married couples don't necessarily make good parents — successful parenting depends on the ability of the people involved to have a loving and caring relationship with their children. Tell your friend you feel happy with your parent, and that he should stop looking at people as stereotypes but as individuals. Perhaps he isn't such a good friend!

a boy out. The best relationships are based on honesty and equality and have no set roles. Sometimes one of you will want to be cuddled and cared for, sometimes the other; sometimes one person will have definite ideas about where to go or what to do. You don't have to fit in with someone else's idea of how you ought to behave.

TREATING GIRLS DIFFERENTLY

There is one persistent stereotype that doesn't seem to go away. A boy who boasts about his sexual exploits and has many different sexual partners is regarded as a real man, while a girl who sleeps with a number of different boys is sometimes branded as loose and easy. The message is that girls shouldn't have any sexual desires, or that they shouldn't do anything about them. This is unequal treatment and untrue. Both boys and girls have sexual desires – the real issue for both is learning when and when not to respond to those desires, and how to act intelligently and with caution to avoid doing something they may later regret.

" I'm much better at math and science than most of the boys in our class, but I feel I have to keep quiet. "

Sue, 14 years

ENRICHING EXPERIENCE
If you live in a multicultural area, you will probably mix with people whose backgrounds are very different from your own.

Starting a relationship

People may know instinctively that they want to get to know someone better. Making the first move is a gamble because there is the chance of being turned down. But, without trying, nothing can happen, so why not try?

I knew he liked me, but he just wouldn't say anything. So I went and sat beside him at lunch and got talking, and after that everything was fine.

Jenny, 15 years

THE PERFECT PARTNER

Most people think they have some idea of their ideal type. Quite often, however, they find themselves falling for someone totally different, who they were not initially attracted to at all. Friendship, good conversation, a sense of humor, liking the same music, or an interest in sports could all be the basis of an attraction to a particular person.

SHOWING AND EXPRESSING FEELINGS

You can show that you like someone by seeking out their company, looking into their eyes a bit more than usual when you talk, or touching them casually – a hand on their arm to attract their attention, for example. If someone shows this kind of interest in you, it's up to you how you respond. If you feel the same, you can smile back, hold their gaze, and not move away. If you want to discourage their advances, you can be a bit aloof without being rude, giving them a cue to back off.

Body language works, up to a point, but it is more honest to say what you feel. Once you are over the "getting-to-know-you" stage, misunderstandings can be avoided if you can tell each other, as well as show each other, how you feel.

ATTRACTION

It's no accident that lovers tend to gaze into one another's eyes. The pupil in the eye widens when we look at something that interests or attracts us. Most of us agree on what makes a "beautiful" face, but differ on what we find sexually attractive. Statistically, physical appearance matters more to men, while women are usually attracted by a man's intelligence and sense of humor rather than by his looks.

Pupils narrow

Pupils widen

Of course, you probably won't like everyone who likes you, so you may have to tell someone you're not interested. If someone you aren't really interested in approaches you, remember that it took courage for them to ask you out. It is kinder to be polite if you're not interested than cruelly to reject someone.

COMING ON STRONG

Trying to get too close to someone too soon is usually a big mistake. You can't force someone to like you. Look for cues that you are moving too fast, and slow down. If you draw attention to yourself, tell too many jokes, or praise people profusely because you want them to like you, you will start to look desperate and drive the person away.

At the start of a relationship, it is often hard not to try to take over the other person completely. But relationships need time to grow. Resist the temptation to demand that your boy or girlfriend be with you all the time.

THREE'S A CROWD

It can happen to anyone: you like someone a friend of yours is going out with. What should you do? You could show that you're interested, but the chances are that you will lose your friend this way. You could also ask your friend how serious the relationship is. You have to decide which means most to you – your friendship or a possible future relationship. It can be just as difficult to find that you are interested in a friend of the person you're going out with. Think carefully before you make any advance. Of the three of you, at least one will get hurt, and it could be you.

GOOD RELATIONSHIPS

Falling in love can be thrilling. Your heart pounds, and there are butterflies in your stomach, and you'll long to be together every moment and think about each other compulsively. A good relationship is one that increases the self-esteem and personal happiness of both people involved. It is also one that is based on mutual respect, good communication, and trust. Being good friends is vital in a relationship.

A couple may enjoy going out and socializing with others; or may just be happy being alone together. Being in a relationship gives one the opportunity to listen to someone else's views intently and to learn to resolve differences. It is not always easy to tell the short-term infatuation from the relationship that will last. Everyone is bound to make a few mistakes as they are growing up. Most, in fact, look back later and wonder what they ever saw in that person who once seemed to be the most important person in their life.

I didn't ask this girl out for ages – I was afraid she'd turn me down or laugh. She said yes, though, and she said she'd been waiting for me to say something. I had no idea!
Keith, 15 years

I went out with this girl for a few weeks, thinking this is it! Then suddenly I realized I didn't want to see her any more – she looks fantastic, but she's a bit boring when you get to know her.
Sean, 16 years

Sexual preference

Part of growing up is discovering what your main sexual preferences are. It is very common for teens to be confused about the range of strong sexual feelings they experience. Many worry if they find themselves attracted to their own sex or to both sexes.

EXPRESSING YOUR SEXUALITY

By a very early age our gender identity as a boy or girl is established. What happens later in life in terms of how we experience our sexuality – how we think, feel, and act as a male or female – involves value judgments and choice. Few people go through life without ever having felt attracted to someone of their own sex. Teenagers often have passionate sexual feelings for a friend or a teacher. Girls are just as likely as boys to have homosexual feelings. But feelings and fantasies are not necessarily an indication of what will ultimately be one's sexual preference. For many, this is a practice stage of sexual development, while some will continue to be attracted by their own sex at some times in their lives, and by the opposite sex at others. As one grows to adulthood, it is usual for a steady preference for one sex or the other to emerge, although there are people who will be bisexual.

WHAT CAUSES THESE FEELINGS?

Nobody knows exactly why some people are attracted to their own sex and others to the opposite sex. Some believe sexual preference is learned behavior, while others believe heredity, environment and upbringing play a part. During adolescence, when so much is changing, a passing homosexual infatuation does not mean one will as an adult have a preference for same-sex relationships. It is wise not to overreact to early fleeting stirrings of homosexual attraction.

COMING TO TERMS WITH HOMOSEXUALITY

Because society treats heterosexuality as the norm, young people who experience homosexual feelings regularly may be uncomfortable in talking about them. There is no denying that there is prejudice against homosexuals. Those who are attracted to their own sex will be tempted to keep quiet about it when they hear their classmates use "gay" as a term of abuse. An older teenager who has experienced homosexual feelings for

I think my parents hoped they could cure me of being gay, and that it was all just in my imagination.

Mark, 18 years

FINDING OUT
Once you've accepted your own feelings, you'll discover that there are plenty of other people who feel like you do.

years and who has identified himself or herself as a homosexual will inevitably encounter problems created by other people's prejudice and intolerance. Knowing this, some gay and lesbian people choose to try to ignore their feelings or disguise their sexuality. This can cause a great deal of unhappiness. Those who are sure of their feelings may feel more comfortable telling the truth to those who matter most to them. A consolation is that society in general is becoming more accepting of homosexuality.

INFORMING PARENTS

One hard decision to make for anyone who knows they are gay or lesbian is whether to tell their parents. Understandably, unsuspecting parents may be upset at first and will almost certainly need time to get used to the idea. Many people think that there is only one way to live and be happy and that is their way. Some parents may have strong religious convictions, and some may think that unless their child has a conventional marriage with children, they won't be happy. And whatever their own feelings, they know also that gays and lesbians are often treated unfairly. They'll also be worried about AIDS.

However, the advantages of telling one's parents and not having to keep a very important part of one's life secret are enormous. It is quite possible that some parents may have guessed, anyway. Loving parents can eventually accept that their child is gay or lesbian.

Some will want a trial run before they tell their parents. A close family friend might be a good person to tell first. They can act as a support when broaching the subject with parents. A close friend who can be trusted and who will listen and be sympathetic is also a vital source of support. Teens can also seek a counselor or trusted teacher or seek out a gay and lesbian organization (*see pages 92-93*) for peer group counseling.

BEING TOGETHER
A loving relationship with someone they care about is what most people want, whether they are gay, lesbian, or straight.

When I called the hotline I realized that she was the first lesbian person I had knowingly talked to. It was comforting.

Sue, 16 years

QUESTIONS AND ANSWERS

What is it that gay and lesbian people do?
Sean, 16 years

Gay and lesbians lead normal lives in which they experience the same sexual and emotional feelings as heterosexuals. They want to be near one another, kiss, and make love like heterosexual people. They can show their sexual feelings through sexual activity and loving and caring companionship.

I usually dream about boys, but last night I dreamt I was kissing my girlfriend. Am I a lesbian?
Jane, 15 years

Everyone fantasizes and dreams about sex. Your dream shows that you love your friend, but it does not mean that you are a lesbian. Such dreams are completely normal.

THE LAW

Every state has laws about sexual intercourse. Because the law in many states makes it illegal for a girl under 16 to have intercourse, 16 has been called "the age of consent." For boys there is no legal age of consent for heterosexual sex, but there are laws about homosexual activity - some states have laws making certain homosexual acts illegal for anyone.

Emotional decisions

Being in love is wonderful. It brings with it many confused emotions and exciting sensations, like having chills run up your spine when you hear that special person's voice on the phone. It takes time to learn how to handle the extreme feelings of the teenage years.

MAKING IT WORK

In the first flush of love, you may think your partner is perfect, but after this infatuation passes, you begin to see each other as real people. If there's nothing much between you but sexual attraction, you may soon become bored and easily irritated with one another. Infatuation and a lasting relationship are not the same thing.

Learning how to handle a relationship takes work, and this is one reason why first relationships might be brief. This can be shattering, and rejection can be painful. But you do learn more with each relationship. What you get from a relationship is, more or less, what you put into it.

THINKING OF OTHERS

When you are in a relationship, you'll find yourself thinking about your partner a lot of the time. If their attitude toward you seems to change, don't take this too personally. Your partner may have moods that have nothing to do with you, so ask them what's wrong, instead of becoming offended and sulking. Learning to communicate in a relationship is very important. This means being able to express what you want, as well as finding out about your partner's needs.

BEING OUT OF STEP

Boys and girls tend to be out of step with one another in their teens. Emotionally, girls usually grow up more quickly than boys; a boy of 15 can seem very childish to a girl of the same age. As a result, some girls are likely to be interested in more mature boys. Because of this, girls often come under pressure to have sex earlier than they might want to, especially if they go out with older boys or men.

HOW FAR SHOULD YOU GO?

Movies, magazines, and books often seem to suggest that there's only one road for a relationship to go down, and it ends in bed. This is not the case in real life. Each person is an individual and each must decide how far to go and when to

We really love each other, but I feel I've met the right person at the wrong time. I wish I could just put the whole thing on ice for five years.

Anna, 16 years

HOW TO SAY NO

Saying no when you are confronted with a difficult social or sexual situation takes practice.

Body language gives the other person the hint quite quickly. Straighten up and move back, keeping some distance between you so that you can get your thoughts clear.

Practice saying no in situations where it is justified – if your little brother or sister is being unreasonably demanding, or if someone wants to borrow a pen that you need, too.

Don't give in to bullying by being made to feel different. Recognize that coercion can be subtle. For example, someone might say: "If you don't have sex, you'll be the only virgin in your group."

stop. Some may not want a sexual relationship yet, or not with this person. Some have strong religious, cultural, and personal views about sex outside marriage and should not be afraid to uphold their views. And, in this time, when it is easy to contract a sexually transmitted disease, many teens are choosing to take it very slow. No one ever died from not having sex.

You'll meet plenty of people whom you like, even love, but want nothing more than a kiss or a hug from, and who may feel the same about you. It is possible to have a loving and caring relationship without sex. The most important thing is to make clear what *you* want, and to make your own choices, especially if you think that the other person might have something else in mind. If you don't know what you want, say so and be assertive. You have a right to make up your own mind without being pressured. No one should force you into having full penetrative sex that you don't want or don't feel ready for.

THE RIGHT TIME AND THE RIGHT PERSON

When you have reached the age of consent – and this differs from state to state and country to country – you can have sexual intercourse legally. This doesn't mean it's compulsory, and it is usually too early for most people. While a 16-year-old, for example, is physically old enough to have sexual intercourse and to have a baby, few 16-year-olds are emotionally mature enough to deal with the commitments and responsibilities involved in a lasting sexual relationship.

There are no prizes for starting early; this is one of the hardest areas to be truthful about when your friends start and you don't want to be left out. Don't always believe what you hear – statistics show that by the age of 17 just under half of all boys and about a third of girls will have had sexual intercourse – so someone isn't telling the truth if you hear "Everybody but you is having sex." If you have doubts, or feel you need more advice and guidance (*see pages 92-93*), then you are probably not ready to have sex just yet. Being pressured to have sex can make it difficult to reach your own decision.

BREAKING UP

Breaking up can be much worse if you don't know why it happens. If the person you want to be with won't answer the phone or letters, you may know that it is over, but if they don't talk to you, you might just keep hoping. It is always kinder to be honest and tell someone when a relationship is over.

WHEN TO SAY NO

If you are thinking of having sex for any of the following reasons, it is better to say no.

To prove you love someone or as proof of their love.

To prove you can (everyone can!)

To satisfy your curiosity.

Because you're afraid that you will lose your boyfriend or girlfriend if you don't.

Because you've been talked into it.

Because you are drunk or high on drugs.

Because the other person expects it.

Mom started telling me to go on the pill when she saw I was getting serious with Tony. I know she meant well, but I can make up my own mind about when I want to sleep with someone.
Jill, 17 years

I thought I'd never get over it. Then my friend persuaded me to go out with her, and I met Alan. We are so happy together! I never thought I'd feel like this again.

Melanie, 16 years

Anyone determined to have sex should make sure it is planned and protected (*see page 54*). Statistics show that early sexual experiences are often spontaneous and as a result unprotected. One's first sexual experience can be fantastic or a real disappointment – even if it is with the right person at the right time and in the right place. This first experience is seen as a rite of passage, and an important point in one's life – don't waste it with the wrong person at the wrong time.

WHEN FEELINGS CHANGE

Relationships don't stand still. One person might want to get more serious, while the other still wants to see other people. Part of maturing is learning what to do as a relationship evolves. Some might find it possible to negotiate a way to go on with a relationship like this, while others might find it too painful.

It hurts to discover that the other person doesn't feel as deeply as you do, and it can be just as hard to find that you don't love someone as much as you hoped you might. It takes courage to end things when you still care for the other person, but it might be necessary. Having sex within this relationship won't save it either, nor will it stop your partner from moving on.

LETTING SOMEONE DOWN GENTLY

It's always painful for both people involved when a relationship breaks up. Teenagers often believe that they'll never be happy again, but with time, feelings change. Talking with friends can help. A definite good-bye may hurt, but everything will be easier once a person accepts that the relationship is over. Then it is possible to go forward, stronger and wiser for the experience.

THE AGE OF CONSENT

State laws regarding sexual intercourse vary. Because the law in many states makes it illegal for a girl under 16 to have intercourse, 16 has been called the "age of consent." For boys, there is no legal age of consent for heterosexual sex, but there are laws about homosexual activity (*see. page 41*).

QUESTIONS AND ANSWERS

My friends all keep telling me to keep away from this girl I like at school, because she treated her last boyfriend really badly. But can't things be different for us?
Martin, 16 years

Seeing how people have behaved in other relationships is a clue to their behavior but it doesn't tell the whole story. Perhaps you are hearing a biased account and the truth is very different. Hurt pride can cause people to be spiteful and tell lies. Spend some time getting to know the girl and find out for yourself what she is like.

My boyfriend and I have been together for six months and we get along really well together, but we don't have a lot in common. Does this matter?
Kristy, 16 years

You don't have to call the whole thing off because you don't share a passion for all the same things. Similar personalities, backgrounds, or interests are all pluses in any relationship, but although they help, they aren't essential. As long as you enjoy each other's company, there isn't a problem; it is probably the differences that attract you to one another.

WHAT HAPPENS DURING SEX

Sexual intercourse

The first time

Enjoying sex

Dealing with difficulties

Sexual intercourse

Sexual intercourse, or making love, is an intimate form of contact between two people. Its biological function is to enable a woman to become pregnant, but when couples have sex they mostly do so simply because they enjoy it.

FOREPLAY AND AROUSAL

A couple arouse one another by holding, caressing, and kissing: this is called foreplay. They can stroke or kiss the sensitive areas of one another's bodies – the stomach, inner thighs, buttocks, nipples, and around the highly sensitive genitals. The smell and taste of a partner's skin and genitals enhance sexual excitement.

During foreplay, the body's senses are stimulated, sending messages to the brain, which, in turn, sends messages to the genitals and other parts of the body, preparing them for sex and increasing excitement. Many men and some women can be sexually aroused by the sight of their partner's body and the thought of sex.

WHAT HAPPENS WHEN SOMEONE IS AROUSED

When people are aroused, their heart and breathing rates increase, and their bodies feel super-sensitive. Both sexes also experience changes in their genitals. Arousal increases blood flow into the penis, causing it to extend, darken, and become erect. As the man becomes more excited, his penis reaches its

We spend more time on foreplay before sex than we used to, and we both have better orgasms – they're more intense.

Nick, 18 years

I get really hot during sex, and my heart pounds. It's better exercise than working out!

Leonie, 17 years

QUESTIONS AND ANSWERS

My boyfriend says if I don't have sex with him it means I don't love him. But I don't feel ready, what can I do?
Zoë, 16 years

Follow your instincts. When you are ready, you will know. If he respects you, he will stop asking.

How long should you spend on foreplay before having sex?
Barry, 17 years

Foreplay should be long enough for both partners to become excited enough to enjoy intercourse. Men

sometimes forget that women can take longer to become aroused than men.

A friend told me sex isn't complete without intercourse. But can't you have orgasms in other ways?
Darryl, 17 years

Sex needn't mean intercourse. Some couples regularly have sex without intercourse *(see page 58)*, arousing each other in other ways, and the orgasms they have are just as satisfying. This is also a way of practicing safer sex.

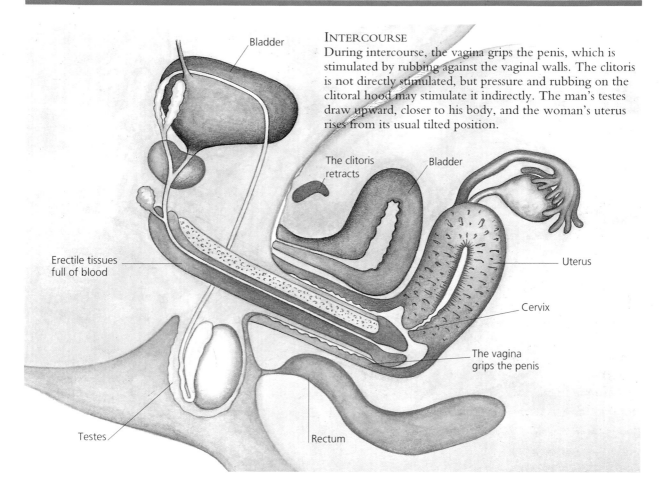

Bladder

INTERCOURSE

During intercourse, the vagina grips the penis, which is stimulated by rubbing against the vaginal walls. The clitoris is not directly stimulated, but pressure and rubbing on the clitoral hood may stimulate it indirectly. The man's testes draw upward, closer to his body, and the woman's uterus rises from its usual tilted position.

The clitoris retracts

Bladder

Erectile tissues full of blood

Uterus

Cervix

The vagina grips the penis

Testes

Rectum

maximum length and thickness. When a woman is aroused, the blood flow to her vulva and vagina increases. Her vagina becomes lubricated with mucus and its inner part expands. Her clitoris and her nipples become erect and more sensitive. As she grows more excited, her clitoris retracts, and her vaginal lips become bigger and darker.

INTERCOURSE AND ORGASM

When both partners are aroused, they may both feel ready for penetration (when the man's penis enters the vagina), though there are other ways of reaching orgasm (*see page 51*) without penetration. Orgasm is experienced by both sexes as a series of deep and pleasurable waves that spread throughout the whole body. Men and women don't necessarily reach orgasm in the same way and at the same time. The man often experiences orgasm as he ejaculates. A woman may not have an orgasm unless the clitoris is directly stimulated. Girls don't always find early experiences of sex orgasmic for this reason. Gradually man and women learn what gives them pleasure so they can let their partner know what they want. After ejaculation, the penis becomes limp and the man's excitement disappears. The woman's body returns to normal more gradually.

When my boyfriend comes, he sort of stops breathing for a few seconds and then makes this strangled sound and starts gasping like he's just run the marathon. I thought there was something seriously wrong with him at first.

Julia, 18 years

The first time

Most people never forget the first time they had intercourse, whether it was better than they expected, a disaster, or somewhere in between. It's impossible to get everything perfect the first time, but it helps if both partners are prepared and understand each other's needs.

THINKING AHEAD

The thought of having intercourse for the first time can be both exciting and frightening. Both of these emotions can make it difficult to relax, and can cause problems.

It is very important for anyone about to have sex to discuss contraception before they get carried away. Both girls and boys must take responsibility to avoid unwanted pregnancy and sexually transmitted disease. Alarmingly, statistics show that many couples don't use contraception or protection against infection the first time. However, there is *always* a risk of pregnancy and infection. Contraceptives are usually available free from a clinic and in some schools, and male condoms can be bought at a drugstore or supermarket.

Having to rush and worrying about privacy are common reasons for nervousness. For the first time, it helps to be somewhere comfortable and not in the back of a car. If your first experience is unplanned and unpleasant, forget it. Look forward to a "first time" having sex when conditions are right.

EXPECTATIONS AND REALITY

Most people want to "get it right," but what they think is right is likely to be based on films or books, and is probably not realistic. One of you might have had experience with another partner, or it may be the first time either person has seen another naked or touched anyone sexually. If the relationship is based on trust and respect and not just physical attraction, it can be wonderful. If it doesn't turn out as exciting as expected, don't worry – no one was ever an expert at anything at the first attempt.

THE IMPORTANCE OF AROUSAL

Men can be aroused just by thinking of sex or seeing their partner's body. A man may be so excited that he ejaculates before intercourse. A nervous man may find it difficult to get an erection. Kissing and caressing together should solve this.

Women generally take longer to become aroused to the point where the vagina opens up and produces lubricating

When we had sex the first time, I didn't enjoy the actual sex that much. What I did like was cuddling up to my boyfriend all night.

Josie, 17 years

IS IT EVER SAFE?

If you are not using any contraception, you can get pregnant even if:
- It is your first time.
- You made love standing up.
- Your monthly period has just finished.
- You wash out your vagina afterward.
- Your partner withdraws before ejaculation.
- You haven't had your first period.
- Your partner puts a condom on just before penetration (there may be some leakage of sperm beforehand).

fluid. The vagina may be closed or dry if a woman is nervous or not aroused. If the man is patient and asks what she likes, and if she can show or tell him, these problems can be avoided. If sex is painful, this is possibly because the vagina is not sufficiently lubricated. If extra lubrication is needed, special gels and lubricants are available at a drugstore. Be informed about what products are best: petroleum-based lubricants will destroy a male condom, for instance. Once a couple feel more confident, lubricant will not be needed.

BEING COMFORTABLE

Some girls feel pain the first time because their hymen is intact *(see page 15)*, and hurts when it is broken by intercourse. There may even be slight bleeding. It was once believed that a broken hymen meant a girl was not a virgin, but often the opening is either quite large or has been stretched in strenuous sports or by tampons. Others feel pain because they find it hard to relax the vaginal muscles – they need time to relax and feel comfortable.

The first time a couple has sex is often not spectacular; it takes time to get to know each other's bodies and to feel comfortable together. It should improve, but only if there is good communication and attention to each other's needs.

Men may thrust too deeply in the vagina; they should try to make sure that they are not hurting their partner. Most men will have an orgasm the first time they have intercourse, but most women will not. Like all things that need practice, sex usually gets better after the first time.

I decided to wait until I was 18 before I had sex for the first time; I didn't feel ready before then.

Peter, 18 years

When I tried putting the condom on I just came right away. But we tried again later, and it was fine: I think I was calmer.

Paul, 16 years

QUESTIONS AND ANSWERS

When you see sex in films, women always have orgasms, even the first time. When I had sex the first time, I was expecting fireworks, but nothing happened. Why not?
Terri, 16 years

Films are just unrealistic: most girls don't have an orgasm the first time that they have sex. It may take you time to learn how to respond to your boyfriend, and take him time to learn how to stimulate you to reach orgasm. Many girls and women do not have orgasms during intercourse at all unless they are very aroused, usually by having their clitoris stimulated at the same time. Sex improves with patience and practice.

I've just had sex with my girlfriend for the first time. I really wanted to look at her, but she said she felt too embarrassed. I don't get it – what's wrong with her?
Damon, 17 years

There is nothing wrong with her at all. Seeing your partner naked is very arousing for you, but some people are not used to being seen naked and feel embarrassed. She may be thinking of all the things she believes are wrong with her body. As time goes on, she will probably feel more relaxed and comfortable, and will start to enjoy you looking at, and being aroused by, her body – and looking at you.

Enjoying sex

Sexual enjoyment is all about giving and receiving pleasure, which means it is about communication. People reach orgasm in different ways, and to enjoy sex to the full, couples must tell one another what they like and – just as importantly – what they don't like.

REACHING ORGASM

Sometimes, a couple reach orgasm at the same time; more often, they don't. It doesn't really matter – whoever comes first can continue to stimulate the other to orgasm. Although orgasms are important to most people, they are not the only sexual sensation – there are plenty of others to enjoy.

VARIETY AND EXPERIMENTATION

Experimenting can be fun, provided that both partners are willing participants. Intercourse is not the only way of enjoying sex – foreplay, for example, can be continued until orgasm. This can be a choice for those who would rather postpone full penetrative sex. Other sexual activities can be as enjoyable as intercourse, and are safer, too, carrying little or no risk of pregnancy (*see page 70*) or of passing on infections (*see pages 80-83*).

TRYING DIFFERENT POSITIONS

Some couples always use the same position for sex; others vary their lovemaking. The many possible positions for intercourse can be divided into two primary groups: face to face and from

We both decided to try out some different positions. Once I fell off the bed, but otherwise it's been a good experience.

Charlie, 17 years

ANAL SEX

This is intercourse with the penis in the anus. Anal sex carries a high risk of infection including HIV if the sexual partner is infected (*see pages 84-85*), and a risk of other infections for women because the anus is full of bacteria that can be spread to the vagina by anal sex.

QUESTIONS AND ANSWERS

I have orgasms from masturbating or from oral sex, but never from intercourse. Will I ever be able to? Tanya, 17 years

Many men and women think that if a man just thrusts away inside a woman long enough she will reach orgasm, but women rarely have orgasms during intercourse unless their clitoris is also stimulated. Some spend more time on foreplay, so that the woman becomes more aroused, and some women rub their clitoris themselves during intercourse. But don't see orgasm as the only goal; there are other enjoyable things about sex.

My boyfriend wants to tie me up when we have sex. I don't really want him to. What should I do? Alex, 17 years

Sex is about doing what you *want* to do, and you should never be forced into doing anything that you don't want to. What your boyfriend wants to do is bondage, which some people – but not all – enjoy. Some enjoy the control of having sex with a person while they are in a submissive position. If you don't feel comfortable with this, and aren't prepared to be submissive, you don't have to do it: tell him firmly that you will not.

behind. In face-to-face positions, a couple can see, touch, and arouse one another. The most common position is with the man or woman on top; this is not necessarily the most satisfactory position for the woman because there is little clitoral stimulation. Other positions include side-by-side, seated, and standing. The chosen position is likely to be one that is comfortable for the individuals.

If the man enters the woman from behind, he can easily stimulate her breasts and clitoris. The most used position is often called the "doggie" position: the woman kneels on her hands and knees, and the man kneels behind her. Other positions include standing and side-by-side.

ORAL SEX

Oral sex means stimulating a partner's genitals with the lips and tongue. Couples may use oral sex as part of foreplay, or may continue to orgasm as an alternative to intercourse. Licking or kissing a woman's clitoris is called cunnilingus, while kissing and sucking a man's penis is known as fellatio. By being in control when stimulating the man, the woman can determine whether the man ejaculates in her mouth. Like all sexual contact, oral sex is more pleasant if the genitals are clean. Oral sex avoids the risks of pregnancy, but a genital infection or cold sores near the mouth can be transmitted during oral sex; there is also a risk of contracting HIV (*see page 84*).

Although I'm on the pill, I still get my boyfriend to wear a condom as well — for safer sex.
Cheryl, 17 years

POSITIONS FOR SEX

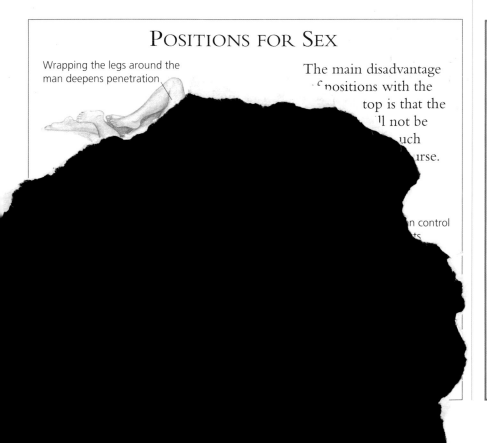

Wrapping the legs around the man deepens penetration

The main disadvantage ⸢ positions with the top is that the ⸢ll not be ⸢uch ⸢rse.

⸢ control

GUIDELINES FOR EXPERIMENTATION

If you want to experiment with your sex life, you must be able to trust each other and you must be very clear about what you want.

■ Never be pushed into doing anything that you really don't want to do.
■ Never try to persuade an unwilling partner into doing anything: it isn't fair.
■ Agree in advance exactly what you want to do.
■ If your partner wants you to stop at any point, do so. You must respect their feelings and wishes.
■ Don't do anything that could be harmful or might hurt either of you.
■ Don't do anything that makes you feel ashamed — it isn't right for you.

Dealing with difficulties

It is not unusual to have sexual difficulties, whatever your age or experience. Sex is a sharing experience, not a test of your abilities, and a couple who have a good relationship can overcome most problems by talking them over.

WHY PEOPLE HAVE PROBLEMS

Any problems you might have will probably be caused by poor communication or inexperience, and most vanish with experience and better communication. Perhaps you are not yet ready for a sexual relationship and for the emotional issues of loyalty and commitment it involves. Some difficulties can be the result of anxiety – especially about being a "good performer" – and disappear once a person can relax. Other problems may result from guilt feelings or past experiences. If you think this is likely, it might be best to see a counselor.

PREMATURE EJACULATION AND ERECTION PROBLEMS

Premature ejaculation means coming too early, even before the penis is in the vagina. If the problem persists, the man can learn control by masturbating and stopping just before orgasm. Failure to get or maintain an erection happens to most men at some time, usually because they are tired or anxious or have drunk too much alcohol. Extra stimulation can help, but it may be better to try again later. Worrying about erection problems only makes them worse. If the problems do persist, talk to a doctor in case there is a medical reason.

NOT HAVING

This is o
womer
for then
Tension
seldom

PA

v

pag

> *We'd had a great night and we were in bed but there was nothing happening – I'd had too much to drink. I was so embarrassed – she said I'd better cut down on beer in the future, or else!*
>
> Greg, 18 years

PREMATURE EJACULATION

This means coming before you want to and it is very common. It is often a shock and a disappointment to a man and his partner. It may happen the first few times you have sex, simply because you are experiencing the reality of sexual contact with another person. As you become used to being sexually excited by the sight and touch of your partner, you will gradually develop control of your ejaculation so that you can come when you want to. If you continue to come too quickly, don't feel a failure. If your partner is sympathetic, talk to her. Try different ways to make love that don't necessarily focus on you coming in her vagina.

CONTRACEPTION

Choosing contraceptives

Contraceptives are used to prevent unplanned pregnancy. They are easy to get, free in many cases, and advice is confidential. From the very first sexual experience, both a man and a woman need to take responsibility for contraception.

RISK OF PREGNANCY

About half of all couples don't use contraceptives the first time they have sex. Some continue not using them, perhaps because they don't know where to get advice or feel too embarrassed to ask. They may think that contraception is the other person's responsibility. Many probably believe that they can get away with it, and some may want a child (*see page 70*). Those who have intercourse without contraception are always taking a risk. Without contraception, the probability of pregnancy is high, because fertility is highest in early adulthood.

WHERE TO GET CONTRACEPTIVES

Everyone is entitled to free, confidential advice on contraception from doctors (*see right*), family planning clinics. and in most schools. Condoms can be bought in supermarkets as well as drugstores and clinics. It may seem that it is premeditated and unspontaneous behavior to think about contraception before becoming sexually active, and many parents may even feel that this will lead to experimentation – but it isn't necessarily so. You and you alone are responsible for your body and what happens to it. Knowing about contraception is part of being responsible and taking control of your life.

Those who do plan in advance can discuss what type of contraceptive to use, and who is going to get it. Some couples visit a clinic or doctor together for advice and guidance. Advice is always confidential, so one can freely ask questions without any worries. Private doctors and doctors at clinics can prescribe most contraceptives. Some prefer not to go to a doctor, and buy condoms on their own.

TAKING THE LEAD
There is nothing to stop anyone from consulting a doctor or clinic about family planning, where condoms are usually free. It is completely unfair for boys to leave the contraception up to girls because they are the ones who get pregnant. Boys as well as girls who are going to be sexually active should ask themselves, "Am I ready to become a parent?"

The doctor will ask or may try to persuade those under 16 to tell their parents that they are using contraceptives; they are not legally required to inform them, but there is a chance they will. It is always best to discuss contraception with one's parents if at all possible – they may be glad to know that you are acting responsibly.

What to ask for

The contraceptives that are supplied only by a doctor or clinic include the pill, cervical cap, diaphragm, intrauterine device, injectables, and implants. A doctor or clinic can also give advice about family planning. Family planning clinics will offer advice on the best method, based on a person's individual needs. Some methods are not suitable for young couples; some methods may affect one's health or may not be appropriate given a person's family medical history or habits, such as smoking. Those who are forgetful, for example, might not do well on a birth control pill that has to be taken at the same time every day.

Some routine tests may be made, such as a blood pressure check, and those who smoke may be advised to give it up. More than likely a pap smear will be taken, and followup visits will be scheduled to check that there are no side effects or problems connected to the contraception being used. Checkups every six months afterwards are advisable.

THE LAW AND CONTRACEPTION

Local laws may govern the age at which an adolescent can expect a medical consultation to be confidential. In some cases, a 16-year-old has a legal right to insist upon confidentiality. Contraception advice and contraceptives are available free from many schools and clinics for those who are reluctant to see a family doctor. Parental permission is not required to purchase any form of contraception.

QUESTIONS AND ANSWERS

I'm a virgin, but I want to start having sex. Can I use a diaphragm?
Janine, 16 years

If you use tampons, you may be able to use a diaphragm. Putting in a diaphragm takes practice, and if you feel nervous about sex at first, you may not want to have to worry about putting it in properly. You will be given a practice cap until you are confident.

Can you go on using the diaphragm when you have your period?
Paulette, 17 years

Yes. In fact, the diaphragm will contain bleeding temporarily while a couple make love. It must be left in place as usual after intercourse for at least six hours because there is a small chance that a girl can get pregnant during her period.

If I squirt spermicide into my vagina just before sex, will that kill the sperm?
Marsha, 16 years

No. Spermicides are sperm-killing chemicals but they are not effective enough on their own. They are used with barrier methods (*see pages 63-65*) as an extra precaution.

Why should there be female condoms if there are already male condoms? Is this a way to put the responsibility onto the woman?
Penny, 17 years

Taking responsibility for contraception is something that, ideally, everyone should do. This is a fairly new method of contraception and, like most methods, it takes time to get used to. Female condoms do protect against infection and unplanned pregnancy.

My boyfriend didn't want to use condoms, because he said they spoiled sex for him. I said no condom, no sex – the risk would spoil it for me.

Paula, 17 years

Types of contraceptives

Contraception has been used for over 3,000 years to prevent unplanned pregnancy. All forms of contraception work by preventing the fertilization of a woman's egg by a man's sperm. This is achieved in various ways.

Methods of contraception can be divided roughly into five groups. Barrier methods physically prevent sperm from swimming into the uterus and fertilizing the woman's egg (*see pages 60-65*); hormonal methods alter a woman's hormonal cycle to prevent fertilization (*see pages 58-59*); the intrauterine device (IUD) prevents the sperm from reaching the egg or may prevent the egg from embedding itself in the uterus (*see page 66*); natural methods are based on calculating the time when a woman is least fertile and abstaining or using another method to avoid conception when she is most fertile (*see page 67*); and sterilization is a permanent surgical means of preventing conception (*see page 67*). On the following pages, the advantages, disadvantages, and reliability of each of the contraceptive methods is given.

Progestogen-only pill

HORMONAL CONTRACEPTIVES
These work by introducing synthetic versions of female hormones into a woman's body. The hormones either stop her from ovulating, or make her cervical mucus thick, preventing sperm from reaching the uterus. The hormones are taken by mouth, as an implant under the skin, or by injection.

Injectable hormone

Hormonal implants

INJECTIONS AND IMPLANTS
Some hormonal methods of contraception can only be administered by a doctor or a specially trained family planning nurse. These are injectable contraceptives and implants that have to be inserted under the skin. Both types are long-term and require no attention from the user.

Ring at open end

Female condom

Polyurethane sheath

Ring at closed end

MALE AND FEMALE CONDOMS
Condoms stop sperm from reaching the uterus. The male condom, made of thin rubber, is unrolled over the erect penis. The female condom, made of thin polyurethane, is inserted into the vagina. Whichever type is used by the couple must be put on, or inserted, before intercourse. Both types are thrown away after intercourse and can be used only once.

Flexible ring

Lubricated sheath

Male condom

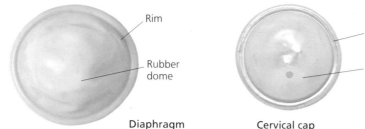

Rim

Rubber dome

Diaphragm

Rim

Rubber dome

Cervical cap

MORNING-AFTER PILL

Contraceptives can sometimes fail. If this happens, one should see a doctor or go to a clinic as soon as possible. The morning-after pill must be taken within 72 hours of unprotected intercourse to be effective. This emergency method must not be relied on as a regular contraceptive, however. It has only recently become available in the United States.

DIAPHRAGMS AND CERVICAL CAPS
These are inserted into the vagina before sex, where they cover the cervix and prevent sperm from reaching the uterus. The diaphragm and cervical cap, made of thin rubber, are used with a spermicide (*see below*), which increases the effectiveness of the method by killing any stray sperm. Both are left in place for several hours and are reusable after cleaning.

Spermicidal sponge

Vaginal suppositories containing spermicide

Spermicidal film

OTHER METHODS

There are other methods of contraception that are not recommended for young people. The intrauterine device, or IUD (*see page 66*), is a small piece of plastic with copper wire wrapped around it. It is inserted inside the uterus by a doctor, and prevents sperm from reaching the egg or a fertilized egg from settling. The IUD is not usually a first choice for young women who have not had children, because of the risk of infection. Sterilization operations (*see page 67*) permanently prevent women from becoming pregnant, or men from releasing sperm. Natural methods of contraception (*see page 67*) rely on knowing when the woman is fertile each month, and are extremely unreliable and difficult to practice.

IUD

SPERMICIDES
These create a chemical barrier that kills or disables sperm in the vagina, so that the sperm don't reach the uterus. They are not an effective contraceptive on their own, however: they must always be used with another contraceptive, such as a cervical cap or diaphragm, to be effective. The spermicide is put into the vagina before intercourse. There are six main types: the spermicidal sponge, which is inserted into the vagina rather like a cap; vaginal suppositories and film, which melt inside the vagina; foam, which is squirted into the vagina; and creams and gels, which are used on diaphragms or cervical caps, or are squeezed into the vagina with a special applicator.

Spermicidal foam

Spermicidal cream

Applicator used with spermicide

Hormonal methods

Because these contraceptives contain synthetic drugs that alter a woman's hormonal cycle, they are available only by prescription. Those who choose to use any of the hormonal methods will be asked to see a doctor regularly to have a general checkup.

WHAT IS THE BIRTH CONTROL PILL?

There are two basic types of pills. The combined pill contains low doses of the hormones estrogen and progestogen. This prevents ovulation (*see page 16*) so conception cannot take place. The progestogen-only pill contains progestogen. This pill causes the cervix to produce thick mucus, preventing sperm from entering the uterus; it may also prevent ovulation.

THE COMBINED PILL

The combined pill is taken each day for 21 days, followed by a seven-day break before starting the next pack. During the break some bleeding occurs. Women who like to take pills without a break can use a 28-pill pack that includes 21 pills with hormones, and seven pills without hormones. Bleeding occurs while these inactive "dummy" pills are taken.

ADVANTAGES AND DISADVANTAGES

The combined pill can be taken by most women, and it usually makes periods lighter and less painful. Because it is so reliable, the pill largely removes the fear of becoming pregnant, and helps many women and their partners feel more relaxed about sex. Before prescribing a contraceptive pill, a doctor will ask about a woman's health and that of her immediate family. This is because the pill may not be suitable for a woman if she, or members of her family, suffer from certain health problems, such as high blood pressure. It is also not suitable for smokers over 35, or very overweight women. Some women suffer side effects, such as headaches, or weight gain. If these do not go away, the woman should consult her doctor. Certain medication and a severe stomach upset – vomiting or severe diarrhea – can prevent the pill from working, and should be treated as a missed pill (*see opposite*).

THE PROGESTOGEN-ONLY PILL

The progestogen-only pill must be taken at the same time every day, without a break between packs. It is therefore not suitable for those who tend to be forgetful.

RELIABILITY

Hormonal methods are 99 percent effective if they are used carefully. Birth control pills are the best known of the hormonal methods and come in two basic forms. Effectiveness of the combined pill is reduced if pills are not taken as prescribed. Used carefully, the progestogen-only pill is only slightly less reliable than the combined pill. Injectable contraceptives are nearly 100 percent effective for the stated length of time – Depo-Provera up to 12 weeks and Noristerat up to 8 weeks.
Implants are nearly 100 percent effective.

ADVANTAGES AND DISADVANTAGES

The progestogen-only pill may cause periods to be irregular or missed — this is normal, but it should be mentioned to the doctor at a checkup. It is also suitable for women who cannot take estrogen. If taken more than three hours late, however, its effectiveness may be lost, and any vomiting or severe diarrhea will also stop it from working. Other methods of contraception would need to be used in this case.

THE INJECTABLE CONTRACEPTIVE

Progestogen is injected into the buttock and is released into the body over the following weeks. It works by preventing the release of an egg from the ovary each month. Injections are needed every eight or 12 weeks. There are two types of injection — Depo-Provera, which lasts for up to 12 weeks, and Noristerat, which lasts up to eight weeks.

Injectable contraception allows sex to be spontaneous and relieves the pressure of worrying about taking pills. The disadvantages are that possible side effects such as weight gain or irregular bleeding may occur until the drug wears off. Bleeding can be heavy at first, but most women have no bleeding after the second injection.

HORMONAL IMPLANTS

This is a fairly new method of hormonal contraception. Implants are plastic tubes, each tube about 1¼ in (34 mm) long and thinner than a matchstick, containing progestogen. Six tubes are inserted under the skin of a woman's upper arm. This is done under local anesthetic by a doctor, and takes about 10 minutes. The implant releases a constant supply of progestogen straight into the bloodstream for five years. Its effect can be reversed at any time by removing the tubes. Any side effects are the same as those for the progestogen-only pill.

MEMORY AID

To help you to remember to take your pill every day you should adopt a set routine. Always take it on waking or on going to bed at night. Follow the instructions and carry your pills with you in case you stay away for a night.

I told my girlfriend I didn't like her being on the pill, because it means that she could sleep with anyone. She told me I was being stupid.

David, 18 years

IF YOU FORGET A PILL

It is important that pills are taken on time and as prescribed. Pill packets come with instructions – read them carefully before starting on them and read them again to see what to do if a pill is late or missed. If in doubt, call your clinic or doctor. In the meantime, do not have sex. Also, do not "borrow" a birth control pill from someone else. Use only your own prescription.

QUESTIONS AND ANSWERS

Because I have painful periods, my doctor is going to put me on the pill. Is this a good idea?
Tracey, 14 years

Your doctor wouldn't prescribe the pill if you are likely to suffer any harmful side effects. Although you are on the contraceptive pill, this doesn't mean that you have to become sexually active right away. The pill is being prescribed to relieve your symptoms.

I am on the pill but I don't have one steady sexual partner, so I want to use a condom to prevent any infection. What should I say to my partner?
Janine, 18 years

It is a good idea to insist on using a condom while you are still experimenting with relationships. Tell your partner that using a condom protects you and him from sexually transmitted diseases.

Condoms

Both male and female condoms are easy to obtain and reliable if used properly. They can help to prevent not only pregnancy, but also the spread of sexually transmitted infections, including HIV. They also reduce the risk of cervical cancer in women *(see page 79).*

THE MALE CONDOM

The male condom is usually made of very thin latex rubber, and fits snugly over the erect penis. When a man comes, or ejaculates, his semen stays inside the condom. Some condoms are made from animal tissues and are sold as a luxury item because they are supposed to "feel more natural." They are not effective enough to protect against pregnancy or infection. Condoms are also known by other names, including sheaths, rubbers, French letters, and johnnies.

Male condoms can be bought in drugstores and supermarkets, and can be obtained from family planning clinics, doctors, and in some schools. They come in different shapes and colors, with or without a tip at the end, and even in different flavors. Many are lubricated with spermicide to make them easier and safer to use. Check all condoms to make sure their expiration date has not passed and that they conform to current national or international safety standards.

THE FEMALE CONDOM

The female condom is a fairly new barrier method that can be bought in drugstores or obtained from some family planning clinics. It is a plastic tube that is bought ready lubricated; it fits inside the vagina, where it forms a lining into which the man directs his penis. One end is closed, and contains a ring to help keep it in place. The other end is held open with a similar ring that lies outside the vagina.

During sexual intercourse, when the woman's partner ejaculates inside her vagina, his semen is trapped inside the condom so that the sperm are prevented from swimming through the cervix and into her uterus.

BUYING AND USING CONDOMS

Some may be embarrassed about buying condoms at first, but stores sell them every day to people of all ages, and they can sometimes be found in dispensers in men's and even ladies' bathrooms. There are many different brands and types, so it helps to keep informed – a clinic can provide free information.

RELIABILITY

Female condoms are a relatively new method of contraception. They are thought to be as reliable as male condoms. Male condoms are between 85 and 98 percent effective, depending on care taken in handling them.

USING LUBRICANTS

Some couples prefer to use extra lubrication with condoms. Only spermicide creams or special gels should be used with male condoms. Products containing oil, such as baby oil, body lotions, and Vaseline, must *not* be used, because they can damage the rubber and make the condom leak. Female condoms are made of plastic, so any lubricants can be used with them.

USING A MALE CONDOM

The male condom is a convenient method of contraception. Putting on a condom need not be embarrassing and awkward. It can be part of the fun of foreplay if couples do it together.

Do not remove the condom until the penis has withdrawn from the vagina. Check it for any leakage and discard carefully after use – if possible, not in the toilet. Do not reuse.

  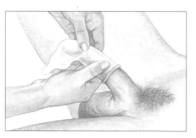

1 Whether you have a condom with or without a tip, squeeze the end to push out the air, so that there is space left for the sperm.

2 When the penis is erect, unroll the condom over the penis to the base. Doing this together can be fun.

3 After ejaculation, the man holds the condom on his penis. Once he withdraws from the vagina, it can be taken off and discarded carefully.

USING A FEMALE CONDOM

The female condom is a fairly recent contraceptive. It is strong and comes ready lubricated. It also allows the woman to take the responsibility for safer sex. After use, check for any leakage and discard carefully.

To insert the female condom, find a comfortable position to relax the vagina

Squeeze the ring at the closed end into a narrow oval

1 Remove the condom from the packaging – it is already lubricated – and, with one hand, spread the labia (*see page 14*). With the other hand, slide the squeezed ring of the condom into your vagina, pushing it as far as possible.

2 With a finger inside the condom, maneuver the ring up past the pubic bone. The ring doesn't have to cover the cervix like a diaphragm does (*see page 64*). When in place, it should hang down about 2 in (5 cm) outside the vagina.

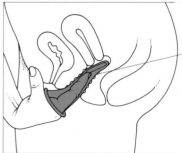

Push the closed end up into the vagina

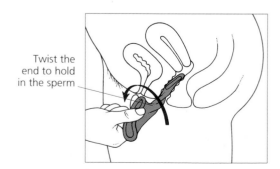

Twist the end to hold in the sperm

3 After sex, when the man's penis has been withdrawn, twist the open end of the condom to seal in the sperm. Pull the whole condom out of the vagina. Check the sheath for any leakages before discarding it. Do not use it again.

With practice, condoms are easy to use properly – try them out on your own first. Girls can practice putting a male condom on a banana or carrot.

Female condoms can be put in place anytime before sexual intercourse. Male condoms can only be put on when the penis is hard, and condoms must always be put on before any genital contact, because semen can leak from the penis before ejaculation. Two male condoms should *never* be used together for "extra" protection: they are likely to rub against each other and tear from friction.

After use, wrap the condom in tissue and throw it away carefully (not in the toilet). There will still be sperm on the penis, so it should be washed immediately and not brought near to the vagina until it has been washed. Condoms can only be used once; they must never be washed and used again because they will no longer protect against pregnancy or disease.

ADVANTAGES AND DISADVANTAGES

Condoms are an effective way to practice safer sex. They reduce the risk of passing on or picking up a number of sexually transmitted infections and diseases (*see pages 80-83*), including the virus that causes AIDS. Condoms should be treated carefully, though: jagged nails, rings, or teeth used to rip open the packet can tear them.

A male condom might split or slip off, especially if the man doesn't hold the condom as he pulls his penis out of his partner's vagina. When using the female condom, the penis could slip outside the condom so that ejaculation takes place in the vagina. In either situation, as soon as possible see a doctor, who may prescribe the morning-after pill (*see page 66*).

QUESTIONS AND ANSWERS

I carry a condom around with me but my friends think that I'm playing easy to get. How can I argue that I am right and that I'm not looking for sex all the time?
Miriam, 17 years

This double standard in which women are regarded differently from men has always existed (*see page 36*). HIV and AIDS have changed views about carrying and using condoms. By carrying one "in case," you are acting sensibly and realistically. You are showing that you care about your sexual health and that of your partner. It's better to be safe than sorry!

If I use a condom, when is the best time to put it on?
Pete, 16 years

The best time to do this is early on while you still have a cool enough head to get everything right. This is another argument for doing it together – having fun and being responsible, rather than rushing. The male condom must be put on when your penis is erect. If you wait too long, you may be too physically close to your partner to stop and open a packet and put the condom on. Putting it on too late may cause you to come early.

Barrier methods

A diaphragm is used with spermicide and is put into the vagina before sex. When the man ejaculates, his sperm cannot swim into the woman's uterus, because the diaphragm blocks its entrance, and the sperm are killed by the chemicals in the spermicide.

DIAPHRAGM AND CERVICAL CAP

Both these contraceptives are made of thin rubber, and both cover the cervix. The more popular of the two is the diaphragm; it is a dome, 2–4 in (5–10 cm) across, with a springy rim. The cervical cap is smaller and fits over the cervix in the same way that a thimble fits over a finger. Diaphragms and cervical caps come in various sizes, and a doctor or nurse has to make sure that the size is right and demonstrate how to use it. Diaphragms and cervical caps are available from doctors or family planning clinics; they are also available from drugstores, but then the size needs to be known.

The diaphragm or cervical cap is removed by hooking a finger over the rim. It can be cleaned in warm water and mild soap, dried, and used again. It should be checked regularly for holes by holding it up to a bright light. The fit needs to be checked by a doctor or nurse about every 12 months. Gaining or losing more than 7 lb (3 kg) in weight, or having a baby, an abortion or a miscarriage, may change the shape of a woman's vagina, making a new diaphragm or cervical cap necessary.

HOW TO USE A DIAPHRAGM OR CERVICAL CAP

Both a diaphragm and a cervical cap must *always* be used with spermicides. With a diaphragm, the spermicide is smeared all over; with a cervical cap, it is smeared on both sides, but not around the rim. A diaphragm or cervical cap can be inserted at any time before intercourse – if it is more than three hours before, some extra spermicide should be inserted in the vagina before intercourse. After intercourse, the diaphragm or cervical cap should be left in place for at least six hours, or sperm left in the vagina may swim into the uterus. For repeated intercourse, more spermicide is needed in the vagina each time, although the diaphragm or cervical cap need not be removed.

ADVANTAGES AND DISADVANTAGES

The diaphragm or cervical cap is used only during sex, and it also helps to protect women against cervical cancer and some sexually transmitted infections. There are no side effects and

---

RELIABILITY

Used carefully, diaphragms and cervical caps are 98 percent effective, but their reliability can drop to 85 percent with less careful use. Spermicide alone is not recommended as an effective contraceptive.

My friend wanted to borrow my diaphragm. I told her no, because diaphragms are like clothes – you need a size that fits you. Anyway, who wants to share something that goes inside you?

Lorraine, 16 years

INSERTING A DIAPHRAGM

The diaphragm is made of rubber. It is placed in the vagina so that it covers the cervix. This means that no sperm can travel into the uterus. Spermicide, which contains chemicals that kill the sperm, is always used as an extra precaution with a diaphragm.

Find a comfortable position to relax the vagina

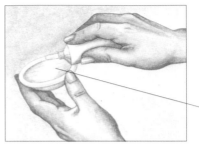

Smear two 1 in (3 cm) strips of spermicide on both sides of the diaphragm

1 Wash hands and remove the diaphragm from its container. Squeeze the flexible rim into an oval shape with the index finger on top to keep the springy rim under control.

2 Smear the spermicide in two strips (about 1 in/3 cm long) onto both sides of the diaphragm and around the rim. It will be slippery and quite difficult to handle.

Insert the diaphragm into the vagina

Check that the diaphragm covers the cervix

3 Insert the flexible rim of the diaphragm as high as it will go into the vagina. The direction is the same as that when a tampon is inserted – upward and backward.

4 Once the diaphragm is in place, it is held over the cervix by its springy rim. Check this by feeling for the cervix through the rubber with a finger. The cervix feels like the end of the nose.

TOXIC SHOCK

A few years ago some women who were using a highly absorbent tampon (no longer available) suffered a dangerous condition called toxic shock syndrome. The tampons were changed less often, and this encouraged growth of a bacterium in the vagina. There are no real risks in using ordinary tampons, a cervical cap or diaphragm, but six hours is the maximum time for leaving a tampon in the vagina (see pages. 16-17).

INSERTING A CERVICAL CAP

The cap is thimble-shaped and smaller than the diaphragm. It stays in place over the cervix by suction. Spermicide should be put inside the cervical cap but not around the rim because this might affect the suction. Like all methods, this requires practice to get it right. Often you will be given a practice cervical cap to help you to feel confident about inserting it.

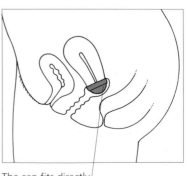

The cap fits directly over the cervix

no health risk from using the diaphragm or cervical cap, although with their use, cystitis (*see page 82*) is more common and there may be an occasional allergic reaction to the rubber. The woman must plan ahead and carry her diaphragm or cervical cap with her. Putting this contraceptive in place takes experience to ensure it is inserted properly. Many people find the spermicide messy and distracting.

Although the cervical cap or diaphragm must be left in the vagina for up to six hours after sexual intercourse, it should not be left there for any longer. Anything that is left in the vagina for too long – for 24 hours or more – which includes a tampon, may lead to a dangerous condition called toxic shock syndrome (*see opposite*).

The first time I tried to put my diaphragm in, it slipped out of my fingers, flew across the room, and bounced off the wall. We just couldn't stop laughing, and it really helped us relax.

Polly, 17 years

USING SPERMICIDES

Most spermicides contain the chemical nonoxynol, which kills not only sperm, but also the organisms that cause many sexually transmitted infections, including HIV. They are not very effective as a contraceptive on their own, however. After intercourse, it is better not to have a bath for about six hours, because this may dilute spermicide or wash it away. A shower is a better option. Spermicide comes in different forms, including the sponge (*see below*); vaginal suppositories, which melt in the vagina; gels or creams, which are smeared over the diaphragm; foam, which is squirted into the vagina from an aerosol; and film, which dissolves in the vagina. All can be bought at drugstores or obtained from a doctor or family planning clinic.

THE SPONGE

The sponge is soft and round, about 5 cm (2 in) wide, and is made of foam soaked with spermicide. It has a dimple on one side, which fits over the cervix, and a loop attached to the other side, used to remove it. Before use, the sponge is first moistened with water in order to release the spermicide. It is then pushed, dimple side up, to the top of the vagina. The dimple should fit over the cervix. The sponge works for up to 24 hours, and it should be left in place for six hours after the last sexual intercourse. It is removed by pulling on the loop. It is not reusable.

WHICH SPERMICIDE?

The sponge is available over the counter, and its spermicide action remains effective no matter how many times intercourse occurs in a 24-hour period. It can be quite expensive, however, since a sponge only lasts one day. Many women prefer to use a form of spermicide that fits easily into a bag or purse.

Other methods

There are other contraceptive options available, but not generally recommended for the young. These include intrauterine devices, permanent sterilization, and natural methods. The morning–after pill can be used in an emergency, not as a regular method.

THE INTRAUTERINE DEVICE (IUD)

Most IUDs (previously known as the coil) are pieces of plastic, 1–1½ in (2–4 cm) long, wound with copper wire. The IUD works mainly by preventing sperm from reaching the egg, or rarely, by preventing a fertilized egg from settling in the uterus. The IUD is inserted into the uterus by a doctor using a special instrument. It can stay there for five years and is removed by a doctor.

An IUD is not chemical, it doesn't interfere with sexual intercourse, and it is effective as soon as it is fitted. However, IUDs may increase the risk of sexually transmitted infection in the uterus or the fallopian tubes – infection that could lead to infertility. This is one reason why they are generally not recommended for young women. Periods can be heavier, and it is possible for the IUD to become dislodged; it should be checked regularly by feeling for the tail of threads at the cervix. There have been some serious problems with IUDs in the past.

RELIABILITY

The IUD is more than 98 percent reliable. Sterilization for women is nearly 100 percent reliable once a woman has had her first period after the operation, and, for men, within a few months – the time it takes for the sperm to be cleared from the tubes. Natural methods are about 80 to 98 percent effective if used properly.

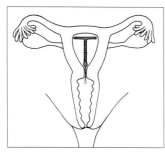

THE IUD IN PLACE
Two fine threads attached to the base of the IUD project a short way into the vagina. The woman can check, by putting a finger in her vagina and feeling for the threads, that the IUD is still in place.

EMERGENCY CONTRACEPTION

Emergency or post-coital (after intercourse) contraception, also known as the morning-after pill, is used when a woman thinks she is at risk of an unplanned pregnancy soon after intercourse. The reason could be forgetting to use contraception, an accident such as a condom tearing or slipping off, or that a woman was not planning to have sex – this includes sexual assault and rape. In such situations, one must contact a doctor or family planning clinic within 72 hours of the unprotected intercourse. The treatment generally consists of two special pills to take immediately, and another two to take 12 hours later. The pills alter a woman's hormonal balance, which delays ovulation or prevents implantation. They can also cause a sick feeling, or vomiting, which could mean that more pills must be taken. This method is about 95 to 99 percent effective. Another method in emergencies for older women is to have an IUD fitted, which can be done up to five days after unprotected intercourse. This prevents the egg from embedding itself in the uterine lining. The IUD can be removed when the next period starts. This is almost 100 percent effective in preventing pregnancy and is chosen if the time limit for the hormonal method has passed or the woman cannot take estrogen.

STERILIZATION

Male sterilization, or vasectomy, is done by cutting the sperm duct, or vas deferens *(see page 25);* this prevents sperm from reaching the penis. Female sterilization is done by cutting or blocking the fallopian tubes *(see page 15),* preventing eggs from reaching the uterus. Neither affects the person's interest in, or ability to enjoy, sex. A man still ejaculates semen (without the sperm) and a woman still has periods. These operations are designed to be irreversible. Doctors generally sterilize only men or women over 30 who have completed their family.

NATURAL METHODS

Often called the rhythm method, the natural method is extremely unreliable because it is so difficult to chart precisely a woman's fertile time, Natural methods depend on careful monitoring, finding out when a woman ovulates *(see pages 16-17).* During the fertile part of the cycle, other barrier forms of contraception or abstinence should be used. To be effective, the methods must be taught by a trained teacher and not tried without instruction.

TAKING TEMPERATURES

Temperature changes, measured with a fertility thermometer at the same time each day before getting out of bed (either orally, rectally, or vaginally), show when a woman is fertile. The fertility thermometer has a narrow range of temperatures, making it easy to read. Immediately after ovulation, the body temperature drops a little and then rises by between 0.2°F and 0.4°F. It remains at this temperature until the next period.

> *My friend had sex without using a contraceptive. She asked me if she could take some of my pills to stop her from getting pregnant. I said it wouldn't work, and she should see her doctor.*
>
> Susan, 17 years

USING THE NATURAL METHOD

A daily record in chart form of temperature and/or cervical mucus must be kept for this method. Day 1 is the first day of bleeding.

Depending on the length of the cycle, ovulation should occur 12-16 days *before* the next period is due.

This chart is based on an average 28-day cycle.

At ovulation mucus resembles the white of an egg

CERVICAL MUCUS METHOD

Changes in the consistency of a woman's cervical mucus *(see page 17)* also indicate ovulation. One can stretch a little vaginal discharge between the thumb and index finger to see the color and consistency. Immediately after a period, there may not be much cervical mucus. After a few days, the cervical mucus may be more noticeable as a discharge; it is thick, sticky, and cloudy. As one is about to ovulate and after ovulation, there is more mucus, and it is clear and stretchy – like raw egg white. When it changes back to being thick and cloudy, this is a "safe" time.

ADVANTAGES AND DISADVANTAGES

Natural family planning has been practiced for centuries, and it has no known side effects. Both the man and woman need to be involved and be prepared to use barrier methods or abstain at other times to be sure. It does require a detailed knowledge of a woman's cycle, and this record keeping is time-consuming and must be precise. Some say that those who practice the rhythm method or natural family planning need to be fully prepared to become parents.

"BEING CAREFUL" OR COITUS INTERRUPTUS

Coitus interruptus or withdrawal is when the man withdraws his penis from the vagina just before orgasm. This is not at all reliable as birth control because some sperm can leak before ejaculation; one sperm is all that is necessary for a pregnancy. Other disadvantages are that this is a difficult thing to do in practice, and the experience for both partners can be frustrating and unsatisfactory.

QUESTIONS AND ANSWERS

What if I were sterilized now and have it undone when I am older and want a family?
Kenny, 16 years

When you are young, a doctor would be very unlikely to consider sterilization unless your health were at risk. If you are sterilized, complicated surgery is required to reverse the sterilization operation. After sterilization, you are still exposing yourself and your partner to sexually transmitted infections and diseases *(see pages 80-83)* if you never use any other form of contraception, such as a condom.

I've heard that if you shake up a bottle of warm cola or any carbonated drink, and squirt it up into your vagina after you have sex, it will stop you from getting pregnant because it washes all the sperm back out. Is this true?
Lucy, 15 years

No, this will not prevent you from becoming pregnant. Washing out the vagina like this is called douching. By the time you start douching after you've had sex, the sperm will already be swimming into the uterus. Douching after sex can cause irritation or an infection in your vagina.

PREGNANCY AND BEING A PARENT

How pregnancy starts

Childbirth

Unplanned pregnancy

How pregnancy starts

The moment of fertilization, when egg and sperm fuse together, is the most significant event in the whole reproductive process. All the material is there for a new individual, who inherits genes from both parents.

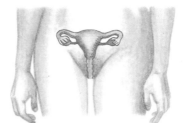

EXPANSION OF THE UTERUS
The uterus is about 4 in (10 cm) long, and 3 in (8 cm) wide. In pregnancy, its capacity and muscle bulk increase until it is about 15 in (38 cm) long and 10 in (25 cm) wide.

About every 28 days – although it can actually be anywhere between 21 and 42 days – from puberty to menopause, an egg, or ovum, is released from a woman's ovaries *(see page 15)*. If she has intercourse around this time, there is a good chance that her partner's sperm will meet and fertilize the egg, beginning the process of conception. The process is complete when the ball of cells that develops from the fertilized egg attaches itself to the wall of the uterus. At first, this implanted mass of cells is called an embryo. Some of the cells develop into the placenta, which anchors the embryo in the uterus wall and delivers nutrition from the mother. A cushioning bag of fluid, called the amniotic sac, forms around the embryo. Eight weeks after fertilization, the embryo has a recognizable form, with face and limbs and all its major organs. It is now called a fetus. The baby will be born about 40 weeks after the first day of the woman's last period.

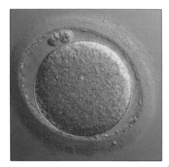

Hundreds of sperm surround the ripe egg, all trying to break through. The sperm release an enzyme, which dissolves the covering of the egg so that one sperm eventually penetrates it. Once this happens, no other sperm can get through. The fertilized egg, called a zygote, has 46 chromosomes – 23 from the sperm and 23 from the egg

BOY OR GIRL?

A baby's gender depends on the sperm. Genetic information, including sex, is carried in chromosomes – there is an identical set of 46 of these in every cell of the body, but eggs and sperm have only 23 each. Sperm can carry an X chromosome or a Y chromosome. The egg only carries an X chromosome. If a Y sperm fertilizes an egg, the baby's cells will be XY, and it will be a boy. If the sperm is X, the baby's cells will be XX, and it will be a girl.

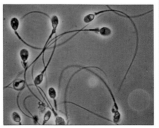

A sperm's head carries the genetic information, and its long tail propels it.

QUESTIONS AND ANSWERS

Can a girl get pregnant the first time she has sex?
Nathan, 13 years

Yes: whether it's the first time or the twenty-first, she can get pregnant if the couple doesn't use contraception.

If a girl misses a period, is she definitely pregnant?
Sarah, 14 years

No. Girls often have irregular periods, so being late, or even missing a period, is not uncommon. The only reliable way to find out is to have a pregnancy test *(see page 74)* if pregnancy is a possibility.

A pregnancy test is able to detect a certain hormone in a woman's urine. This is usually possible within a week of a missed period. However, whatever the result, it is advisable to visit a doctor or clinic to have the result confirmed.

A friend told me that you can't get pregnant if you have sex during your period – is she right?
Alison, 15 years

No. Ovulation can happen shortly after a period, and sperm can live to find an egg for up to three days, so a girl certainly can become pregnant if she has sex during her period.

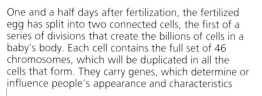

One and a half days after fertilization, the fertilized egg has split into two connected cells, the first of a series of divisions that create the billions of cells in a baby's body. Each cell contains the full set of 46 chromosomes, which will be duplicated in all the cells that form. They carry genes, which determine or influence people's appearance and characteristics

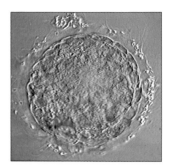

Three days after fertilization, more cell divisions have produced a solid mass of 64 separate cells. This ball of cells, which is called a morula, is no bigger than the period at the end of this sentence. It is still traveling down the fallopian tube and will not reach the uterus for another 24 hours

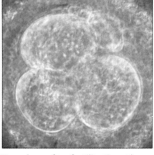

Two days after fertilization, the journey down to the uterus continues. A second split has taken place, producing four cells. From now on, the cells will divide about twice every day

Fallopian tube

Thickened by hormones, the uterine lining is ready to receive the egg

An egg has around 12-24 hours in which to be fertilized after ovulation

Ovary

THE STAGES OF CONCEPTION

During intercourse *(see pages 46-47)*, up to 500 million sperm are released from the penis. The sperm swim into the uterus and toward the ovaries – only a few thousand will make it this far. If they find an egg, they will surround it, and there is a good chance that one of them will fertilize it. The fertilized egg divides into a mass of cells as it travels down the fallopian tube. It attaches itself to the inside of the uterus, and at this site, the placenta begins to grow. The uterus keeps its lining, which is usually shed in menstruation, so the first sign of pregnancy is normally a missed period. Over the next 266 days, the tiny ball of cells develops at a rapid rate into a fully formed baby.

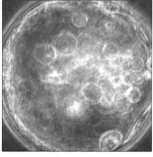

One week after fertilization a hollow space has formed in the center of the ball of cells, now called a blastocyst. After floating in the uterus for two or three days, it starts to embed itself in the wall. When the blastocyst is fully implanted, conception is complete

Childbirth

After about 40 weeks, a pregnancy comes to an end when the baby is born. The sequence of events that leads to the birth is called labor – divided into three stages – during which the uterus contracts with increasing strength and pushes the baby and placenta out.

Regular contractions of the uterus are a sign that labor has begun. It is time to contact the doctor and go to the hospital where arrangements have already been made for the birth. A nurse usually carries out routine examinations. The father or a close friend or relative is usually present throughout the labor. Labor is painful, as contractions of the uterus increase in frequency and intensity. The woman can feel tired, and frightened at this time, but breathing exercises help. During the birth, she may experience extreme pain, although procedures learned at prenatal classes or painkilling drugs will help lessen the pain and reduce fear. The support and encouragement of those with her is very important. During the second stage of labor the baby is born; the doctor assesses its health and hands the baby to the mother. Returning home can be a letdown. After all the congratulations comes the responsibility of taking care of the new arrival. Parents may feel exhausted from lack of sleep, and mothers can feel especially lonely during the first months. Support from a partner, family, and friends is important at this time. It can also be helpful and reassuring to meet other young parents to share ideas and problems.

DEPRESSION

Many new mothers feel helpless and have crying spells after giving birth. This is caused by sudden changes in the hormone levels and the feeling of anticlimax after birth; it is sometimes called "baby blues." If this feeling persists, and the mother is still feeling depressed four weeks after the birth, she should see a doctor: she could be suffering from postpartum depression.

DEVELOPMENT OF THE FETUS

At 16 weeks, the mother will notice changes to her breasts. The fetus has started to move. Its heartbeat can be heard. By 20 weeks, the mother begins to look pregnant, and she can feel the fetus moving inside her. At 32 weeks, the fetus is completely formed, and if born now, it has a 50 percent chance of survival. In the remaining 8 weeks it will put on fat, becoming plumper and less wrinkled.

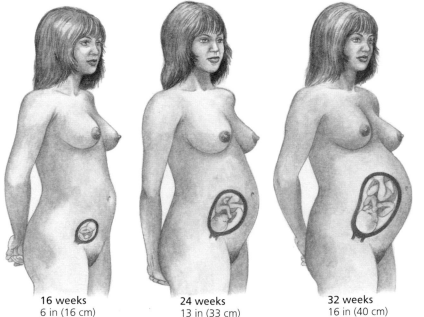

16 weeks
6 in (16 cm)

24 weeks
13 in (33 cm)

32 weeks
16 in (40 cm)

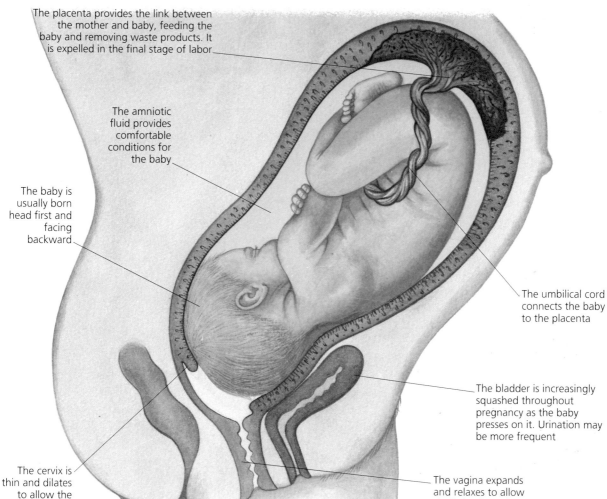

The placenta provides the link between the mother and baby, feeding the baby and removing waste products. It is expelled in the final stage of labor

The amniotic fluid provides comfortable conditions for the baby

The baby is usually born head first and facing backward

The umbilical cord connects the baby to the placenta

The bladder is increasingly squashed throughout pregnancy as the baby presses on it. Urination may be more frequent

The cervix is thin and dilates to allow the baby through

The vagina expands and relaxes to allow the baby through

THE PELVIC GIRDLE

During birth, the baby has to pass through a narrow opening in the pelvic girdle, a ring of bone consisting of the hip bones and lower spine, held together by tough ligaments. In fact, the baby is only able to squeeze through the narrow opening because hormones (also released throughout pregnancy) relax the ligaments, making the pelvic girdle wider and more flexible so that it "gives" as the baby is born.

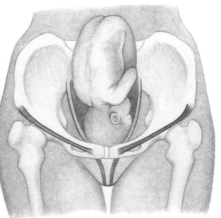

This is a front view of the baby's position in the pelvic girdle, with the uterus left out for clarity.

READY FOR THE BIRTH
Labor has three stages. The first stage generally lasts between 12 and 14 hours, although this time can vary. The uterus contracts strongly and frequently. The bag of fluid surrounding the baby bursts, and the cervix opens up (dilates) to allow the baby's head to pass through. The cervix should be fully dilated before the second stage begins. As the woman pushes downward and her uterus contracts more strongly, the baby is born. After delivery, the umbilical cord is clamped and cut. During the final stage, which lasts about 15 minutes, the placenta is pushed out of the uterus.

Unplanned pregnancy

It's easy to think that this can't happen, but it can be devastating to find out that it has. Once a young woman is pregnant, it may be hard to think of anything except how to tell one's parents, but there are many other decisions that also need to be made.

WHAT TO DO FIRST

To help you to sort out your feelings about the pregnancy, ask yourself the following questions first:
- Do you want the baby?
- Will your parents be supportive of your decision?
- Do you want your partner to be involved?
- Do you think your partner will stand by you?
- Is there someone you can confide in?
- Would you consider an abortion?
- Would you consider adoption?

FACING UP TO BEING PREGNANT

A girl discovering that she is pregnant may feel frightened, angry, and fearful about the future. The first step is to think through all the issues concerning the pregnancy, the baby, and what the future holds. It is very important to act quickly and to seek help and advice.

The choices facing a pregnant girl are not easy. She should not be pressured into doing what someone else thinks is right. Whatever choice she makes, it has to be right for her. Her partner may want to share in the decisions, but might not be ready for the responsibility, or be much help. He may be another complication in her life. He may not want to know. In the end, what happens must be the girl's choice. Her partner's agreement is not legally necessary for the continuation or termination of a pregnancy. Once a baby is born, if the father's name is on the birth certificate, he has legal rights and responsibilities that may include financial support of the mother and the baby.

TELLING THE MOTHER'S PARENTS

Every pregnant girl needs support and advice, especially in making the decision about telling her parents. Even in the closest families this can be difficult. Some find that talking first to a trusted family member or friend helps, and that they can suggest how to approach one's family. For a girl who can't tell her parents, the best place to turn to may be a family planning clinic, health center, or counseling service (*see pages 92-93*). The people there are trained to offer help and advice; they won't pass judgments or criticize. But in seeking advice, be careful to go to an organization that does not try to coerce a girl either into having the baby or seeking a termination.

BEING TOGETHER Once the baby is born, many girls find that they can cope as well as women twice their age, and enjoy motherhood.

CHOOSING TO HAVE THE BABY

A girl who is in a stable relationship, or who has family willing to help and support her, might keep the baby. This would mean rethinking one's whole future. Babies are not babies for long: a girl deciding to have a baby should try to imagine how she will feel bringing up a child for the next 16 or so years. Those who are very young, or on their own, may find this very difficult economically and emotionally. The opportunity for a girl to continue her schooling under these circumstances will depend to a large degree on her family and how they support her and the baby – whether financially, or by providing housing and childcare. The cooperation of the school system will also be important.

Having the baby and giving it up for adoption is another option. It is difficult for a girl to know how she will feel when the baby is actually born: some mothers find that they cannot give the baby up. Others decide to go through with it, although they often change their minds once the process is under way.

Once the pregnancy starts to show, some girls decide to leave school and make arrangements to continue with their education at home until the birth. Those who want to continue their studies after the baby is born may find that their family can help arrange childcare, or there may be a program in their school or neighborhood for young mothers and babies.

BEING A SINGLE PARENT

Bringing up a child alone is not easy. It can be harder still when all one's friends are still carefree teenagers. Money and housing are often problems. Family support can make a significant difference. Family members may be able to help out financially, but, just as importantly, they can provide emotional support and practical help. Even when parents are upset or angry about an unexpected pregnancy, they are still family, and it is worth trying to build bridges and maintain a good relationship with them.

HAVING THE PREGNANCY TERMINATED (ABORTION)

Abortion is the medical term for the termination of a pregnancy. Abortion raises many issues. It is legal in Canada and has been legal in the US since 1973. It is performed by a variety of methods. Most people have a view on whether it is an appropriate course of action or not. Remember, though, it is the girl's body involved, and it is her decision to make.

The earlier an abortion is performed, the safer it is. An abortion cannot be performed after 24 weeks except under exceptional circumstances. Vacuum aspiration, also called "D & C," is the most common method of abortion used until about 12 weeks. Under general anesthetic, the cervix is dilated

> *The worst part was telling Mom and Dad. Once I'd done that, it was easier to think clearly about what I wanted to do.*
>
> Amy, 16 years

PREGNANCY TEST

A variety of pregnancy testing kits are available from drugstores. One type consists of a strip impregnated with chemicals. This is held in the woman's urine for a few seconds, and if it changes color, she is pregnant. These kits are 99 percent accurate, but results should be confirmed by a doctor or at a clinic. There are a number of agencies that offer free pregnancy testing services, and they can also provide free advice about contraception if you are not pregnant *(see pages 92-93).*

SIGNS OF PREGNANCY

A missed period.
Tingling and tender breasts.
A strange metallic taste in your mouth.
Wanting to urinate more frequently.
An increase in white vaginal discharge.
Feeling tired.
Suddenly craving or disliking certain foods.
Nausea.

and the uterine lining is sucked out through a small plastic tube. This takes about 10 minutes.

In more advanced pregnancies (12-20 weeks), abortion can be accomplished by the insertion of a prostaglandin suppository against the cervix. This hormone stimulates the pregnant uterus to contract much as it does in labor. Abortion often occurs within several hours, although repeat insertions may be necessary to complete the process. This can be upsetting because it is like a real birth, so the earlier the abortion is arranged, the better. In later pregnancies, the cervix is dilated under general anesthetic and an instrument is used to scrape out the fetal tissues.

Before a girl becomes pregnant, she may have strong views on whether or not she would ever have an abortion. But she could feel differently once she is actually pregnant, and so could her partner. A girl thinking of having an abortion should see her own doctor or a doctor at a family planning clinic as soon as possible so she can make an informed decision early in the pregnancy.

THE AFTERMATH

After an abortion a girl may feel relieved, or she may not feel as pleased as she thought she would. Even when a girl believed this way was the correct course of action, she may experience a great sense of loss. The best thing to do is to talk to someone sympathetic, such as a friend or a counselor at a family planning clinic. Don't hold feelings in – seek support at this difficult time. It is also important to seek advice on the type of contraception to use in the future (*see pages 56-57*).

ABORTION LAW

Abortion is legal in Canada, and in the US since 1973. Many states require a 24-hour waiting period between counseling sessions and the abortion, parental consent for girls under 18, and counseling by a doctor on alternatives to abortion. In some states, judicial approval can replace parental consent when the young woman involved cannot or will not obtain parental consent. Parental consent is required for a minor's abortion in 23 states. Other states have similar laws that are not being enforced because of court injunctions.

QUESTIONS AND ANSWERS

My boyfriend's always been a bit wild. I would really like to have a baby with him. Do you think it would settle him down?
Angela, 17 years

It's just as likely to make him leave. Have a baby when your relationship works, not to make it work.

I am pregnant, and I don't want to tell the baby's father because it is all over between us. My parents think I should. Is telling him the right thing to do?
Lee, 18 years

This is a difficult decision if your relationship is over but you have decided to keep the baby. If possible, your ex-boyfriend should really be told about the baby as he is the father. What you decide to do, however, is still up to you and not to him.

I think I'm pregnant. I still live at home: if I go to a clinic for a test, will they tell my parents?
Tina, 16 years

No: if you are pregnant, it will be up to you to tell your parents. In the case of abortion, however, some states require parental consent.

SEX AND HEALTH

Taking care of your body

Diseases and infections

HIV and AIDS

Taking care of your body

In adolescence, your body changes in ways that affect not just your appearance, but your health and personal hygiene too. Your skin produces new smells, your genitals secrete new substances, and you have to start taking care of your body in a different way.

PERSONAL SCENT

Everyone has their own smell. If you are clean and healthy, it's natural and pleasant, and a part of you. Animals secrete scent chemicals called pheromones, which help to attract mates. It is possible that we secrete pheromones, too, and that when we are attracted to someone, we may be responding to them by secreting these substances.

When body secretions have been exposed to air for a while, they become breeding grounds for bacteria and have an unpleasant smell. Almost everyone uses deodorants and antiperspirants (*see page 10*) to counteract underarm odors. Daily washing of the genital area is also essential. A different, strong smell could be a sign of infection (*see pages 80-83*).

LUMPS AND BUMPS

With adulthood and changes in your shape, you will probably start to develop a new awareness of your body. Every now and again, check for signs of anything different or out of the ordinary. For example, breasts normally feel uneven, and before and during a period they can feel larger than usual and more lumpy and tender. You can get to know your breasts by checking them each month at the same time just after your

> *I hate it when people wear loads of perfume or aftershave – I always think they must be covering up some other smell. If you wash, you shouldn't need all that stuff.*
>
> Gurinder, 17 years

HAVING A PAP TEST

You lie down on a flat surface with your knees bent and your feet together. You then let your knees drop to the side. The doctor or nurse inserts a speculum into your vagina. This metal instrument holds the vaginal walls apart while the examination is being carried out. It won't hurt, though it can feel cold and you may feel pressure. A spatula is inserted through the speculum and scrapes cells from the cervix. You may not feel this. The sample of cells is put on a glass slide and sent to a lab to be analyzed. Your doctor or the clinic will tell you when to call for results. Keep a note in your diary so that you remember to have another checkup (usually every three years).

CHECKING THE TESTES

Testes should be examined regularly. The best time is just after a hot bath or shower, because the skin of the scrotum will be loose, making examination easy. Roll each testis between your thumb and fingers, gently moving the skin and feeling the entire surface. You are looking for changes in the texture, feel, size, and weight – the back of each testis is naturally lumpy (*see page 25*).

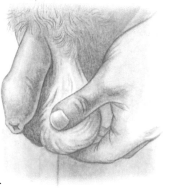

period. A painless lump or changes in skin texture are symptoms of one of the most common female cancers, though breast cancer is rare in young women. Early treatment improves the chances of successful treatment. If you note any changes or anything unusual, check with a doctor.

Cancer of the testes, while rare, is one of the most common cancers in young men. It can be cured if treated early. Regular checkups are a good idea. If you have a painless lump or swelling that wasn't there before, see a doctor to put your mind at ease.

THE PAP TEST

This is a screening procedure for cervical cancer that is carried out regularly on women who have ever been sexually active from the age of about 20, or within one to three years of having regular intercourse. This test is also known as a cervical smear. A doctor or nurse at a surgery or family planning clinic can do this. Abnormal cells on the cervix develop slowly and regular pap tests allow these to be treated, usually with lasers. Cervical cancer has been linked to early sexual activity, genital warts, and smoking.

> *When my breasts first started, they were really lumpy, and I used to worry all the time that there was something wrong.*
>
> Chrissie, 15 years

CHECKING THE BREASTS

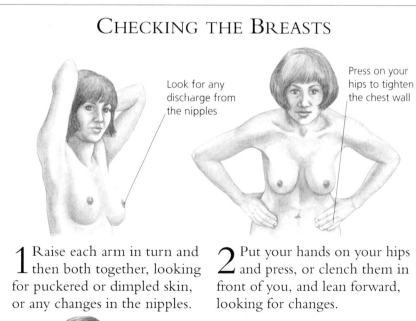

Look for any discharge from the nipples

Press on your hips to tighten the chest wall

1 Raise each arm in turn and then both together, looking for puckered or dimpled skin, or any changes in the nipples.

2 Put your hands on your hips and press, or clench them in front of you, and lean forward, looking for changes.

Press gently

3 Move your fingers over the entire surface of each breast. If you have large breasts, support them with the other hand. Feel for lumps and any changes in skin texture.

PERSONAL HYGIENE ESSENTIALS

For girls

- Wipe from front to back after a bowel movement, to avoid spreading germs forward from the anus.
- See your doctor if you have a different-smelling or colored discharge: you might have an infection that could be treated *(see pages 80-83).*
- Don't use douches or vaginal deodorants. they are unnecessary and can irritate the vagina and cause infection.
- Wash the vaginal area daily but avoid soaping between the vaginal lips, because soap may irritate the vulva.
- Take regular baths or showers during your period.

For boys

- If you are uncircumcised, pull your foreskin back to wash away the secretions (called smegma) that may accumulate underneath it.
- Take regular baths or showers.
- See your doctor if there is discharge from your penis.

Diseases and infections

Those who are sexually active can pass on or pick up a sexually transmitted disease (STD), so it is essential to take precautions. Sex is never free of the risk of unplanned pregnancy or an infection. Every sexually active person must be responsible and practice safer sex.

It was my first sexual experience and I was sure I'd gotten a sexually transmitted disease. It turned out to be just an irritation and the ointment cleared the itching up in 24 hours.

Pippa, 16 years

HOW DO YOU KNOW YOU'VE BEEN INFECTED?

Both sexes may have burning soreness or itching on or around the genitals, pain or discomfort when passing urine, or lumps, sores, blisters, or warts on or around the genitals. Men may have a clear or white discharge from the penis. Women's vaginal fluid may become heavier, change color, or have an unpleasant smell. Women may need to urinate more frequently. Sometimes, however, women have no symptoms.

Infections that are not sexually transmitted can cause similar symptoms, and sometimes infections don't cause symptoms at all. So if someone you've had sex with tells you that they have an infection, you should visit a doctor or a clinic, even if you have no symptoms.

VISITING A CLINIC

Clinics that treat sexually transmitted diseases may be independent or part of a hospital complex; call your local hospital or consult the telephone directory to find out where the nearest one is (*see pages 92-93*). Anything you tell the doctor or the clinic is confidential, but part of their job is to try to stop infections from spreading. They may ask you the names of your sexual partners, so that they can be contacted and treated. This can be done anonymously.

If you are worried about HIV (*see page 84*), the doctor or clinic can help you decide whether to have a test. If your family doctor does the test, it goes in your medical files. You might need to give someone access to these and not want them to know about the test. A test at a clinic is confidential.

WHAT HAPPENS AT A CLINIC?

At many independently run clinics, you don't need an appointment – you can walk in. The staff won't criticize you or give you a lecture. You will be examined and given tests, including a blood test. Once the disease or infection is identified – some results are given right away while others may take a few days – you will be given a course of treatment. Always finish any course of treatment, even if the symptoms

SAFER SEX

Always use a condom to protect your own and your partner's sexual health.

Remember that a condom only reduces the risk, it doesn't eliminate it.

Casual sex or a lot of partners increases the chances of meeting someone with a sexually transmitted disease.

If a partner or ex-partner tells you they think they have an STD, seek medical advice, even if you have no symptoms.

Alcohol and drugs can make you less careful than you should be about sex and more inclined to take chances.

go before your medication is gone, otherwise some germs may reinfect you. Many of those tested find out they have no disease.

WHY GO FOR TREATMENT?

With the exception of HIV *(see pages 84-85)*, STDs can be treated. Sometimes a disease or an infection does clear up by itself, but without treatment it can reappear. An untreated one can also spread, causing permanent damage to both you and your partner's health, and you may pass it on to someone else in the meantime. Some STDs can affect your chances of having children. Treatment is easiest if it is started early.

People who think they have caught a sexually transmitted disease often feel frightened or ashamed. They may feel too embarrassed to go to a clinic or see their doctor. Don't worry. Doctors and clinics deal with these problems all the time and will understand your feelings.

It can be difficult to tell someone that you have passed an infection on to them, or that you have an infection you could only have caught from them. But it is essential that your sexual partners know: they might have no symptoms and no idea that they have an STD. A clinic may be able to trace people for you and inform them anonymously.

I thought I had something really awful and I was seriously sick, but the clinic gave me antibiotics, and it cleared up in couple of weeks.

Craig, 16 years

SYMPTOMS

If you notice anything different around your genitals and you are sexually active, then you may have a sexually transmitted disease. Refer to the following pages for a list of common infections and diseases that can affect the sexual organs. Common symptoms include:

- a white or different discharge from the penis – chlamydia, gonorrhea, NSU
- itching around the genitals – genital herpes, pubic lice, yeast infection
- sore, itchy genitals – vaginitis, yeast infection
- pain when urinating – chlamydia, gonorrhea, NSU
- lumps, sores, warts or blisters around the genitals – genital herpes, genital warts, syphilis
- an unusual discharge (frothy or yellow, for example) from the vagina – bacterial vaginosis, chlamydia, gonorrhea, yeast infection, trichomoniasis, vaginitis

- an unpleasant, smelly discharge – bacterial vaginosis, trichomoniasis
- frequent and/or painful urination – cystitis
- abdominal pain and tenderness – pelvic inflammatory disease

IF IN DOUBT

Practicing safer sex *(see left)* is a way to reduce the risk of a sexually transmitted disease, but if you suffer any of the symptoms listed above, it is best to abstain from any sexual contact until you have visited your doctor or a clinic to find out whether there is a problem or not. About half of the people who visit clinics have no sexually transmitted disease.

VAGINAL DISCHARGE

It is normal to have some vaginal discharge – this is the way the vagina cleans and lubricates itself *(see page 14)*. Normally, this discharge is colorless and doesn't smell, although it dries to leave a yellow or brownish stain on underwear. If it begins to have a bad smell, or to look different, perhaps frothy, this may indicate infection. Leaving a tampon in for too long can cause a foul-smelling vaginal discharge *(see Toxic shock, page 65)*.

Diseases and Infections

NAME	SYMPTOMS	TREATMENT
Bacterial vaginosis	A grayish, frothy discharge with a fishy odor, caused by a bacteria naturally present in womens' bodies that has multiplied out of control. Men can also have the germs, but usually without symptoms.	Antibiotic drugs or creams to insert into the vagina. If untreated, this infection may cause fertility problems.
Chlamydia	In men, pain on passing urine and a discharge from the penis. Women may have a vaginal discharge or no symptoms. There may be pelvic pain during sex.	Antibiotics. If untreated, this could lead to infertility and other problems in women and men.
Cystitis	Frequent and painful urination, maybe only a trickle, which may smell strong and contain traces of blood. This is an infection of the bladder caused by bacteria that are naturally present in the body. Cystitis is common in women, because a woman's urethra is short and the bacteria are able to reach the bladder from the rectum (*see page 15*). If a woman has strenuous sexual intercourse, this can trigger a state called "mechanical stress," resulting in cystitis. Men have a longer urethra, so cystitis in men is rare.	Drinking plenty of water (with a teaspoon of bicarbonate of soda added to each glass) at the first sign of the symptoms can help keep your urine flowing. Drink about two glasses of liquids every hour. If symptoms do not disappear, or you are uncomfortable, your doctor may prescribe antibiotics.
Genital herpes	Tenderness, tingling, and itching of the genitals, followed by blisters, which may burst to form painful sores. There is often pain on urinating, and sometimes a feeling of illness and a raised temperature. This disease is caused by the herpes simplex II virus. It can be caught through intercourse and is different from the herpes simplex I virus that causes cold sores on the mouth. The first outbreak usually clears up in about two weeks, but the virus stays in the body and may lead to further outbreaks.	The virus cannot be killed, but antiviral drugs and painkillers help heal sores and reduce pain during attacks. Sex must be avoided, or condoms used, during attacks. Women who have genital herpes should have regular Pap smears because there may be an increased risk of cervical cancer.
Genital warts	Soft warts appear on and around the anus, the penis, or the entrance to the vagina and cervix. They may go undetected because they are small, or disappear of their own accord. These are also called venereal warts. Untreated, they may multiply rapidly, so early treatment is advisable.	They are removed by repeated application of a lotion or by surgery, but they tend to recur. Any woman who has had them, or whose partner has had them, should be sure to have an annual Pap smear (*see page 78,*), because of the link between genital warts and an increased risk of cervical cancer.
Gonorrhea	Men suffer pain on passing urine and have a discharge from the penis. Women contract the disease more rarely, and may have a vaginal discharge, or no symptoms.	Antibiotics. If untreated, the disease can cause infertility in men and women, so a woman's partner must be checked, too.
HIV and AIDs (*see pages 84-86*)		

NAME	SYMPTOMS	TREATMENT
Nonspecific urethritis (NSU)	This inflammation of the urethra mostly affects men, who may have pain on passing urine or a discharge from the penis: these symptoms can be mild. Women may have a slight vaginal discharge or, often, no symptoms. This is one of the most common sexually transmitted diseases, called nonspecific because its cause cannot always be identified.	Antibiotics. If untreated, infections can cause serious complications such as a rare form of arthritis. In women, there may be later complications such as pelvic inflammatory disease.
Pelvic inflammatory disease (PID)	Symptoms include abdominal pain and tenderness, often immediately after or during sex. Periods may become irregular and painful. There may also be fever, backache, and vomiting. This is an infection of the female reproductive system. It cannot be passed on to sexual partners, but it is often a result of an untreated infection such as chlamydia or gonorrhea.	Antibiotics and, in some cases, painkillers and bed rest. If the woman has an IUD in place, it should be removed if the infection does not respond to treatment. If left untreated, chronic pelvic pain or an abcess can develop.
Pubic lice (crabs)	Bloodsucking, crablike parasites, the size of a pinhead, which live in the pubic hair, where they cause itching. Pubic lice are sometimes passed on by sharing bedding, clothes, and towels, although usually by sexual contact.	The white, shiny eggs cannot be removed by normal washing: a special over-the-counter medication or antibiotic may be prescribed. Towels, clothes, and bedding must be washed in very hot water to prevent reinfection.
Syphilis	The first sign of syphilis is a painless, but very infectious, sore at the site of infection, commonly the genitalia, rectum, tongue, or lips. This heals on its own in a few weeks, but the germs remain in the body and develop.	Antibiotics. If untreated, the disease will progress to cause a rash, mouth sores, and general aching. If not treated, the disease can be fatal.
Trichomoniasis	A frothy, yellowish, foul-smelling vaginal discharge in women. Men may suffer symptoms similar to those for NSU, but often have no symptoms. Trich, as it is known, is caused by parasites that infect the vagina in women, and the urethra in men.	Antibiotics.
Vaginitis	Irritation and sometimes discharge. It can be caused by various bacteria, usually thrush, trichomoniasis, or bacterial vaginosis. Allergies to spermicides or to scented soaps can also cause inflammation.	Antifungal or antibiotic drugs, depending on the cause, or avoiding the cause of the irritation.
Yeast infection	A white, curdy discharge, genital itching, redness and swelling of the vulva, and soreness on passing urine. This is not caused by sexual contact, but by a yeast or fungus that is naturally present in the vagina. This infection is very common in women. A woman can pass it to a sexual partner through sexual contact, although this is rare. The glans of the penis may become inflamed.	Antibiotics and creams. A yeast infection thrives in warm and airless conditions, so if a woman has an attack, it is wise to wear cotton underwear and avoid pantyhose and tight pants.

HIV and AIDS

HIV is a virus that causes the illness known as AIDS. Anyone can contract this virus through unprotected sexual intercourse with an infected person or by using infected needles. It is estimated that around 12 million people worldwide have contracted HIV.

> *When my dad told me my uncle was HIV positive, I just couldn't believe it. I didn't know what to say to him at first, but he acted just the same, so I do, too.*
>
> Ben, 12 years

THE IMMUNE SYSTEM

The body has an immune system that is its defense against infection. However, if the human immunodeficiency virus (HIV) enters the body, the cells in the body's immune system are invaded and cannot destroy the virus. HIV stays alive within the cells of the immune system, and may lie dormant there for years. At present, there is no known way to kill this virus once it enters the body. A blood test will detect HIV. If there is HIV, the person is said to be HIV positive. Being HIV positive does not make people ill. Someone with HIV may look and feel well, and stay this way for a long time – often for years. But they are infectious to others, and will be for the rest of their lives.

THE ONSET OF AIDS

When HIV is active, the infected cells in the immune system die, and the virus is released into the blood to infect other cells. As the immune system is weakened, the person loses weight, tires easily, and becomes more vulnerable to all sorts of infections, such as skin disorders, ulcers, yeast infection, and diarrhea. Eventually, serious problems, such as herpes, tuberculosis, pneumonia, and cancer, develop.

When a person becomes ill in this way, they are said to be suffering from acquired immune deficiency syndrome, or AIDS. Once a person reaches this final stage of the disease, they usually die of a major infection within a year or two.

HOW DOES HIV SPREAD?

HIV is found only in bodily fluids, and of these blood, semen, saliva, and vaginal fluids have been shown to transmit infection. The virus enters the body through a sore or cut in the skin, or an injection, or through the membranes that line the mouth, the vagina, or the anus. A baby can contract HIV from its mother through the placenta in the uterus, or possibly through breast milk after birth.

The virus cannot survive for long outside the human body. It is perfectly safe to live with someone who has HIV or

HOW HIV IS SPREAD

It can be spread by bodily fluids through:
  Unprotected sex.
  An open wound.
  Shared needles.
  Mother to unborn child.

It cannot be spread by:
  Toilet seats, showers.
  Food, dishes, etc.
  Coughs, sneezes, sweat, tears.
  Hugs, handshakes.
  Insect bites.

AIDS, to share their food, to use the same silverware and dishes, to touch or hug them, and even to sleep in the same bed as them. It is not safe to exchange bodily fluids through unprotected sex, or by sharing toothbrushes, razors, or, in the case of drug users, hypodermic syringes, with anyone who is, or may be, HIV positive. Doing so puts one at serious risk of contracting HIV.

THE SEARCH FOR A SOLUTION

There is no real cure for even the mildest virus, such as the common cold. At present, there is no cure for AIDS and no vaccine against it. Various drugs have been tried in the hope that they can slow down the progress of AIDS; however, the search still goes on for a cure.

The other area of research is the attempt to find a vaccine. Worldwide vaccination for smallpox wiped out the disease in this century: if a vaccine against HIV can be developed, AIDS might also be overcome.

SAFER SEX

Everyone can avoid doing things that put them at risk. Many people have already changed their behavior to reduce the risks of infection; many still take risks, however. While you can never completely eliminate the chances of catching any infection, you can do a lot to protect yourself against being infected by HIV.

Kissing, touching, hugging, or mutual masturbation are usually safe, unless open sores are present. Oral sex is slightly more risky, because bleeding gums and mouth sores are quite common and can provide a point of entry for the virus (*see page 51*).

Sexual intercourse is still the most common means of infection. There is a higher risk with anal intercourse, because the lining of the anus tears more easily than that of the vagina, providing a way in for the virus. The risk can be reduced during intercourse by wearing a condom (*see pages 60-62*).

MINIMIZING THE RISKS

Most people know that unprotected sex carries risks and that the more sexual partners you have, the higher the chances that one of them is HIV positive. But even with people you know, there is a risk. Whatever risks your partner takes or has taken in the past, you are taking too. Anything that involves blood can be risky: drug addicts who inject drugs have contracted HIV. Addicts who share needles or use dirty needles are putting themselves at risk.

Everyone should avoid sharing items such as razors, and

He made such a fuss when I asked him to put on a condom — you'd think I was asking him to come to bed wearing his boots. He put it on, though.

Debbie, 17 years

LIVING WITH HIV

Many people with HIV stay well for years. The people around them may never know that they are HIV positive. People who are ignorant about AIDS are often frightened and can be cruel, so people who are HIV positive may be happier if only those close to them know. If you know someone with HIV, you can still be their friend. Just treat them normally, not fussing over them too much, but remember that they may sometimes tire easily or get depressed. If they want to talk about it, encourage them, and listen sympathetically. If they don't want to talk about it, accept that, too.

PROTECTING YOURSELF

Use condoms (*see pages 60-62*) to protect you and your partner's health.

Be honest about your past.

If either of you has done things that put you at risk, get an HIV test.

Don't take drugs intravenously – if you do, don't share needles.

Remember that drinking alcohol can make you less careful than you should be.

Don't share personal items such as razors.

even toothbrushes – people often have mouth sores or minor cuts on their gums without even being aware of them. Tattooing and ear-piercing could also carry a small risk if instruments are not sterilized: ask about the hygiene methods used (*see below*). Having a blood transfusion should no longer be dangerous, because blood is now carefully screened.

When the disease first appeared in the developed world, most of its victims were gay or bisexual men, so some people used to think that AIDS was a disease solely of gay men. This is not true. This prejudice can encourage heterosexuals to think that they are safe. It is better to behave in ways that will reduce the risks for everyone instead of assuming that if you are female or heterosexual, you are unlikely to be infected.

HAVING AN HIV TEST

If you are worried about HIV and AIDS, you should talk to a special counselor in a clinic or contact a special hotline (*see pages 92-93*). Many clinics will not test you without this counseling, because the implications of the test are greater than people imagine.

The test is *not* for AIDS. The test determines whether you have antibodies to HIV in your blood. Usually, the antibodies appear within six weeks of infection, but they can take up to six months to show up, so you may test negative but be asked to return for another test in six months. During this time, you should not do anything that puts you or any partner at risk.

QUESTIONS AND ANSWERS

Someone told me I shouldn't have my ears pierced because I might get HIV from the needle they use. Can this really happen?
Nicky, 14 years

This could happen if an unsterilized needle was used, which might have been previously used on someone who had HIV or AIDS. The same is true for the needles used for tattoos and acupuncture. But if you go to a reputable jeweler or store, there should be no risk: their needles should be sterile, or they should be using disposable needles. Don't be embarrassed to ask about hygiene methods before you have the piercing done, and if you're not happy, go elsewhere.

What does an HIV test involve, and if there's no cure, what's the point in anyone taking it?
Pete, 16 years

A small blood sample is taken and tested. The results are available in a few days – in some clinics on the same day. If the result is positive, the person infected will need to take steps to avoid passing the virus on to anyone else. They should tell anyone who needs to know: their partner, their doctor, their dentist, and their family. Because it can take from six to eight weeks from the time of infection for the antibodies to appear, the test is usually not considered reliable until six months after exposure to the infection.

PROBLEM AREAS

Sex and the law

Child sexual abuse

Sexual harassment

Rape

Sex and the law

Whatever happens to your body should only happen with your consent, and because you want it to happen. There are laws designed to protect people from abuse by others.

THE AGE OF CONSENT

The law protects children until they are old enough to make their own decisions about sex. The age at which you are considered old enough to do this is called the age of consent. If you are under the age of consent *(see page 44)* and someone has sex with you, even if you agree to it, they are committing an offense. The age of consent varies from state to state.

SEXUAL OFFENSES

Some behavior is always against the law. Incest (sex with close relations such as a parent or an uncle or aunt) is always illegal, regardless of age. Anything that offends or harms others, such as sexual harassment *(see opposite),* or that forces someone to have intercourse or commit a sexual act against their will *(see page 91),* is also against the law.

PORNOGRAPHY

Pornography is any material designed to arouse the viewer sexually. Some people claim that lightly clad people in advertisements are pornographic, while others claim that they are harmless. In most countries, the law allows some kinds of material, but bans others. "Hard-core" porn shows sexual acts with violence and depicts its subjects as objects to be dominated or humiliated. In most countries, such material is illegal.

Pornography has been shown to affect people's attitudes; it can change the way that we view other people. People in real life are unlikely to be as willing or as adventurous.

PROSTITUTION

Prostitution is the sale of sex, by men or women. In most countries, it is either illegal, or made very difficult by laws that a prostitute cannot avoid breaking. Few of these laws protect the prostitute, who leads a dangerous life, exposed to the risks of HIV infection and other sexually transmitted infections, and of violence. In the US and Canada, prostitution is illegal.

Child sexual abuse

Child sexual abuse is any activity in which children are used by other people for sexual pleasure. It includes not only intercourse, but any kind of sexual touching.

WHO ABUSES?

Usually the abuser is a friend of the family, a relation, or someone known to the child. Sometimes a child is abused by a parent, a sibling, a stepparent, or stepbrothers or stepsisters.

It is difficult to know exactly how many children are, or have been, abused. When adults are questioned about their childhood, a large number (and twice as many women as men) say that they were abused. Thousands of children call telephone hotlines every year to confide that they have been, or are being, sexually abused.

WHAT IS ABUSE?

If you're not certain about what someone is doing, or whether it is abuse or not, ask yourself the following questions to help you make up your mind. Does what is happening make you feel uncomfortable? Are you being sworn to secrecy so that nobody else knows about it? Are they doing it for their pleasure, with no regard for how you feel? Do they threaten you or ignore you if you try to stop them? Do they say that something bad will happen if you tell? If the answer to any of these questions is yes, then you are being abused.

WHAT SHOULD YOU DO?

No matter who is abusing you, try to tell an adult what is happening. Even though you feel fearful about what will happen, telling someone is the best thing to do. This is easy advice to give, but it is often difficult to follow, especially if a member of your family is involved.

It is important for you to realize that when an adult abuses a child, it is *always* the adult's fault, *never* the child's. It may take time for you to summon up the courage to tell someone what is happening, but nothing is likely to change unless you do.

A parent is the best person to tell, if you can. If you can't, tell a grandparent or another close relative whom you trust, a mature friend, or a sympathetic teacher at school. Or you can call one of the telephone hotlines or organizations *(see pages 92-93)* and talk in confidence to a specially trained counselor. They can advise you on the next step to take.

WHAT HAPPENS NEXT?

If the police or social services are told that a child is being sexually abused at home, the first thing they must do is make sure that the child is safe. If necessary, the authorities remove the child from the home, at least for a time. This "breathing space" gives everyone a chance to decide what should be done for the best interest of the child and to seek professional help for both the child and the abuser, if possible.

The police will decide whether to charge the person concerned or not. They must check on everyone's story and collect evidence. Sometimes they can't bring charges – this doesn't mean that a crime

has not been committed. If the case does go to court, the victim may have to appear in court and give evidence. By telling someone, the abused person may have prevented the abuser from doing the same thing again.

Reporting sexual abuse is a difficult thing to do, but it is necessary. It can also be traumatic, and for this reason, most victims find counseling helpful.

Sexual harassment

This is unwanted pestering of a sexual nature. It doesn't have to be physical – comments, whistling, or obscene telephone calls are also sexual harassment.

WHAT TO DO ABOUT IT

Sexual harassment is not about attraction, it is about belittling someone. It is often done by people in positions of power. If you have been harassed, remember that it was not your fault. You are not alone: many people are harassed every day. Even if you are scared, don't keep it to yourself, but tell someone you trust. Sharing the experience will often make you feel better. Most harassment is illegal, so report incidents to someone in authority or to the police so that the perpetrator can be caught.

If the sexual harassment happens at school, take the names of any witnesses and tell a parent and a teacher or the principal. If your complaint is ignored, inform the board of education; if the harassment involves a criminal offense, notify the police. If you feel you have a valid complaint, do not be persuaded to drop the matter. You may have to sign a statement naming your harasser in order to have any action taken.

WHISTLES AND COMMENTS

Harassment of this sort is common. You may feel angered and humiliated, but depending on where you are and who you are with, you can either try to ignore it – responding may encourage the harasser – or be assertive and tell the harasser that you don't accept this behavior. If anything like this happens at school, report it. Students, and even teachers, sometimes comment on teenagers' physical development. If you don't like this, tell the person, and if they go on, report it. If someone makes unwanted sexual suggestions, tell them to stop, ask others if it has happened to them, and report it to someone in authority.

FLASHERS AND PEEPING TOMS

Flashers are men who expose their penises in public. Get away as fast as you can. In all cases, tell a parent or teacher and the police. Flashing is a crime.

Voyeurs are people who try to watch others when they are undressing or naked, or having sex. They are also known as "peeping toms." If you ever see someone spying on you, tell a parent, and report it to the police. Voyeurism is a crime.

UNWANTED TOUCHING

Crowded places, such as trains or buses, give some people the chance to touch or rub themselves against you. Draw attention to what is going on by loudly telling the offender to stop, and tell a parent or other adult as soon as you can. Contact the police: this kind of harassment is a crime.

OBSCENE TELEPHONE CALLS

Also called nuisance, or dirty, phone calls, these are upsetting and illegal. Callers may be silent, or ask intimate questions, or make sexual threats. If you receive an obscene call, put the phone down calmly – don't slam it down. Don't talk to the caller, and never give your name. Tell a parent, and contact the police and the telephone company. Calls can usually be traced easily, so if the caller persists, they can be caught and prosecuted.

CURB CRAWLERS

Curb crawlers are drivers who harass pedestrians by driving slowly behind them, sometimes making obscene suggestions. Ignore any comments and walk away from the car. If possible, memorize the license plate and make of car and pass the information on to the police. Curb crawling is an offense.

Rape

If someone forces you to have sex against your will, it is rape – whether you are a man or a woman. Other forms of sexual attack are known as indecent assault.

WHAT IS RAPE?

Rape is a frightening and horrible experience, and often rape victims feel guilty, even though they have done nothing wrong. They may feel dirty, as though they have been somehow "spoiled." Because of these feelings, the first reaction may be to tell nobody and to pretend that nothing has happened.

YOU MAY KNOW YOUR ATTACKER

Most rape victims know the person who rapes them. When a girl is raped by someone she knows, it is often called "date rape." Many such rapes happen at or after parties, when one (or both) of the people involved has had too much to drink. If the girl says no, and the boy insists, this is still rape. If she finally gives in, she may feel raped because she didn't want to do it, although the boy could claim that she had consented. There is sometimes a fine line, however, between date rape and sexual misunderstanding. Boys and girls often expect different things: each assumes that the other knows what they want (or don't want), but they can't read each other's signals. Girls must be clear about what they want and make it clear that they mean it when they say no. And boys have to accept and believe a no as readily as they would a yes.

WHAT TO DO IF YOU ARE RAPED

It isn't always easy to tell anyone, let alone the police. You may be afraid of the person who raped you, or fear you won't be believed. But, if you keep silent, it may be harder for you to get over what has happened. It also allows your attacker to go unpunished, and they may rape someone else. Tell your parents, a relative, or a close friend. They should report the rape to the police at once. You may be able to talk to a specially trained policewoman, who will make it as easy for you to talk as she can.

Even if you feel that you just want to forget the whole thing, it is sensible to collect some evidence. Forensic evidence, such as tiny fragments of skin under your nails, can be vital in securing a conviction. It is important that you be examined, either by a police doctor or by your own doctor, within 24 hours of the rape. The doctor's report is essential evidence if the police are to prosecute your attacker.

It will help you if you can talk about it to someone else, especially someone who has had a similar experience. Contact a rape crisis center or a telephone hotline about this *(see pages 92-93),* or ask your doctor to refer you to a counselor.

Useful addresses

ABUSE & ASSAULT

Childhelp USA, Inc.
6463 Independence Avenue
Woodland Hills, CA 91367
Tel: 1-800-4-A-CHILD

Local Rape Crisis Centers (consult telephone directory)

National Committee for Prevention of Child Abuse
332 S. Michigan Ave, Ste. 1600
Chicago, IL 60604-4357
Tel: (312) 663-3520

National Council on Child Abuse and Family Violence
1155 Connecticut Avenue NW
Ste. 400
Washington, DC 20036
Tel: 1-800-222-2000

ADOPTION

Adoption Families of America
3333 Highway 100 North
Minneapolis, MN 55422
Tel: (612) 535-4829

National Adoption Center
1500 Walnut Street
Ste. 1701
Philadelphia, PA 19102
Tel: 1-800-TO-ADOPT

National Committee for Adoption
1930 17th St. NW
Washington, DC 20009-6207
Tel: (202) 328-8072 (National Adoption Hotline)

COUNSELING

American Psychiatric Association
1400 K Street NW
Washington, DC 20005
Tel: (202) 682-6000

Anxiety Disorders Association of America
6000 Executive Boulevard, Ste. 513
Rockville, MD 20852
Tel: (301) 231-9350

The Coalition on Sexuality and Disability
122 East 23rd Street
New York, NY 10010
Tel: (212) 242-3900

National Depressive and Manic Depressive Association
730 North Franklin, Ste. 501
Chicago, IL 60610
Tel: (312) 642-0049

National Mental Health Association
1021 Prince Street
Alexandria, VA 22314-2971
Tel: 1-800-969-NMHA

DRUGS

Alcoholics Anonymous
General Service
475 Riverside Drive
New York, NY 10115
Tel: (212) 870-3400

American Cancer Society
1599 Clifton Road NE
Atlanta, GA 30329
Tel: (404) 320-3333

Families Anonymous
PO Box 528
Van Nuys, CA 91408
Tel: 1-800-736-9805

National Council on Alcoholism and Drug Dependence
12 West 21st Street
New York, NY 10010
Tel: 1-800-NCA-CALL

800-Cocaine
PO Box 100
Summit, NJ 07902-0100
Tel: 1-800-262-2463

EATING DISORDERS

The American Anorexia/Bulimia Association
c/o Regent Hospital
425 E. 61st Street
6th fl.
New York, NY 10021
Tel: (212) 891-8686

ANAD-National Association of Anorexia Nervosa and Associated Disorders
PO Box 7
Highland Park, IL 60035
Tel: (708) 831-3438

FAMILY RELATIONS

Family Resource Coalition
200 South Michigan Avenue
Ste. 1520
Chicago, IL 60604
Tel: (312) 341-0900

Family Service America, Inc.
11700 West Lake Park Drive
Milwaukee, WI 53224
Tel: (414) 359-1040

National Council on Family Relations
3989 Central Avenue NE, Ste. 550
Minneapolis, MN 55421
Tel: (612) 781-9331

Parents without Partners, Inc.
c/o Smith Bucklin Associates
401 North Michigan Avenue
Chicago, ILL 60611
Tel: (312) 644-6610

MEDICAL CONCERNS

National Alliance of Breast Cancer Organizations
1180 Avenue of the Americas
New York, NY 10036
Tel: (212) 719-0154

National Herpes Hotline
Tel: (919) 361-8488

National STD Hotline
Tel: 1-800-227-8922

SIECUS (Sex Information and
Education Council of the US)
130 West 42nd Street
Ste. 2500
New York, NY 10036
Tel: (212) 819-9770

Local Hospital Clinics

AIDS Hotlines

PREGNANCY &
CONTRACEPTION

American College of
Obstetricians and Gynecologists
(ACOG)
409 12th Street SW
Washington, DC 20024-2188
Contact : Adolescence
Tel: (202) 638-5577

Informed Homebirth
PO Box 3675
Ann Arbor, MI 48106
Tel: (313) 662-6857

National Abortion Federation
1436 U Street NW, Ste. 103
Washington, DC 20009
Tel: 1-800-772-9100

National Organization of
Adolescent Pregnancy and
Parenting
4421A East-West Highway
Bethesda, MD 20814
Tel: (301) 913-0378

Planned Parenthood Federation
of America
810 Seventh Avenue
New York, NY 10019
Tel: 1-800-829-PPFA

GENERAL

U.S. Department of Health and
Human Services
Public Health Service
Centers for Disease Control and
Prevention
National Center for Health
Statistics
6525 Belcrest Road
Hyattsville, MD 20782

Index

Acknowledgments

Dorling Kindersley and the authors would like to thank:
Sashola Mahoney, Mark Noble and Candida Ross–MacDonald
for help with the text; the young men and women for being
models; Antony Heller and Maryann Rogers for production
assistance; Camela Decaire for editorial assistance.

Special photography
Antonia Deutsch

Illustration
Coral Mula

Index
Jane Parker

Picture research
Clive Webster

Additional photography
Stephen Bartholomew, Andy Crawford, Tim Ridley,
Hanya Chlala (jacket front)

Picture credits
Comstock: 44, 46;/R. Michael Stuckey 3b
The Image Bank:/Werner Bokelberg 9
Oxford Scientific Films, Mantis Wildlife Films: 70c, 71tl
Pictor International: 30, 40
Science Photo Library: 66, 67; /Andy Walker, Midland Fertility
Services: 71ct, 71b; /CNRI: 71tr; /John Walsh 70b
Telegraph Colour Library: 87; /R. Chapple 32, 37b; /Marco
Polo 33b; /Paul von Stroheim 87
Zefa: 3r, 29, 34, 45, 77; /Norman 2; /Wartenberg 3

tlt=top b=bottom l=left r=right

CANALS OF KILDARE

STARTING AND FINISHING
POINT
Robertstown, County Kildare
(790249). The village is situated
2 miles (3 km) south of the
R403/L2.
MAPS
The OS half-inch to the mile
Sheet 16 covers the area and
should be useful for the route to
Robertstown, but is on so small a
scale that it is of marginal use on
the walk. A leaflet with a sketch-
map covering all the Kildare canal
walks is available from Cospoir
— see Appendix.
LENGTH
8 miles (14 km)
ASCENT
Negligible.

Kildare is a flat inland county, and one not normally associated with walking. Nonetheless a system of walking routes has been laid out using as a centrepiece the canals that run through the county on their way from Dublin to the west and south-east. These routes traverse a country of pleasant villages and wet fields bounded by straggling unkempt hedges. Much of their length follows shallow, rarely used canals, arched by high humped-back bridges, whose banks support wildfowl, dragonflies and a variety of flowers. If you find that canal banks are a trifle tedious, take heart; the first stretch of canal bank is followed by sections of country road, forest and bog-land, which should refresh you before the final length of bank.

ROUTE DESCRIPTION (Map 1.2)

Following the gaudy signpost of the Kildare Way, cross the prominent Binn's Bridge in Robertstown *(1)* to reach the north side of the canal, thus leaving the main part of the village. Take the road beyond, continuing straight ahead along a narrow road beside the canal where the main road swings R. Just before Lowtown Marina, cross Fenton Bridge, pass around the Marina buildings *(2)* and cross the high footbridge beyond, where a signpost announces far-off and exotic destinations culminating in St Mullins 70 miles (112 km) away.

Turn L beyond the footbridge and walk along the towpath, passing one road-bridge (do *not* cross it). At the second bridge continue straight ahead onto a metalled road, pass Ballyteige Castle *(3)* and a lock; just beyond it, turn R onto a side-road, thus following the purple arrows of the 'Robertstown Local Walk' (you follow these to the end of the walk).

Take this narrow road, further on a rough farm road, initially through an area of scattered houses and later through a state forest, and past turfworkers' billets on the R *(4)* (both forest and billets appear by their unkempt and desolate appearances to be reverting to the gentle care of nature). Pass a turn on the L and at a T-junction turn L to pass to the R of the end of a raised bog *(5)*, with the cooling tower of Allenwood Power Station *(6)* ahead. At the next T-junction turn L onto the main road (not R as instinct for home would rightly suggest), and a few steps along turn R up a side-road, so reaching yet another stretch of canal. Turn R here to follow the towpath to the next bridge, Shee Bridge. Cross this bridge and continue along an overgrown towpath (now on the L bank) past Bond Bridge (do *not* cross this one), so reaching again the canal bank opposite Lowtown Marina. Return along the same side-road as the outward journey to reach Robertstown, turning R over Binn's Bridge to reach the village.

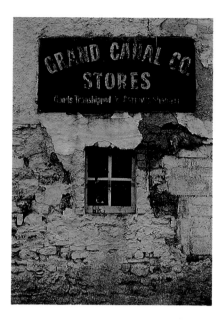

Sign on the old stores

1   *Robertstown*

The village owes its origin to the Grand Canal, work on which commenced in the middle of the eighteenth century. The large, imposing building in the village was originally a hotel owned by the Grand Canal Company, and is at present used by local tourist interests.

2   *Lowtown Marina*

Lowtown lies at the junction of the Grand Canal and the Barrow Line, so canals radiate from here to Dublin, the River Shannon to the west, and the River Barrow to the south. From Lowtown water levels are controlled and the necessary paperwork to operate the canal is issued.

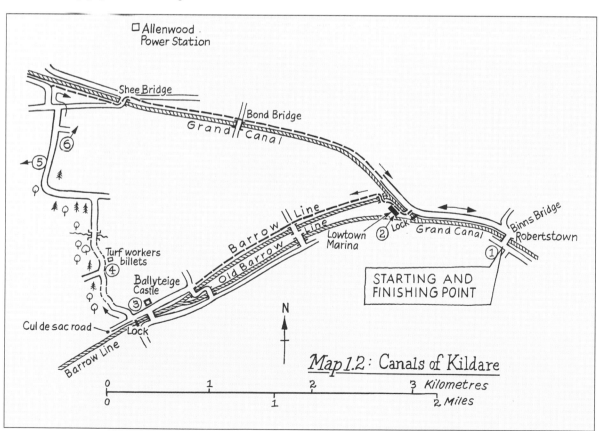

Left: *The bridge at Robertstown*   *Lock on Grand canal*

3   *Ballyteige Castle*

This is a typical example of an Irish fortified house of the fourteenth to sixteenth centuries.

4   *Turfworkers' Billets*

These were built during the fuel crisis of the 'Emergency', as World War II is still euphemistically called. They were intended as accommodation for workers harvesting peat from nearby bogs, but were never completed.

5   *Lullymore Bog*

On the L is Lullymore Bog, a typical midlands raised bog, and part of what was the Great Bog of Allen before it succumbed to the cutting machinery for nearby peat-burning power stations. Its dome shape is caused by the accumulation of sphagnum, which is able to draw up water so that the bog surface can rise above the water-table.

6   *Allenwood Power Station*

This power station burns sod peat from nearby bogs, Ireland being one of the very few countries in the world to have this type of fuel. The station is still open, having been given a reprieve from closure in the late 1980s.

CORRIES OF THE COMERAGHS

In the townland of Lyre (264126). The starting point is difficult to find and requires careful attention to the following details. Take the R671/T27 (Dungarvan to Clonmel road) turning onto a minor road opposite Melody's Pub in Ballymacarbry village (the village is well signposted). Drive straight ahead for 2.1 miles (3.4 km), turning R uphill here. Turn L at an offset crossroads after another 0.5 miles (0.8 km), continue straight on past a R turn, the first on this stretch of road, after another 2.4 miles (3.8 km) and park considerably near a farmhouse on the L after another 0.3 miles (0.5 km). Have courage, most navigational problems are now behind — but take care not to get lost on the drive home.

MAP

OS half-inch to the mile Sheet 22. Luckily the route is such that it does not rely overheavily on the availability of a good map.

LENGTH

$6\frac{1}{2}$ miles (10.5 km)

ASCENT

1500 ft (460 m)

The central section of the Comeraghs (pronounced '*Come-err-ahs*'), between the Sgilloge Gap and Coumfea 3 miles (5 km) to the south-west, is a dull, boggy plateau which greatly contrasts with the virtual ring of fine corries surrounding it. This walk takes in three of the corries, holding in all six lakes and several small lochans. Each corrie is backed by grassy slopes about 700 ft (210 m) high, here and there broken by protruding horizontal sandstone, while higher up the otherwise smooth skyline is disrupted by an occasional jagged pinnacle. In a surprisingly remote area this is a walk of constantly changing vistas and sudden revelations, with lakes cupped in deep hollows unexpectedly coming into view over heathery hillocks and rolling moorland.

ROUTE DESCRIPTION (Map 2.3)

With the farmhouse on your left walk along the road to the T-junction. Turn R and cross through a gate on the L 150 yards (135 m) along (a truly enormous flat boulder will be visible in the field beyond it). Walk downhill diagonally R towards the river (the Nier, pronounced and sometimes spelt *Nire*) and follow it upstream, crossing what appears to be a major tributary at a clump of trees, but is in fact the Nier itself. Continue straight ahead (thus *not* following the Nier) along an intermittent path beside the stream to walk to the R of a ruin that lies beyond the junction of two more tributaries. The trick here is to pick the correct tributary among the complex gathering of tributaries on the bleak moorland hereabouts: you may need to take a compass-bearing south-east on the lower Sgilloge Lough in order to find it. Walk on the R bank and note, for reassurance, the fence running parallel to the stream on the other bank.

A path develops along the bank of this tributary, and where the fence swings R across the path, look out R for the lower Sgilloge Lough, the least impressive of all the lakes on this route. Continue on a path along the near shore over hummocky ground to the upper Sgilloge Lough *(1)*, which is surrounded by a great amphitheatre cut out of the cliffs with a narrow stream cascading down into its south-eastern corner — a good place for a rest.

The rule from here to the next corrie is to follow the contour of the hillside with the cliffs and high ground close on the L. At the upper Sgilloge Lough swing to the R to walk along the shore. Then walk to the so-far unvisited south side of the lower Sgilloge Lough and continue round the high, grassy ground on the L into the dull moorland at the lower edge of the next corrie, that holding Coumalocha (2). Once into the arms of the corrie swing

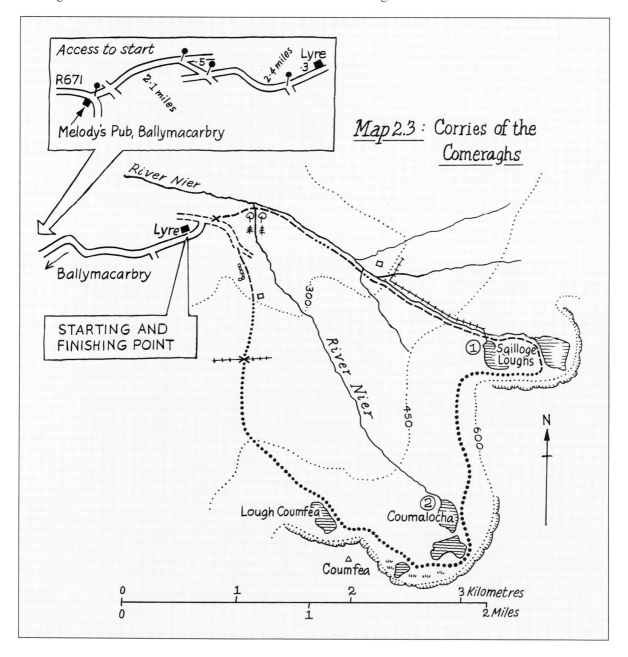

R away from the cliffs to visit the lower lake, and then walk along the shore to the next lake, which is very close by. This is the more impressive, though both are lovely. Walk from here over steep little heathery hummocks to the third lake in this corrie, the one nestling under the north-facing cliffs. This lake is backed by an evil-looking swamp that has been fenced in, presumably to keep sheep out.

Continue along the foot of the cliffs to Lough Coumfea, passing on the way the formidable pyramid of the mountain, also called Coumfea (2340 ft/713 m), soaring skyward and so much more impressive from below than on top. Walk the length of the lake on its R-hand side and continue north-west and north along a broad ridge towards fields on a bulge ahead. Before this bulge, cross a gate in a fence and then descend gradually towards the river R (it is the Nier again), keeping well above the thickly vegetated banks. Look out along here for the ruins of an old stone shelter 200 yards (180 m) from the near bank. From this shelter walk parallel to the river, following a path to a corner of wall. Take a track from here downhill (still parallel to the river), continuing straight ahead where it joins a farm road coming in from the R. Follow this round the hill L and back to the start.

The 'truly enormous flat boulder'

1 *Corries*

Corries, the deep hollows gouged out of the sides of the mountains, are a notable feature left from the Ice Age, and this is a good example of one. They were formed as the climate worsened at the onset of the cold. Snow gathered in north- and east-facing hollows sheltered from the prevailing winds and the sun. The snow solidified and accumulated over the years, eventually hollowing out a cliff-rimmed bed. Later still the solidified snow began to creep downhill, forming a glacier, to join other glaciers on the lower ground.

The hummocky ground below the corries on this route are moraines, rough unsorted rubble left behind by the snout of a glacier on its retreat at the end of an ice age.

Probably the finest corrie in Ireland, backed by cliffs 1400 ft (430 m) high, is at Coumshingaun, just to the east.

2 *The Dark Fisherman of Coumalocha*

Even though it is said to be haunted, fishermen are not afraid to spend the night at this lake. The spectre arises from the lake in the dead of night, takes the rod from fishermen who have caught no fish, catches trout for them and returns silently to the depths. This kindly ghost is called the Dark Fisherman of Coumalocha. If you are fishing, it is advisable not to rely entirely on him.

Opposite: *The River Nier*

2·4

THE LUGDUFFS

STARTING AND FINISHING
POINT
At the Visitor Centre at
Glendalough (124968). This is
reached by taking the R755/T61
to Laragh and then the
R756/L107 to Glendalough. The
Visitor Centre is on the L, and is
well signposted.
MAPS
The OS 1:50 000 Sheet 56 is
recommended. The OS Wicklow
District and the National Park
maps (at 1 inch to the mile and
1 : 25 000 respectively) are also
satisfactory, the latter depicting
the paths and tracks best of all.
LENGTH
8 miles (13 km)
ASCENT
1750 ft (540 m)

Glendalough, the village and valley, is a well-known monastic site and beauty spot. On both sides of the valley's two lakes and farther on to the west to bound a higher valley, Glenealo, run lines of delectable hills, steepening in places towards Glenealo into majestic cliffs. The southern line of these hills, a long ridge of hummocky peaks, collectively called the Lugduffs, gives an easy but spectacular stroll from Glendalough. This ridge is especially impressive on an eastern extension of the Lugduffs that directly overlooks the Upper Lake at Glendalough. After the Lugduffs, the walk descends into Glenealo, whose remote and gentle charms contrast sharply with the tourist bustle of Glen-

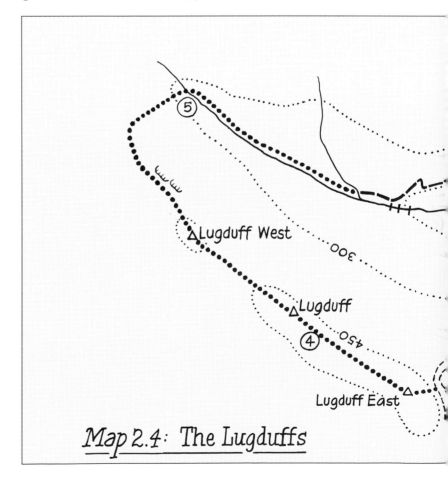

Map 2.4: The Lugduffs

dalough itself. The walk ends, as it began, along the scenic wooded shores of the Upper and Lower Lakes.

ROUTE DESCRIPTION (Map 2.4)

Turn L outside the Visitor Centre car-park, cross the village bridge on a sharp L bend, and turn L off the road to walk through the monastic site *(1)*. Cross the bridge beyond it and turn R onto a pleasant tree-lined forest road *(2), (3)*, which passes to the L of the Lower Lake. Directly ahead beyond the lake rises the wooded Spink, towering over the Upper Lake — a fine initial target to aim for. Take the second forest road steeply uphill, crossing a bridge (signed 'Poll an Easa'), branching L off it to take a path close to the cascade on the L.

At the top of the path rejoin the forest road and continue upwards to a multiple junction of forest roads. Turn sharp R here steeply uphill onto a forest road sign-posted 'Prezen Rock'. Follow the road to the first bend L, leaving it here to climb a stile on the R. Follow the path beyond diagonally uphill to the top of

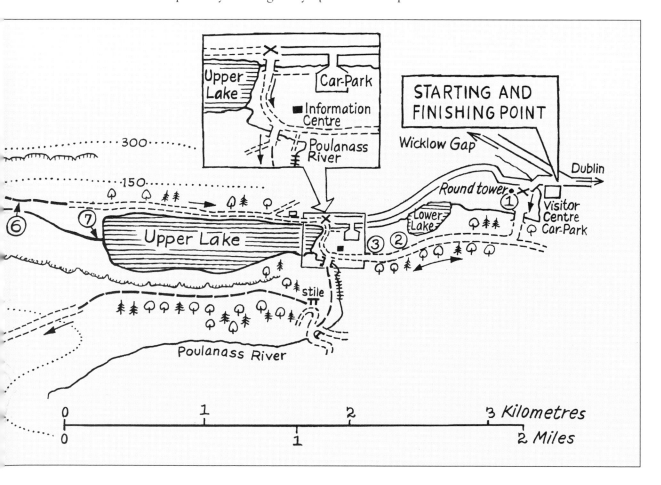

the Spink, where at the edge of the cliffs and with the magnificent trough sheltering the Upper Lake at your feet, you will doubtless conclude that the climb was well worth the effort.

Walk up the eroded path along the Spink so that the cliffs are on the R, continuing beyond the Upper Lake on what by here has become a track. Where this levels out (and here, in defiance of the maps, there are only scattered trees and clear-felled areas in the basin on the L) head directly towards the eastern end of the Lugduffs, picking up if fortunate an intermittent path.

Before starting along the Lugduffs, a word on navigation. The features on the Lugduffs do not lend themselves to determining your exact position, nor is it necessary that you should know it. However, if you do wish to know your position, the reservoir of the pumped storage station across the valley to the north provides a capital 'fix' (it has no other desirable attributes from a hillwalker's point of view).

Walk to Lugduff East and then to Lugduff itself over ground which, though soggy in places, allows good progress and offers magnificent views, south over the Lugnaquillia massif and north to Camaderry and beyond *(4)*. Lugduff (2154 ft/652 m), the highest of the family, is recognizable, apart from its cairn, by the great white quartzite boulders on the western side of its summit.

Walk onward to Lugduff West, after which a decisive drop into the col towards Conavalla marks the end of the Lugduffs. Turn R (north) in this col to reach the western end of the Glenealo Valley *(5)*. Cross the main stream in the valley and turn R to walk downstream on the L-hand bank along an intermittent path. At the start of the distinct drop into Glendalough the stream gathers force to drop in a series of waterfalls interspersed with tiny lakes that are partly hidden by thick vegetation. Around here the unpromising path graduates into an unexpectedly good track zigzagging down towards the Upper Lake, with steep ground clothed by occasional areas of trees on the R and boulders, scree and cliffs on the L.

Follow this track past the old mining ruins *(6)*, where it falters for a short distance, and then along the shore of the Upper Lake *(7)*. Just beyond the Upper Lake, cross a wooden bridge R, then follow the track beyond it parallel to the lake. Turn L at the fork and follow this forest road, the first of the day, back to the start.

The Upper Lake, Glendalough

43

Glenealo River

1 *The Monastic Site*

The monastic site at Glendalough is built around a monastery founded in the sixth century, which flourished as a place of learning and a focus for pilgrims until the twelfth century. The Round Tower dates from about the eleventh century and acted as a campanile and early-warning system against both foreign and native aggressors. Other buildings, mostly churches, are scattered along the valley to the east and west.

2 *Wicklow National Park*

Much of the area immediately south and west of here, covering 9400 acres (3800 hectares) and including nearly all the area covered by this walk, is in the Wicklow National Park. A separate area to the north covers 6900 acres (2800 hectares). It is hoped that eventually these two areas will be joined up and the total area greatly extended. There is an Information Centre for the park just before the climb to Poll an Easa.

3 *The Oakwoods*

The oakwoods here are probably a remnant of the great forests that once covered nearly all of Ireland. They were depleted in the Middle Ages to provide fuel and charcoal for mining.

4 *Bog Oak*

Watch out along the ridge of the Lugduffs for stumps of 'bog oak', partly exposed on the surface and in the peat hags (see p.14).

5 *The Large Mammals of Glenealo*

Herds of deer — sika, red and hybrids of the two — roam the entire area, grazing on the heath and bog vegetation. Of the three, the red deer is in danger of being overwhelmed by interbreeding. A band of feral goats also grazes in the Glenealo Valley and the adjacent mountains.

6 *Mining in Wicklow*

Mining for lead and copper was carried out in the nineteenth century and even for a short time in the 1920s. The zigzag track was originally a mining track. The metals occur along a metamorphic zone between the granite to the west and the older shales and slates to the east. Similar workings are evident in the glacial valleys north and south of here.

7 *The Disappearing Lakes*

The western shore of the Upper Lake has moved 130 yards (120 m) eastward in the last 80 years because of the wash-out from mining spoil, augmented by silt from the Glenealo River. In post-glacial times only one lake occupied the valley floor, but silt from the Poulanass River eventually split the lake in two.

SLIEVE BEARNAGH

At a car-park on the L of the
minor road (312314). From
Newcastle take the B180
(Hilltown road) forking L off it
onto the unclassified but labelled
Trassey Road 2.2 miles (3.5 km)
west of Bryansford. Drive onward
for 0.8 miles (1.3 km) to the car-
park.
MAPS
Northern Ireland OS 1:50 000
Sheet 29, or 1:25 000 Sheet
'Mourne Country'.
LENGTH
7 miles (11 km)
ASCENT
2850 ft (870 m)

Though the initial walk becomes a little tedious with long views
precluded by an increasingly narrow slabby-sided glen, the first,
sudden glimpse into the Silent Valley and across to the great arc
of peaks around it makes the effort seem trivial. Slieve Bearnagh
is the high point, literally and metaphorically, the sets of huge
boulders on its summit adding a touch of the spectacular to an
already impressive scene. The subsequent views, over the Meel-
mores and down by Fofanny Reservoir, are more gentle. The
walk ends as it began on the Ulster Way. An easy introductory
walk to the best of the Mournes.

ROUTE DESCRIPTION (Map 2.5)

Turn L out of the car-park *(1)*, pass the house on the L, and cross
the gate L just beyond it to follow the Ulster Way *(2)*. Continue
straight through another gate, thus leaving the Ulster Way, and
walk up a wide track, ignoring R and L turns which lead to quarry
workings *(3)*.

The Hare's Gap between Bearnagh and Slievenaglogh is the
first target, and before it the track becomes not so much intermittent as indecisive, spreading heedlessly over a wide area, so
that the gate at the gap in the Mourne Wall *(4)* ahead is a useful
landmark. At the gap cross this gate *(5)*, so revealing the splen-
dours of the Silent Valley and the high peaks of the Mournes
beyond it.

Beyond the gate, turn immediately R to follow the Mourne
Wall or, failing that, keep close to the steep slabs where
the wall is not continuous. Climb to the two sets of gigantic
piles of granite crowning the summit of Slieve Bearnagh
(2425 ft/739 m), the first of which is called the North Tor and
the other, a little way off, the Summit Tor. A good place to rest,
explore among the boulders and admire the excellent views.

Descend steeply from Slieve Bearnagh towards Slieve Meelmore, the Mourne Wall still on the R, taking a short path that
veers away from the Wall to avoid the Bearnagh Crags. At the col
continue along the Mourne Wall (not the other wall, which veers
L from it *(6)*) to reach the top of Slieve Meelmore
(2310 ft/704 m), crowned by one of the occasional towers along
the Wall *(7)*.

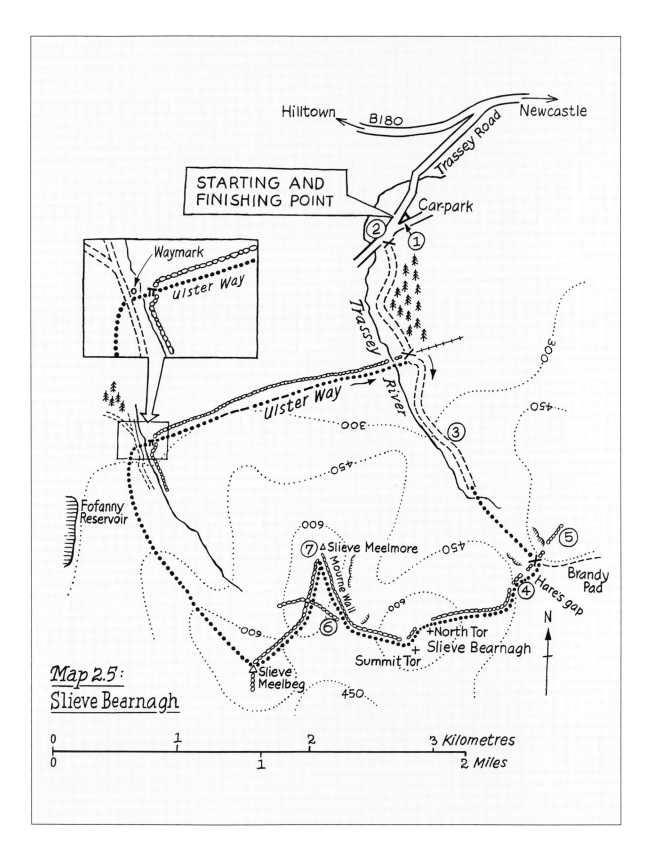

STARTING AND FINISHING POINT

Hilltown

B180

Newcastle

Trassey Road

Car-park

②

①

Waymark

Ulster Way

Trassey River

Ulster Way

300

300

450

③

300

450

Fofanny Reservoir

600

⑦ △Slieve Meelmore

450

⑤

Brandy Pad

Mourne Wall

600

④ Hare's gap

600

⑥

+North Tor

+ Slieve Bearnagh

Summit Tor

N

△Slieve Meelbeg

450

Map 2.5:
Slieve Bearnagh

0   1   2   3 Kilometres

0   1   2 Miles

Hare's Gap (and the Mourne Wall)

From Meelmore follow the Wall down to the col and thence up to Slieve Meelbeg (2323 ft/708 m). Leave the Wall here to follow an intermittent and short-lived path down the north-west spur of Meelbeg with the Fofanny Reservoir prominent on the L and a wooded shore on the gentle slope behind it. Towards the bottom of the spur, veer R off it to meet an Ulster Way waymark, and follow the Way across a stream and over a stile.

Continue on the Ulster Way, with a wall on the L, all the way to the second gate of the day. Surprisingly, in an area of generally clear paths, this section of the Ulster Way is intermittent and the ground underfoot wet. At the gate, turn L and follow the Way back to the metalled road. Turn R for the car-park.

1   *The Cecil Newman Memorial*
    The simple stone memorial in the car-park commemorates Cecil Newman, a planner, who worked in the Northern Ireland Civil Service. He was among the first to recognize the necessity of planning for the mountain areas, particularly the Mournes.

2   *The Ulster Way*

This was the first Long Distance Route in the island, and is still by far the longest. The route is about 440 miles (700 km) long and goes right round Northern Ireland, taking in a wide variety of terrain. Most of it is waymarked.

3   *The 'Plug and Feathers' Method*

Look out along the way for wedge marks along the edges of granite stones. To split the quarried stones, rough holes were made in a line across the stone, and the plug (a small iron wedge) inserted between the feathers (two thin strips of steel).

4   *The Mourne Wall*

This sturdily built wall, the most noteworthy granite wall in a land of such walls, is 22 miles (35 km) long and encloses the catchment area of the Silent Valley Reservoir. It was built as late as 1910–22 by local unemployed men using locally quarried stones, which were transported by handbarrows, no animals being used. The route of the Wall was until recently that of the Mourne Wall Walk, which attracted annually such huge numbers (several thousands) that it has wisely been abandoned.

5   *Diamond Rocks*

A few hundred yards north-east of here are the Diamond Rocks where, if you have an abundance of patience, knowledge, skill and above all luck, you may chance upon almost worthless lodes of 'precious' crystalline stones such as topaz and quartz.

6   *The Stone Walls of Mourne*

Drystone walls, of which the Mourne Wall is the most notable example, are a common feature of the Mournes. Local farmers neatly constructed them of undressed granite stones and boulders. They served as a boundary for sheep pastures.

7   *Meelmore and Meelbeg*

'More' means big in Gaelic and 'beg' means small, but Meelmore is lower than Meelbeg by 13 ft (4 m). It is doubtful if the people who named the two mountains realized or would have cared about this seeming error. They probably named them on the basis of the apparent bulk as seen from where they lived.

The Tors on Slieve Bearnagh

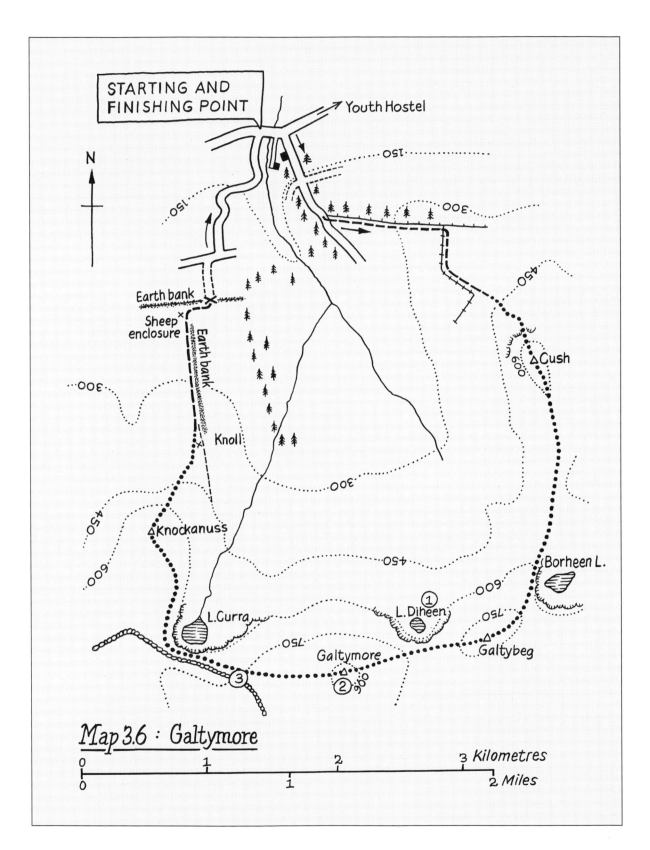

STARTING AND
FINISHING POINT

Youth Hostel

N

150

150

150

300

Earth bank

Sheep
enclosure

Earth bank

450

Knoll

△Cush

600

300

300

450

△Knockanuss

450

600

Borheen L.

L.Curra

①
L.Diheen

600

750

750

Galtymore

750

Galtybeg

△

750

③

②
900

Map 3.6 : Galtymore

0   1   2   3 Kilometres

0   1   2 Miles

3·6

GALTYMORE

STARTING AND FINISHING POINT

At a turn-off on the south side of the southernmost of the two Glen of Aherlow roads (872281). From Cahir take the N24 (Limerick road) branching L off it after 6 miles (9.5 km) to follow signs for Ballydavid Wood Youth Hostel. Do not turn L up the side-road to the Hostel; instead continue along the Glen of Aherlow road. Pass Condon's Pub on the R and across a bridge 1.7 miles (2.7 km) beyond it. Park on the waste ground on the L just beyond the bridge.

MAPS

The only maps available are the OS half-inch to the mile series, and both Sheets 18 and 22 are needed for this walk. The coverage of the Galtees is inconveniently divided between these two sheets; they have no overlap, thus contributing to the cartographic deficiencies of the area.

LENGTH

8 miles (13 km)

ASCENT

3400 ft (1040 m)

The northern slopes of the Galtees rise abruptly as a series of broad spurs from the rich agricultural dairy lands of south Tipperary. South of these spurs the otherwise smooth form of the high east–west grassy ridge that forms the backbone of the range is disrupted by a line of surprisingly deep and dramatic corries. By ascending one spur and descending another the walk includes the highest peak of the range and its one Munro, taking in on the way the rims of three of the best corries in the range.

ROUTE DESCRIPTION (Map 3.6)

Cross back over the bridge and take the second turn R, a narrow, metalled road. Keep on this where forest roads leave to R and L. On emerging from forest on the L (it continues on the R), and with Cush ahead displaying great blocks of rock on its otherwise smooth R flank, cross a fence L to walk uphill along a rough path with fence and forest close on the L. Cross one fence near the crest of the hill and turn R to follow the path towards Cush. Continue upwards where the fence swings R and climb steeply over grass, and near the summit between conglomerate boulders, to Cush (2109 ft/643 m).

Continue along the narrow ridge of Cush, and beyond it drop to the boggy col towards Galtybeg (only at this point will the two summits of Cush become evident). Climb over grass beyond the col, fairly steeply at first and then more steeply, as far as Galtybeg, with the impressive corrie holding Borheen Lough on the L. Galtybeg (2629 ft/801 m) commands excellent views, the tiered cliffs of vertical rock in the next corrie, that of Lough Diheen *(1)*, each topped by a precarious ramp of grass, being particularly impressive. Drop to the col and from there climb to Galtymore (3018 ft/920 m), signalled by a cairn, the lower part of an OS obelisk and a white cross and memorial plaque *(2)*. The view from here is exceptionally wide north and south, towards the plains of Tipperary and beyond in one direction and towards the Knockmealdowns in the other.

Continue to the western end of the summit ridge to a large cairn, dropping sharply beyond it to come within sight of a high wall *(3)*. Veer R to walk parallel to it, the corrie of Lough Curra

The Galtees across the Glen of Aherlow

on the R. Where the corrie rim veers R away from the wall follow the rim over the short climb to Knockanuss (2166 ft/660 m), descend along the spur north-west, veering R off it to pick up an earthbank near a small grassy knoll. Follow the earthbank down to enclosed land at a sheep enclosure. Turn R at another earthbank just beyond it and L through the first gate. Beyond it follow a track, which gradually improves to a metalled road as it gathers tributary lanes on its meandering route down-hill. Follow the metalled road to the main road and the starting point.

1   Lough Diheen
    The corrie lake north-east of Galtymore attracted the rather gullible attention of the Halls, a husband and wife team who travelled around Ireland in the early 1840s. They uncritically re-told local stories that the lake was unfathomable, that if only a slight breeze blew across it the area round the lake became intensely cold, no matter how warm the day, and that in spite of its apparent narrowness a stone could not be thrown across it even when a champion in this simple sport

Cush and Galtybeg

hurled it. All this they, or rather the locals, attributed to a Pooka (ghost) which inhabited the lake. (A note for those interested in the inconsequential: the lake is about 80 yards (70 m) across, a considerable distance even for a champion stone-thrower.)

2   *The Plaque on Galtymore*

The plaque on the summit commemorates James Blake and Richard Hayward. James Blake was a local who, as the plaque states, died while trying to rescue a woman bather in Tangier. Richard Hayward was from far-off Belfast. He wrote many books and guides between 1922 and his death in 1964, mostly, but not exclusively, about his native Ulster. It is not clear why the two men are jointly remembered in this way.

3   *The Stone Wall*

This wall was built late in the nineteenth century to keep cattle away from the steep ground on the northern side of the hills, and also perhaps to define grazing boundaries. It is quite unusual for such a substantial wall to be built at this considerable height.

A TRAVERSE OF THE MOURNES

STARTING POINT
At a car-park (345219) on the
mountain (that is, north) side of
the C313 that runs from the
Silent Valley east along the edge
of the range. Take the A2 for
1 mile (1.6 km) north of
Annalong, turning inland here,
signposted 'Silent Valley 5', and
drive straight ahead for 2.3 miles
(3.7 km). Alternatively, take the
C313 east from the gates of the
Silent Valley Reservoir for 2.5
miles (4.0 km).
FINISHING POINTS
At Donard Park (375306), a
major car-park at the south (that
is mountain) side of Newcastle.
The shorter route returns to the
starting point.
MAPS
Northern Ireland 1:50 000 Sheet
29, or 1:25 000 Sheet 'Mourne
Country'.
LENGTH
6½ miles (10.5 km) for the short
route, 9½ miles (15 km) for the
long.
ASCENT
2100 ft (640 m) for the short
route, 3950 ft (1200 m) for the
long.

A traverse of the Mournes, south to north, is a moderately long
but satisfying undertaking since it includes perhaps the finest
peak, Slieve Binnian, and a selection of the best scenery in the
range. This scenery is particularly good to the west — down
into the Silent Valley and across to the great outcrops of Bearnagh. It must be admitted that the three peaks to be traversed
north of Slieve Binnian are fairly undistinguished, and though
they fall in impressive slabs to the east, they are a little dull on
their western flanks. For this reason, a short route for returning
to the start from Binnian is given. However, if you persevere
with the longer route your efforts will be rewarded by good
views to the town of Newcastle and northwards over lowlands
and the coast beyond.

ROUTE DESCRIPTION (Map 3.7)

Take the track at the R of the car-park. Just over a ½ mile (1 km)
further up, pass through the far-right gate and continue along the
track with a wall of gigantic boulders on the L (Mourne Wall).
Keep close to the Wall where the track veers R, and climb
steadily upwards all the way to the point where the Wall prudently, but only temporarily, discontinues at steep slabs almost
at the top of Slieve Binnian. Cross the end of the Wall
here and veer L under the slabs to reach the huge horizontal
granite Summit Tor dominating the top of Slieve Binnian
(2451 ft/747 m) (1).

From Binnian the route is quite simple. Take the path from the
summit, first to the L of the huge boulders of the North Tor, and
then continue downwards to the col facing Slievelamagan.

Short route Take a clear path R, which runs to the R of Blue
Lough and thence to the main track of the Annalong Valley.

Long route Climb up the pathless — and relatively dull —
slopes of Slievelamagan (2310 ft/704 m), drop to the col north of
it and ascend Cove Mountain (2145 ft/655 m) keeping to the L of
the direct route to avoid steep ground. From Cove, drop to a

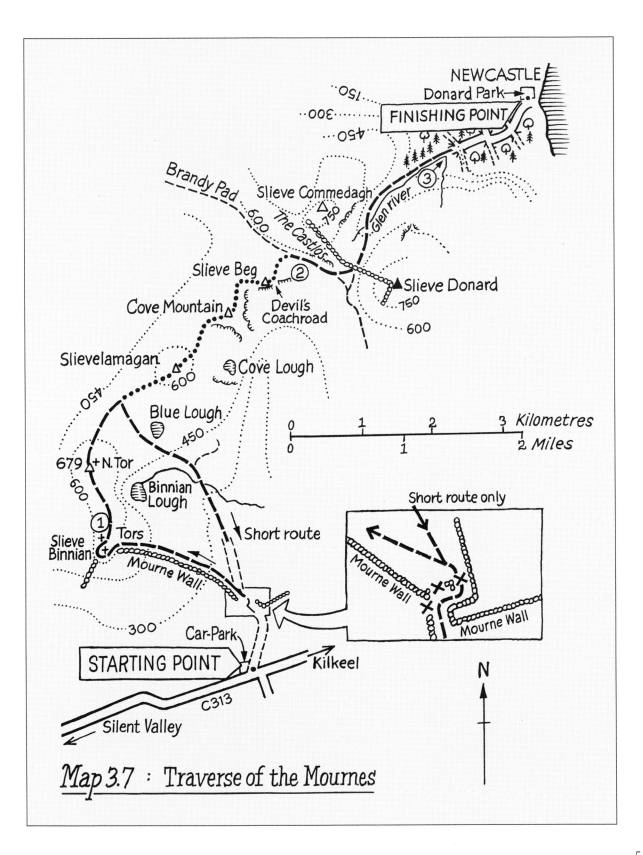

Map 3.7 : Traverse of the Mournes

Slieve Binnian from the south

sandy col towards Slieve Beg (about 1940 ft/590 m) and climb the peat-hagged slopes to the summit, a slightly unnecessary manoeuvre but worth it for the views it gives down cliffs pierced by a steep and narrow gully R, called the Devil's Coachroad. Drop a little to the col north and turn R onto the Brandy Pad *(2)*, the path which runs east–west across the southern slopes of Slieve Commedagh. Take the Pad under the cliffs of the Castles on the L, and beyond them leave it to climb L to the high pass between Commedagh and Slieve Donard. Cross the Mourne Wall at the pass and descend between cliffs towards the source of the River Glen, picking up a path that crosses the quickening stream R to L at its upper reaches *(3)*.

The aim now is to follow the stream down into Newcastle. Take the path downstream, crossing into forest at a stile. Cross over to the R bank at the second bridge down, and back to the L at the third, so keeping all the way to a path. Where the path joins a track further down on level ground turn R onto it, to keep close to the stream on the R. Keep on the track to the car-park just ahead.

1   *The Reservoirs of the Silent Valley*
   The Silent Valley to the west cradles two major reservoirs. The larger, Silent Valley Reservoir dates from the 1930s and the smaller Ben Crom Reservoir to its north dates from 1957. Both reservoirs serve Belfast and surrounding areas.

2   *The Brandy Pad*
   In the eighteenth and early nineteenth century the Brandy Pad was a favoured route of smugglers transporting wines and spirits, tobacco, tea, silk and (strangely) soap, all of which would have been landed from the Isle of Man onto deserted beaches. The goods were loaded onto ponies and taken under cover of darkness over the mountains west to Hilltown.

3   *The Ice House*
   The igloo-like stone structure on the opposite bank, located just before forest is reached, is an 'ice-house', which once functioned as a primitive refrigerator. Since the owners of the ice-house lived down in Newcastle, a certain amount of forethought would have been needed in deciding what was required from it.

Ben Crom Reservoir and Slieve Bearnagh (centre)

57

LUGNAQUILLIA AND THE GLEN OF IMAAL

In the Glen of Imaal at a junction on a side-road (982948). Take the N81 to the junction on the east (L from Dublin) for Donard and go straight through the village, watching out for the slightly offset crossroads here. Pass the Youth Hostel and drive straight ahead for another 1.6 miles (2.6 km) to a side road R and a cryptic and oddly worded Army injunction on a signboard on the L reading 'WALKING ROUTE FOLLOW'. Park carefully on the grass around here. (A note for the faint-hearted: this starting point facilitates an escape route from the pass between Imaal and Glenmalure.)
MAPS
The OS 1:50 000 Sheet 56 map is recommended. The Wicklow District one-inch to the mile map, though not quite as useful, is adequate.
LENGTH
15½ miles (25 km)
ASCENT
3400 ft (1050 m)

Lugnaquillia at 3039 ft (925 m) is the highest mountain in Ireland outside Kerry, the qualification admittedly being extremely significant. It stands at the centre of a series of spurs reaching starfish-like in all directions and so allows a good variety of routes up one spur, down another. Though the summit is an unimpressive grassy plateau, the views it provides are excellent, particularly to the north. The high-level gradual descent in this direction, included in this route, extends and modifies these views and turns a simple mountain climb into an impressive circuit.

ROUTE DESCRIPTION (Map 4.8)

Facing away from the Army board, take the side-road south through an area of scattered trees past the memorial on the L *(1)*, over a bridge spanning the Little Slaney River and up to the hamlet of Seskin. Turn L here along a rough road which ends at a T-junction. Continue straight ahead through a gate onto a track marked by an occasional Army waymark. Walk steadily upwards on this track, which further on narrows to a path to reach the top of Camarahill (1567 ft/480 m), an undistinguished outlier of Lugnaquillia.

Drop slightly beyond Camarahill, after which continue the steady climb, which steepens onto a rocky shoulder as the summit plateau of Lugnaquillia nears. Walk across the short grass to reach the huge cairn marking the summit at 3039 ft (925 m). The mountain indicator here points to an impressive array of peaks, including some in Wales. To obtain the widest panorama it is necessary to walk a little way from the cairn, an effort far outweighed by the consequent dramatic, broad views.

The descent from Lugnaquillia is an easy and scenic one. Walk north-east and then north-west, with the shoulder of Cannow to the L, so keeping to the high grassy ground. Along this initial stretch pick up a good path which continues all the way down to the boggy ground facing Camenabologue. On this gradual

SAFETY NOTE

The area enclosed by this route is a military artillery range. Do not diverge to the L of the route. If firing is taking place, the whole area (including this route) will be out of bounds. Though firing is infrequent it is imperative that you check with the Army authorities before setting out: Tel: 045–54626 or 045–54653.

descent watch out for the rounded hills to the R of the path, whose high ground may mislead the unwary into wandering east. On a more cheerful note, look out also for the great whale-back peak of Tonelagee prominent ahead, and the tiny Art's Lough across a valley to the R of the route *(2)*.

From the low point climb Camenabologue (2495 ft/758 m) through a rocky area, and northwards beyond it descend through peat hags to the indistinct pass between the Glen of Imaal and Glenmalure *(3), (4)*, a pass marked by Army signposts. Here you may wish to return directly to the starting point. If so, take the clear path directly west following a line of Army waymarks down through open moorland, along an untidy forest road and through an area of pleasant deciduous trees to the start.

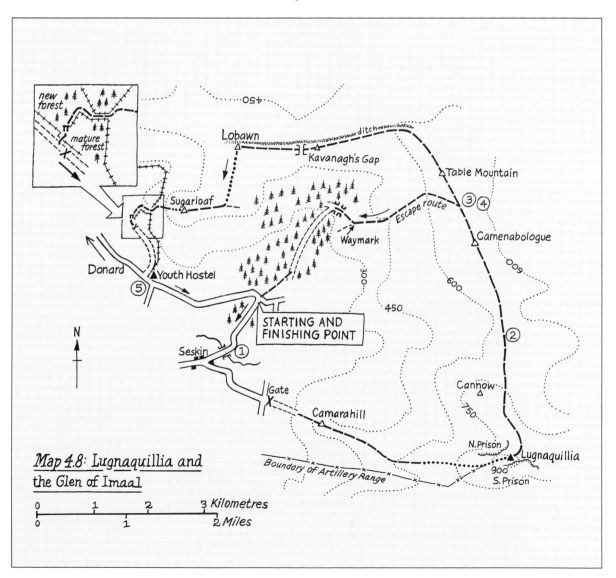

Map 4.8: Lugnaquillia and the Glen of Imaal

For the full route continue north at the pass to the cairn on Table Mountain (2302 ft/702 m), a mountain which lives up to its unflattering name all too well. Continue north-west from Table across a broad, windswept expanse of bogland, aiming for the long spur running west on the northern side of the Glen of Imaal. Along the initial stretch from Table, a wide but intermittent ditch develops, a useful aid in navigating all the way to Lobawn.

Once on the spur the route is generally downwards, the two rises being an unusually green unnamed hill east of Kavanagh's Gap and the rise to Lobawn itself (2097 ft/636 m), a grassy peak crowned by a WD (War Department) pillar. From Lobawn head on a dog-leg south and then west to Sugarloaf (1817 ft/554 m), following a clear path on the westward stretch. The descent from Sugarloaf is steep and gorse-impeded. Aim a little north of west and at forest turn L downhill to a point where the boundary fence is supplemented by horizontal wooden poles. Beyond these, two lines of fencing run directly into the forest (it is important to find this point). Cross the boundary fence and walk between the two lines of fencing on a narrow path, and beyond it keep close to the fence on the L. Turn L with this fence to a grassy track which can be reached using a stile.

Turn L onto the track and follow it on the level, and later downhill, first through deciduous and then through coniferous trees to a metalled road. Turn L here for a direct walk to the starting point (5).

1   The Memorial in the Glen

The memorial here honours four officers and 12 other ranks of the Irish Army who were killed at Leitrim Mountain near here in 1941. Twenty others were injured, 12 of them seriously. The accident occurred when a fuse failed during a demonstration of the operation of an anti-tank mine. Curiously, the report of this major accident in the local newspaper merited as much space as cake-making competitions in nearby villages.

In 1979 three children were killed and nine injured in a shell explosion in this area while they were throwing 'scrap metal' around. Since then, security around the range has been greatly tightened.

Looking across the top of Glenmalure

The Glen of Imaal Artillery Range has been used by both the British Army in its time, and later by the Irish Army. On the walk you will see several 'WD' pillars, indicating the boundary of War Department territory.

2   *River Basin and Glacial Valley*
The contrast here between the broad, shallow river basin to the west (Imaal) and the deep, narrow glacial valley to the east (Glenmalure) is very striking. In this range as elsewhere glaciers tended to form on the north and east of the mountains, where shelter from the prevailing westerlies and the sun allowed snow to accumulate.

3   *The Pass between Glenmalure and Imaal*
Until the last century, coach and horse could use the track between the two glens and there was frequent communication between them. The track is now almost non-existent near the top of the pass to the east.

4   *Three Lakes*
The two lakes seen ahead are called 'Three Lakes'. If there ever was a third lake it has long since dried up.

5   *Irish Elk in Ballinclea Bog*
The skull and much of the antlers of an Irish elk (*Megacerous hibernicus*) were dug out of the bog near here during drainage operations in 1983. The elk, which lived 7000–10 000 years ago, was about the size of a horse, with antlers 12 ft (3.7 m) across.

Summit of Lugnaquillia

Introduction

This region comprises the large, sprawling county of Donegal and the area to its south in Sligo, which is geographically close but geologically far distant from it. Backing a rugged indented northern coast, the core of the region consists of the great ranges of hills, much of them over 2000 ft (610 m), stretching in parallel lines south-west to north-east; Errigal to Muckish, and the Derryveagh and Glendowan Mountains. Each range is bare and unforested and each separated from its neighbours by lowland bog or lake. The clear-cut orientation of these hills reminds one of the Scottish Highlands and no wonder, since they belong to the same mountain-building epoch. Indeed, not only the hills echo Scotland; the people of Donegal have more than a touch of the Scot about them in accent and in their forthright manner, accentuated by the seasonal migration to Scotland that has long been a tradition here.

South of this core area, in a wide band across the centre of Donegal, are lower and less rugged mountains degenerating in more than a few places into windswept moorland. In the southwest of Donegal is a great area of mountain bulging westward which includes the massive cliffs of Slieve League and, fronting Donegal Bay, a tangle of muted mountains and high ground which has just a trace still of the south-west to north-east trend of north Donegal. A route along the sea-cliffs at Slieve League has been omitted. Of course the cliffs are spectacular but it is essentially an unchanging spectacle with a dull landward side. In addition, access is difficult.

The scarplands and tiny but rugged hills of Sligo (and Leitrim) across Donegal Bay are quite different to any part of Donegal, or to anywhere else in Ireland for that matter. This is a gentle and less wild area with strong literary and poetic associations, though the attractions for the walker are far from minor.

Seven walks in this area have been included. One representative sample from the Sligo area was essential, and the plateau of Ben Bulben, the name widely associated in both poetic and mountaineering terms with the whole area, gives as good a walk as any and better than most. The Bluestacks, the highest group in the south of Donegal at just over 2000 ft (610 m) was perhaps an odd choice, given their gently moulded summits and semi-aqueous

fringes. Nevertheless, it is an area whose subtle pleasures are reserved for those who are prepared to persevere.

Lough Eske from the Blue Stacks

The remaining five routes encompass the great heartland of north Donegal. The lake and Castle of Glenveagh, the focal point of a National Park, provides a rare opportunity for a short walk combined with a visit to an elegant house and gardens. Two routes, the circuit of the Poisoned Glen and the climb to Slieve Snaght, are both in the lofty Derryveagh Mountains. The former route approaches the range from the north, so taking in the scarred cliffs almost surrounding the wild, strangely-named defile. The latter's goal is the great dome-shaped peak, at 2240 ft (683 m) the highest in the range. The approach is from the south where the frowning cliffs of the Bingorms confront the low and boggy shores of Lough Barra.

Errigal and Muckish are the two best-known mountains in Donegal. And deservedly so, because they are two fine peaks. Taken separately they do not form good, looped walks, but together they give a tough but highly attractive route. Lastly, on the rugged, indented coastline facing north against the Atlantic is a walk on Horn Head peninsula, one of several impressive promontories in the region.

GLENVEAGH

At Glenveagh Castle (021209) in Glenveagh National Park. The entrance to the National Park is on the R251/L82 and is well signposted. A bus takes visitors from the Visitor Centre near the entrance as far as the Castle — cars are not allowed. There is a small charge for this service. The bus does not operate in winter.

MAP
The Park authorities issue an adequate one inch to the mile map at the entrance. If not available Northern Ireland OS Sheet 1 or Republic of Ireland OS Sheet 1 (both half-inch to the mile) suffices.

LENGTH
6 miles (9.5 km) for the short route; 7 miles (10.5 km) for the long.

ASCENT
400 ft (120 m) for the short; 1100 ft (340 m) for the long.

ACCESS
Walking off paths may be restricted in winter to facilitate deer culling. For details telephone 074–37090.

Glenveagh Castle, the focal point of Glenveagh National Park, and the starting point of this walk, is an oasis of sophisticated civilization in a desert of natural wildness. The Castle and its gardens stand on the shores of Lough Veagh, which in turn occupies a long, straight, beautiful valley, almost entirely unwooded except for a plague of rhododendrons on the hillside. The whole atmosphere of the area is as much Scottish as Irish, a feeling enhanced by the red deer that roam the hillsides. Both the routes given explore the narrow main valley and even narrower side valley, in which mixed woodland softens the otherwise bleak valley floor. Both give views of the spectacular three-tiered Astelleen waterfall. The long route, in addition, samples the high moorland, so giving long views of neighbouring peaks for comparatively little effort.

ROUTE DESCRIPTION (Map 1.9)

Short route From behind the Castle *(1)* walk south-west on a clear track to the end of Lough Veagh; that is, keep it on the R *(2), (3)*. Just beyond it, past a small cottage tucked into the bank on the R, turn back L steeply uphill onto a side track not shown on the map issued by the Park authority. Keep on this to walk through a mixed wood and later into a narrow, open valley. Turn back where the track loses itself in rough wet country and retrace your steps to the Castle.

Long route Walk along the lake as described above, but continue straight ahead on the main track where the side track branches L. Pass to the R of the stalking cottage. Where the track swings L and then R and immediately passes a copse of beeches on the L, the first point where rhododendrons do not block the upper slopes, ascend L up a steep, wet, pathless hillside. At the top, between the two muted peaks of Farscollop ('Scollops' on the Park authority's map), cross the narrow, flat saddle and descend on the other side into a very wet side valley of the main valley.

Turn L and walk along an initially treeless, pathless stretch which further on gives way to a mixed wood in a narrow steep-sided valley. Follow the track which gradually emerges, keeping to it as far as the main track. Turn R onto this for the Castle.

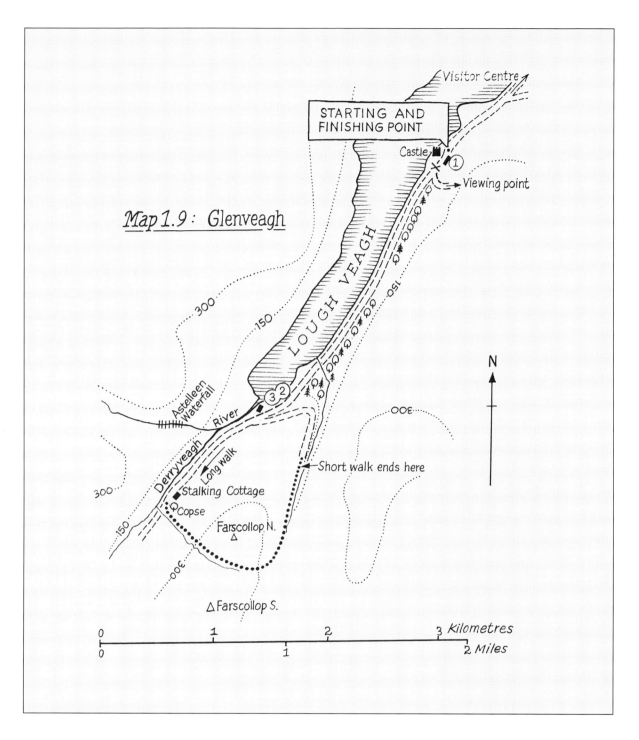

Map 1.9: Glenveagh

1   *Glenveagh National Park*
    The Park covers 24,600 acres (10,000 ha) and includes a long
    line of mountains running north-east from Slieve Snaght as
    well as lower ground to the south-east of Lough Veagh. Part
    of Errigal is a detached segment. The Interpretative Centre

Lough Veagh

near the entrance car-park gives a fine overview of all aspects of the Park, including its geology and fauna and flora.

The Castle, a castellated four-storey mansion made from rough-hewn granite, was built about 1870 and it and its extensive gardens were donated to the state by its American owner in 1981. Both Castle and gardens are open to the public. It is a tribute to the attentive work of the planners and gardeners that a variety of exotic plants from as far away as Chile, Madeira and Tasmania thrive here in such unpromising and unlikely surroundings, sheltered by pines and rhododendrons. Sculptures and other formal features counterbalance the otherwise informal layout of the gardens.

2   *Derrybeg Bog*
The small bog at the south-west end of Lough Veagh is slightly dome-shaped like a raised bog, but its vegetation is more akin to that in a lowland blanket bog; that is, it is dominated by grass and sedge, and not shrub and moss as in the raised bogs. This bog has been classified as being of national importance.

3   *The Glenveagh Evictions*
Glenveagh was the scene of a notorious series of evictions in 1861. The landlord, John George Adair, evicted all 254 of his tenants in that year after a steward was murdered and sheep stolen. People horrified by these evictions paid the passage of the former tenants to Australia, where they founded a settlement named after their far-off native place.

Opposite: *A stream in Glenveagh*

2·10

SLIEVE SNAGHT

STARTING AND FINISHING
POINT
Just north of Lough Barra on the
R254 (Doocharry to Church Hill
road) (938134). Park near the
farmhouse that has a thick shelter
belt of trees, the only one for
miles, on both sides of the road.
MAPS
Northern Ireland OS Sheet 1 or
Republic of Ireland Sheet 1 (both
half-inch to the mile). The entire
route is also shown on the
Glenveagh National Park one-inch
to the mile map and this is better
than either of the half-inch ones.
LENGTH
5 miles (8 km)
ASCENT
2000 ft (610 m)

Slieve Snaght is a fine peak, a great granite dome whose rocky flanks glisten in the fleeting sunlight which frequently follows rain. At 2240 ft (683 m) it is the highest of the Derryveagh Mountains, a range which exhibits to perfection the north-east to south-west orientation of the mountains of north Donegal. The peak can be approached from the north at Dunlewy, a route which entails a long walk-in, or from the south by a shorter approach, the one chosen here. A minor road runs through countryside of desolate splendour giving a long but memorable drive to the start. The route penetrates the south-west end of the great barrier of the Bingorms, a fine line of cliffs, crags and gullies. After climbing Slieve Snaght and exploring the tangled terrain of dyke and lakelet to its north-east, the route descends gently around this barrier's northern side.

ROUTE DESCRIPTION (Map 2.10)

From the farmhouse, walk south-west (that is, with high ground on the R) for 350 yards (300 m) along the road to a bridge, cross it and turn immediately R onto a rough, intermittent path along a stream, the Sruhanerolee River (1). Follow it into the wet upper basin, keeping to slightly higher ground L to avoid the soggiest terrain. Climb up beside the high waterfall at the end of the basin (not the waterfall on the R), keeping to the shelving slabs if you have sufficient friction and nerve.

At the top of the waterfall, cross the stream to head north-east to Slieve Snaght (there is no need to continue to the top of the col), a stiff ascent with several crags to surmount or evade and at least one intermediate cairn and several false summits to cause disappointment. Slieve Snaght, crowned by a fine cairn, gives excellent views in all directions, those north and north-east to Errigal and the Aghlas being particularly good.

From Slieve Snaght continue in approximately the same direction north-east to the side of Lough Slievesnaght, a lake tucked into a bleak but highly scenic rocky mountainside. From its northern end take the conspicuous grassy ramp towards the southern Rocky Cap Mountain, so avoiding long and steep crags to the L.

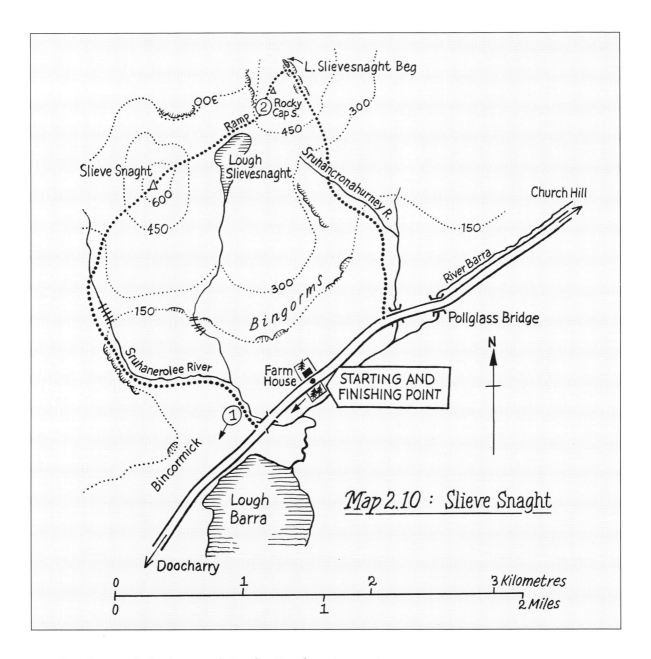

Map 2.10 : Slieve Snaght

After the initial climb towards Rocky Cap there is a curious area of tiny dykes cradling lakelets *(2)*. Some sections of the walls of the dykes are in the form of rough, square granite blocks, with one rock in particular protruding precariously over a dizzying void. Walk to the small cairn on the southern Rocky Cap (about 1700 ft/520 m) and continue towards, but not to, the northern top. At a lake with crags falling directly into its near side (Lough Slievesnaghtbeg), a larger one than those so far encountered around this peak, turn R (i.e., south-east) thus heading along a narrow valley.

Continue down into a wide, wet basin following the Sruhan-cronahurney River, the major stream. Veer R from the stream as you descend, to emerge onto the road at a bridge initially hidden by cliffs R, and turn R for the starting point.

1   *Lough Barra Bog*
South-west of Lough Barra and partly visible on the ascent is Lough Barra Bog, a lowland blanket bog with numerous pools and lakelets that make it hazardous to explore. The river that flows through it is a habitat for Greenland white-fronted geese, golden plover and merlins.

The Sruhanerolee River

2   The Dykes

The narrow, straight and often long trenches which are crossed on this and Route 13 mark the lines of igneous dykes. During a geologically recent volcanic era hot magma was thrust vertically up from below the earth's crust to cleave the pre-existing rock, here granite. The upthrust rock, also granite, proved to be less durable than the metamorphozed pre-existing rock and has been worn down quicker by erosion, thus leaving the present-day trenches.

These dykes are well displayed on an aerial photograph at the Visitor Centre at Derryveagh National Park.

Peat cuttings

HORN HEAD

At a side turn on Horn Head
peninsula (017382). Take the
signposted road off the N56 at
Dunfanaghy, drive across Horn
Head bridge and park at the side-
road on L, 0.7 miles (1.1 km)
further on.
MAPS
Northern Ireland OS Sheet 1 or
Republic of Ireland OS Sheet 1
(both half-inch to the mile) are
adequate.
LENGTH
$7\frac{1}{2}$ miles (12 km)
ASCENT
800 ft (240 m)
SAFETY NOTE
The initial part of the route is
difficult to follow in summer
when the bracken is high. In
addition, the pleasant walk along
the beach at the start is severely
restricted when the tide is in. If
this is the case take the road, not
the rough country behind the
beach, to avoid an impassable
stretch of vegetation.

On a rugged coastline dominated by cliff-bound headlands and
long, surf-fringed inlets, Horn Head peninsula is probably the
most spectacular. Bounded on the east by Sheep Haven and the
headland of Rosguill, and on the west by a long sweep of desolate
shoreline reaching to Bloody Foreland, it offers excellent long
views of sea-cliff and coastal scenery backed on the landward side
by the high peaks of Muckish and its western neighbours.

The walk, one of several that can be easily devised on the
peninsula, is along the more rugged eastern side. It starts quietly
enough at sea-level. Gradually the tempo quickens along a low
ragged coastline and over a shaggy headland until finally one faces
the towering quartzite cliffs of Horn Head itself rising sheer
626 ft (191 m) from the surging ocean. The return is more
placid; an easy stroll by road through the rough moorland at the
centre of the peninsula.

ROUTE DESCRIPTION (Map 2.11)

Continue along the road that you arrive on *(1)* and descend to the
beach where the road rises and continues straight ahead. Walk
along the beach noting thick vegetation centred on a small stream
which issues onto the beach *(2)*. Beyond it, climb the low, grassy
slope and continue parallel to the shore, keeping it on the R.

A word about the long stretch from here to Horn Head. There
are numerous paths wending here and there, each offering some
help to the walker but none giving a definitive route. In the wild,
rough and rising ground to the Head you must navigate without a
sure path, a not over-difficult task given that the sea is always to
be kept on the R and that, in case of difficulty, there is generally a
road not too far off on the L.

Follow a wall which runs parallel to the shore to an inlet on
the R, and then continue past an amphitheatre sheltering an array
of plants, which thrive in the comparatively calm ecosystem.
Beyond this are a few curious, flat-topped islands and peninsulas.
At the last of these, Duncap Isle, the coast swings from north to
west to reveal Traglisk Point with the ruined Signal Tower on its
shoulder. After this turn, climb along the shoulder of Croaghnamaddy and beyond it continue along what is now a high cliff *(3)*

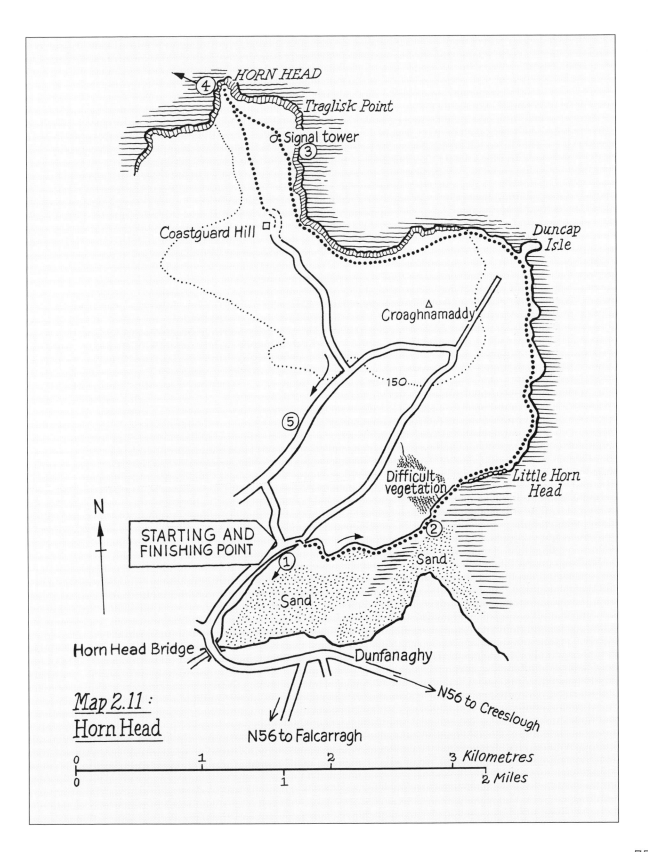

HORN HEAD

Traglisk Point

Signal tower

Duncap Isle

Coastguard Hill

Croaghnamaddy

150

Difficult vegetation

Little Horn Head

STARTING AND FINISHING POINT

Sand

Sand

N

Horn Head Bridge

Dunfanaghy

N56 to Creeslough

Map 2.11:
Horn Head

N56 to Falcarragh

| 0 | | 1 | | 2 | | 3 Kilometres |

| 0 | | 1 | | 2 Miles |

past the Signal Tower. From here the two projecting peaks of Horn Head itself are a short distance away over short grass *(4)*.

To return, retrace your outward route keeping more to the R of the Signal Tower, over rough, boggy ground, and ascend towards (not to) the blockhouse on Coastguard Hill. Take the track which curls round the near side of the hill and walk the short stretch to a metalled road. Continue straight ahead where a road comes in on the L (this is the Horn Head scenic drive and is not shown on the maps) *(5)*. Turn L at the junction marked 'Horn Head 4 km' (the previous sign which measured the distance at 3 km is 1 mile/1.6 km away) and follow it downhill to the starting point.

The start of the walk

1 *The New Lake*

Horn Head peninsula was an island until as late as the eighteenth century, when the sand dunes to the south-west of the present peninsula developed. The area south of Horn Head bridge was a tidal estuary until the twentieth century, when it was sealed by westward-blowing sand encouraged by over-cutting of the marram sand at Tramore Strand. The OS maps still show the estuary, and not the freshwater New Lake which formed as a result.

2 *A Treacherous Coast*

Note the ribs of wrecked ships half-buried in the sand around here.

3 *The Seabirds of Horn Head*

The vertical or near-vertical quartzite cliffs here are a favourite nesting area for a variety of birds, including kittiwakes, guillemots, razorbills and puffins. Other birds which breed around here include the peregrine falcon, raven, rock pipit and chough.

4 *Tory Island*

Tory Island, one of the most remote of the inhabited islands off the Irish coast, is visible from the Head on clear days, 9 miles (15 km) away to the west, its almost entirely cliff-bound southern side making it unmistakable. The islanders, who number about 200, are Gaelic-speaking. The East Town, on the near side from Horn Head, is a *clachan* (see p. 15) reputedly the most authentic in Ireland.

5 *Fuchsia*

The shrub fuchsia grows in unusual profusion along the hedgerows here, which are as thick and abundant as the fields they enclose are narrow and barren. Its red or purple bell-like flowers last from July all the way through to October.

Opposite: *Muckish from Horn Head*

2·12

BEN BULBIN

STARTING POINT

On a minor road south of the Ben Bulbin plateau (714424). From Sligo take the N15, turn R at the church in Rathcormack (signposted 'Glencar 4½'). Turn R at the T-junction after 1 mile (1.6 km) and park 1.4 miles (2.2 km) further on near the prominent guesthouse on the L.

FINISHING POINT

On the same minor road as above at a crossroads at 689436. From the starting point, drive back along the road for 1.9 miles (3.0 km), to a slightly offset crossroads with a metalled road R and farm road L.

MAPS

Northern Ireland OS Sheet 3 or Republic of Ireland OS Sheet 7 (both half-inch to the mile). (OS 1:50 000 Sheet 16 is scheduled for end 1991.)

LENGTH

6½ miles (10.5 km)

ASCENT

1700 ft (520 m)

SAFETY NOTE

The Ben Bulbin plateau is featureless, so it is difficult to fix one's position in bad visibility. It is also mostly surrounded by cliffs and steep ground. Fortunately, *most* of the cliffs are immediately evident because they are sheer and abrupt. Most also drop directly from the top of the

Ben Bulbin, an area immortalized by W. B. Yeats, is one of a group of plateaus to the east of Sligo town. From the lowlands the slopes below each plateau appear as a steeply rising grassy bank topped by a fearsome layer of dark limestone, so fearsome and forbidding that it is something of an anticlimax to discover that the plateau itself is flat moorland. It is as if the land that the maps optimistically labelled 'here be dragons' turn out to be solely the abode of slugs. However, the walk reaches the Ben Bulbin plateau by traversing one of the great gullies that cleave it open, on the way giving excellent views over scenic Glencar. Once there, one can admire a wide sweep of coast and the neighbouring section of the plateau's rim, though not the out-of-sight section at one's feet. The return is by an easy grassy slope and pleasant country roads.

ROUTE DESCRIPTION (Map 2.12)

Go through the gate on the L of the guesthouse as one faces it and up the lane. Cross another gate further up and continue on to a derelict house. Here the lane ends so continue upwards across two rough fields, climb the steep but short rise beyond them and carefully cross the wall on the L into open country.

The good track into King's Gully is the next objective. With a plentitude of false trails hereabouts, perhaps the best plan is to head diagonally upwards *(1)* towards the gully, avoiding numerous rocks that have fallen from the cliffs above (especially if they are still moving). Once on the track, take it into the R side of the gully *(2)* and where it swings sharply back R continue straight ahead on a path, which peters out at about the same point as the gully softens to a steep but narrow valley.

Cross this valley onto the Ben Bulbin plateau *(3)*, a region of soft boggy ground and occasional peat hags, and head north-west (a compass bearing is advisable) to climb a rounded hill. Beyond it descend slightly to a narrow neck of high ground, keeping to the R of the promontory to admire the long stretch of coast round Donegal Bay.

Keep the cliffs on the R to Ben Bulbin (1722 ft/525 m). This has an OS obelisk which, if you didn't know that it was on a lofty plateau, so that the walker is unlikely to encounter cliffs low down on the descent, a disheartening experience. Nonetheless, care should be taken to avoid steep ground when coming off the plateau in poor visibility.

site, would appear to be inexplicably located in a flat boggy field. From Ben Bulbin continue round the plateau, sheer cliffs still on the R. Where they relent, drop gradually over rough ground to the upper end of a fence by an infant stream in a hint of a valley (in bad weather head to the R of the direct route, to make sure that you hit the fence). Follow the fence directly downhill on its far side to a grove of hawthorn and below it cross a gate on the R. Take the track beyond past a L turn (ignore it), and at a metalled road just ahead turn L (this may be better described as continuing

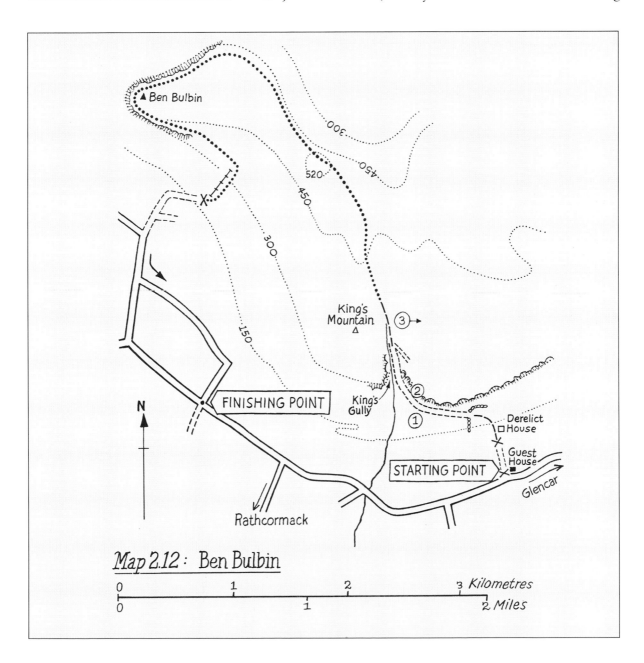

Map 2.12: Ben Bulbin

The prow of Ben Bulbin

straight ahead). Take the first side-turn L and follow it parallel to the rim of the plateau, and then directly away from it. The end of the walk is at the minor road (see STARTING POINT) which, given the really minor roads you have just walked, will now probably appear quite major.

1   *Drumcliff Church*
    Sligo and the surrounding area was beloved of Ireland's national poet, W. B. Yeats, and it is in the little churchyard at Drumcliff 'under bare Ben Bulben's head' that he is buried (the spelling of 'Ben Bulbin' varies). The church tower is easily visible on this ascent at the north-east corner of Drum-cliff Bay. Many of Yeats's most famous poems describe and indeed immortalize this area.

2   *Flora on the Limestone Cliffs*
A wide variety of rare Alpine plants grows on the precipitous slopes of the limestone cliffs. For instance, this is the only site in the British Isles where the fringed sandwort grows. Other plants which thrive in this calcareous environment are mountain avens, alpine saxifrage and maidenhair fern.

3   *A Prehistoric Landscape*
A few miles to the east of here, on a continuation of the gently sloping plateau in County Leitrim, a huge prehistoric landscape of house sites, field systems and burial monuments has been discovered. This whole complex lies under blanket bog at 1300 ft (400 m), compared with present-day settlements which are seldom found higher than 500 ft (150 m). The complex is thought to have been inhabited by Neolithic people 5000 years ago.

Ben Bulbin and the King's Gully

81

2·13

THE POISONED GLEN
HORSESHOE

STARTING AND FINISHING
POINT
At the hairpin bend on a side-road
off the R251/L82 at Dunlewy
(930192). Dunlewy, to
paraphrase the comment about
Los Angeles in a form appropriate
to this smaller context, is '20
houses in search of a village'.
From the Youth Hostel, drive east
0.9 miles (1.4 km), turning R
here towards an unroofed church
— it is a prominent landmark —
from the R251, whether
travelling east or west. Park at
the hairpin bend near the church.
MAPS
Northern Ireland OS Sheet 1 or
Republic of Ireland Sheet 1 (both
half-inch to the mile) are
adequate. The Glenveagh National
Park one-inch to the mile map
covers the entire route and is
better than either.
LENGTH
7½ miles (12 km)
ASCENT
2800 ft (850 m)

The Poisoned Glen, a morass of ominously green and watery vegetation, is almost surrounded by a line of bare rocky cliffs riven by deep dykes. The circuit of these cliffs is short in distance but not in time as the dykes extend as narrow but steep-sided rocky gaps in the plateau behind the cliffs, thus necessitating much exhilarating but time-consuming descending and climbing. The long views are excellent, dominated across Dunlewy Lough by the fine cone of Errigal which displays sometimes one, sometimes two of its tiny summits, and on a more practical level acts as a useful landmark for navigation.

ROUTE DESCRIPTION (Map 2.13)

From the church *(1)* take the track at the hairpin bend to a bridge 150 yards (135 m) away *(2)*. Cross it, turn L and follow the stream for about a ½ mile (1 km), at which point bogland on the R is a little less wet than further back. Leave the stream half R, striking directly towards Maumlack, carefully crossing the deer fence *(3)* marking entry to Glenveagh National Park on the way. Maumlack (1589 ft/484 m) is topped by an elegant, squared-off cairn. From the summit, walk east to keep to the high ground and then turn R (south) and drop to boggy terrain at Lough Beg. Climb over rough rocky ground to the unnamed peak directly to its south.

Here one enters a region of dykes, about which a general comment may be useful. The choice of route across this pathless region is infinite. However, the closer you are to the cliffs on the R, the harder the dykes are to negotiate — and the more spectacular the scenery. To the L, away from the cliffs, progress is faster but duller. The route described favours the R approach.

Cross the first dyke, climb the rocky promontory beyond it, and cross the second dyke along which the deer fence runs. Luckily the third dyke is also unmistakable because of the string of lenticular little lakes running along it. From this dyke climb steeply through crags, passing rock-bound Lough Maumbeg on

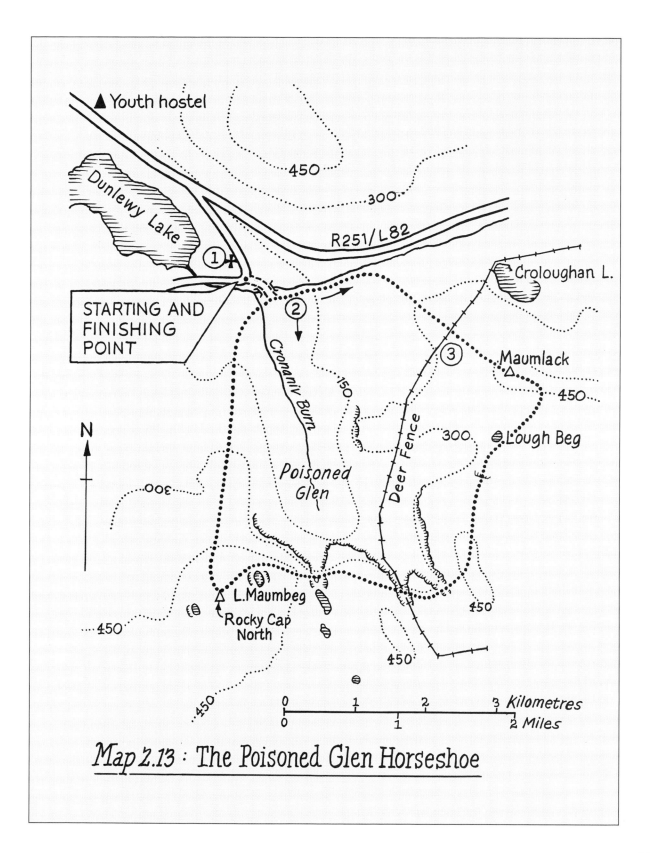

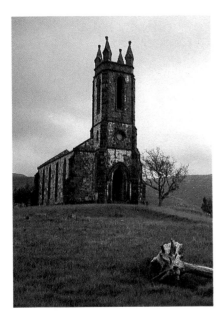

The Church at Dunlewy

the ascent to the northern summit of Rocky Cap, a peak to the north-east of Slieve Snaght which is unnamed on the maps. This peak has an undulating top so the summit cairn, and there is only one, is useful. (NB If you encounter a second lake on this mountain you are on the way to the southern top and should retrace your steps.)

From Rocky Cap descend north along a spur directly towards Dunlewy (use the church as a target) down steep ground at first, then through a flat and boggy stretch with many tiny lakes, and finally over a surprisingly steep shoulder to the valley floor. Cross the Cronaniv Burn, walking upstream if necessary to ford it, turn L and walk back to the only bridge of the day and the hairpin bend.

1   *The Abandoned Church at Dunlewy*
This Church of Ireland church was built in 1844, but was in full use for only a few years thereafter. After that, one service was held per *year* until 1955 when it was de-roofed and the door walled up. Even in the 1920s Arthur Fox, a scholar from Cambridge, noting that only three families worshipped there, added enigmatically that for that reason he 'would not be over-eager to worship in it'.

2   *The Poisoned Glen*
From along this stretch of the route the glen is unmistakable on the R. The name is said to be derived from the poisonous Irish Splurge (genus Euphoria), which grew along the stream that drains the glen (very ineffectively). However, this explanation is somewhat implausible since it also grew in many other places. The valley is a glacial trough; a glacier originating in the Derryveagh Mountains to the south spilled over the cliffs surrounding the glen before heading first north and then along the lakes to the west of here.

This area was one of the last in which the golden eagle bred; they were still being recorded as late as 1910. Alas, 20 years later eagles had departed from here and from Ireland generally. Some thought has been given recently to attempting to re-introduce them, but it is very likely that this would be unsuccessful as long as farmers continue to use pesticides.

3   *The Deer Fence*
This fence is 28 miles (45 km) long, and thought to be the longest fence in the country. Erected in the 1890s it encloses most, but not all, of the National Park. The herd of 650 red deer which roam within the enclosed area is the largest in Ireland, but it has been introduced, and is not native as in Killarney.

Opposite: *The Poisoned Glen*

THE BLUE STACKS

At the end of a side-road
(973871) off the minor road
circling Lough Eske. The junction
off the minor road is at the
northern end of Lough Eske and is
marked by a 'walking-man' signpost. Park carefully where the side-
road continues as a rough track.

MAPS
The Republic of Ireland OS half-
inch to the mile Sheet 3 is barely
adequate given the complicated
nature of the terrain. The
Northern Ireland OS half-inch to
the mile Sheets 1 and 3 are both
needed to cover the route and are
therefore not recommended.

LENGTH
$6\frac{1}{2}$ miles (10.5 km)

ASCENT
1900 ft (580 m)

SAFETY NOTE
Even good maps — and there
aren't any as yet — could not
show the complexity of the
ground over much of this route.
The wet hummocky bogland
slows progress and numerous low
crags cause detours. In addition,
their degree of severity is very
difficult to evaluate in bad
weather. In poor visibility it
would be advisable to go no
further than Lough Belshade, so
keeping to a path (of sorts) all the
way.

The Blue Stacks are a gently moulded, little-frequented range
sheltering shyly behind low foothills near Donegal town. Because
of their boggy surrounds, some might strongly assert that they
are deservedly little-frequented and should remain so. But this
evaluation is a little unfair. This walk takes in small-scale attractive scenery whose prelude and postscript is plain moorland: the
narrow waterfalls that cascade over the foothills of the range, the
rock-rimmed splendour of Lough Belshade, and the expanses of
pink granite slabs facing the summit of Ardnageer. A short but
not easy walk with much variety.

ROUTE DESCRIPTION (Map 3.14)

Walk up the track, the Ulster Way (Donegal) (1), towards the
deep cleft ahead. Where it swings L follow the Way straight
ahead (2) avoiding, or at least postponing, a soggy stretch by
climbing through boulders on its R.

Follow the stream, rejoining the Way for a short distance
further up, into a flat valley which retains water to an unprece-
dented degree even for these watery parts. Noting the large and
distinctive U-bend in the river, continue upstream for a further
130 yards (120 m) and then branch L upstream along a tributary,
taking a subsidiary path, the first, which avoids many hummocks
but which is just as wet as the surrounding hillside.

This path ends at Lough Belshade (3), a high lake bounded on
its further side by magnificent boiler-plate slabs beyond which
rise the rocky undulating mounds of the Blue Stacks. Walk along
the southern shore of the lake (the path, initially intermittent,
soon expires) and then follow the stream issuing into the south-
west corner for a little way before striking north towards
Ardnageer. (A none-too-consoling word about the summits
hereabouts. They are difficult to find because of the numerous
subsidiary summits, and to identify on the maps because few of
them are indicated and fewer still named. The heights are the
surest guide to identification on the maps.)

This stretch towards Ardnageer provides numerous obstacles
to a quick advance. It is a bewildering complex of tiny lakes,
rocky crags, boggy patches, and most memorably great slabs of

smooth, pink granite at all angles from flat to vertical. Beyond this area climb Ardnageer (2061 ft/628 m) which is a distinct rise onto a high, hummocky plateau. There is a summit cairn, but if you are still in doubt watch out for the long slab of white quartzite rock, which is unique in this area and lies 220 yards (200 m) to the west of the summit.

Cross broken ground *(4)* to reach a great wedge of high rocky country stretching south-east between Ardnageer and Croaghgorm, and come gradually off its R (i.e., west) side to avoid the crags at its nose. Descend steeply to Lough Gulladuff, and walk to the R of the stream issuing from it, which is gathering sluggish tributaries here before its precipitous descent by a low waterfall

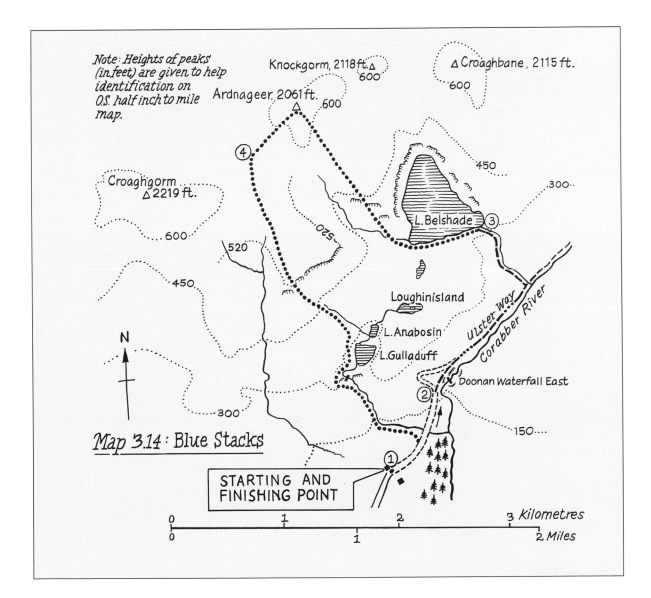

Map 3.14: Blue Stacks

Lough Eske from near the start

into lower ground towards Lough Eske. Veer prudently a little way from the stream to avoid small cliffs at the waterfall. Lower down, follow the stream closely to the forestry plantation bounded on its near side by the Ulster Way, up which you toiled earlier. Turn R onto the Way to return to the starting point.

1   *The Ulster Way (Donegal)*
    This section of the Ulster Way runs from Lough Derg in the south-west of County Donegal to Falcarragh on the north coast, and traverses much of the best of the Donegal highlands. It is 45 miles (75 km) long and is mostly unway-marked. (A note for those perplexed by the fact that the *Ulster* Way is in the Republic of Ireland: Donegal is in the province of Ulster but not in Northern Ireland. Donegal also extends farther north than any point in Northern Ireland.)

2   *Hydro-electricity on the Corabber River*
    If rivers are to be harnessed for electricity this scheme shows the way to do it. Water is stored unobtrusively at Lough Belshade. A pipe runs underground below the steep slope under your feet, parallel to the Corabber River, and the power-house is hidden in the forestry plantation passed earl-

88

Lough Belshade

ier, on the ascent. There is virtually no disturbance beyond the end of the track, which is a little way upstream. During construction, much of the heavy equipment was flown in by helicopter to avoid extending the track for lorries.

3   *The Treasures of Lough Belshade*
The Gaelic form of this name, 'Loch bel sead,' means 'the lake of the jewel'. This is thought to refer to an incident in 1593 when English troops captured the Abbey in Donegal. Before they arrived the monks fled, taking with them the treasures of the Abbey which they hid on an island in Lough Belshade — unfortunately no one knows which.

4   *The Crashed Plane*
A British war-plane crashed in the valley north of here in World War II and its wreckage can still be seen near a narrow stream. During the war, planes based in Northern Ireland just to the east of here headed for the North Atlantic over the narrow neck of neutral Irish Free State territory (as the Republic was then called) with the secret agreement of the Irish government. This avoided a lengthy detour round the north of Donegal. This plane, a Sunderland flying-boat on a reconnaissance mission, crashed killing six of its crew.

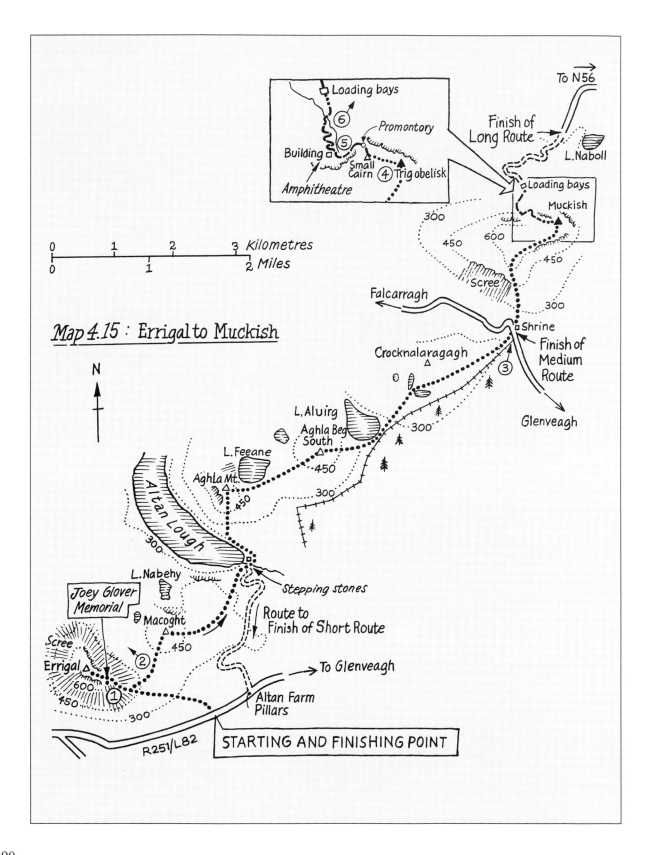

Map 4.15 : Errigal to Muckish

4·15

ERRIGAL TO MUCKISH

STARTING POINT

On the R251/L82 east of Dunlewy at 940196. Drive 2.6 miles (4.2 km) east from the Youth Hostel and park at a walking signpost on the L featuring a startlingly buxom wench. If driving west, watch out for the gate pillars labelled 'Altan Farm' on the R and park at the signpost a $\frac{1}{2}$ mile (1 km) further on.

FINISHING POINTS

For the short route: At the starting point above.

For the medium route: At Muckish Gap (999269), at a shrine on the highest point of an unclassified road running south-east from Falcarragh to Glenveagh.

For the long route: At the end of a side-road off the N56 (008302). Take the N56 west from Creeslough for 1.8 miles (2.9 km), then turn L onto the side-road (if coming from the other direction turn R just beyond the cemetery on the L of the road). Drive straight ahead for 3.6 miles (5.8 km) and park where the metalled road ends.

MAPS

Northern Ireland OS Sheet 1 or Republic of Ireland OS Sheet 1 (both half-inch to the mile). The first half of the route is also on the Glenveagh National Park one inch to the mile map.

Though they are otherwise sharply contrasted, Errigal and Muckish have this much in common: they are easily recognized. In fact, they are two of the most easily recognized mountains in Ireland. They do not have much else in common. Errigal is a graceful quartzite cone with long scree slopes falling from a tiny double summit. Muckish is a long, gently sloping upland, a rock-strewn plateau standing high and conspicuous above the surrounding hills and low boglands.

Their locations, aloof from other high mountains, make it a little difficult to provide good looped walks encompassing each of them separately. The solution is to combine them in a long south-west to north-east walk also taking in two of the Aghlas, a fine trio of peaks that lie between them.

This is the route of the Joey Glover Marathon (see p. 93) except that the marathon goes north-east to south-west. The advantage of walking in the direction given here is that it allows an early 'out' for the faint-hearted, *after* the finest peak — Errigal — has been climbed (a second drop-out point at Muckish Gap is also indicated) and, no trivial consideration, it means that the strong prevailing westerlies are behind the walker.

It is hardly necessary to add that the coastal and mountain views on this route are superb and the underfoot terrain mostly (but not wholly) good. All that — and two options to drop out, should you be so foolish as to take either of them.

ROUTE DESCRIPTION (Map 4.15)

Take the rough path across bogland towards Errigal following posts where the path is indistinct. At drier, steeper ground where the posts cease, follow the clear path upwards to a small cairn on a mound (useful later on in the route). Higher up climb, with steep scree on the R, to the Joey Glover memorial pillar *(1)*. Walk onward from here along a narrow path with ground falling steeply on both sides to the first summit of Errigal (2466 ft/752 m), which has the foundations of an OS obelisk. The second summit at about the same height is 30 yards (27 m) further on, reached by a narrow path. These are reputed to be the smallest summits in Ireland, a claim few would dispute. The

LENGTH

6½ miles (9.5 km) for the short route: 9 miles (14.5 km) for the medium route; 12 miles (19 km) for the long route

ASCENT

2800 ft (850 m) for the short route; 4800 ft (1460 m) for the medium route; 6100 ft (1860 m) for the long route

SAFETY NOTE

The full walk is long with strenuous climbing, so an early start is essential. The cliffs and scree slopes at Mackoght and the Aghlas are not well represented on the maps, but are easy to avoid. The descent from Muckish requires your full attention at a time, late in a long day, when attention may be flagging.

views, especially towards the Derryveagh Mountains, are superb.

Retrace your steps as far as the small cairn mentioned above, and strike out from here to the L (2) to Mackoght (about 1600 ft/500 m) across rough, pathless country broken by occasional avoidable rocky outcrops. From Mackoght the next goal is the R-hand (i.e., eastern) end of Altan Lough. Bear R of the direct line to avoid cliffs and scree on the north-east side of Mackoght and also to avoid a shelving bogland, gentle on this side but craggy and steep where it overlooks the lough. The lough marks the first decision point.

Short route Take the clear grassy track on the near side of the stream entering the lough, walk to the R251/L82 at Altan Farm pillars, turn R and walk to the starting point.

Medium route If you wish to continue, cross the stepping-stones at the stream entering the lough, and with the curious castle-like derelict building on the L climb Aghla Mor keeping initially close to the lake to avoid a small drop further up on the direct route. Aghla Mor (1916 ft/581 m) — the alternative name 'Wee Errigal' might be more appropriately applied to Mackoght — has scree slopes to north-east and south-west and these come close together towards the summit to give a fine hogsback peak.

With these scree slopes in mind, retrace your steps a little and then descend steeply to the peat hags on the south side of Lough Feeane, and walk along the broad saddle south of the lake. Climb through the boulder field to the more southern (of two) Aghla Begs (about 1900 ft/580 m). From here swing slightly R of the direct approach again, to reach the south side of Lough Aluirg where there is but a narrow passable strip between the lake on the L and the forestry plantation on the R.

The next section poses a navigational problem. The hummocky, wet high ground to the north-east contains an indistinct peak, Crocknalaragagh, and three lakes, which are better navigational landmarks than the mountain. Across the entire area runs a meandering fence which, if it remains as it is at present, leads to the central lake. But will it? Perhaps it will collapse, be moved or be augmented by other fences, so leading to errors. The best plan is probably to rely on one's own resources. Aim for the small area between the two eastern lakes by climbing steeply at first and then walking over flat boggy ground. Ignoring Crocknalaragagh, walk between the two lakes and climb a little to gain a distinct ridge (it has forest further down, close on its R) that runs all the way down to Muckish Gap (3). This is the second drop-out point and marks the end of the medium route.

Long route If you intend to complete the long walk cross the road, go round to the L of the mound which shelters the shrine to take the rough path which ascends a spur terminating about 1000 ft (300 m) above on Muckish plateau. Walk across the gently sloping plateau, keeping to its south-east edge to avoid rocky ground, to reach the OS obelisk marking the summit *(4)*.

The next task, an essential one, is to find the way down, which both here and at the quarry below requires you to keep to paths that give a safe way down the rough steep ground. From the obelisk head west for about 220 yards (200 m) to a small cairn and follow a faint path half R which originates about here and bends L over a promontory bounded by cliffs and steep ground to R and L.

This path ends at the quarry, which takes the form of a small semi-amphitheatre in a spot likely to excite considerable awe *(5)*. It consists of a tiny sandy plain, rusting mining artifacts and curious light-brown towers fronting the partly man-made cliffs which half surround the quarry. The only sound, as likely as not, is the harsh caw of the ravens fluttering overhead.

Let not awe cause a hasty descent. Walk to the ruined building at the centre of the rim of the quarry and take the miners' path which is to its R (facing out) and to the L of a small stream. The path follows stumps of iron fence posts and decayed wood poles which occasionally peter out. In case of doubt, remember that the path runs wholly *between* two streams and crosses a sand run at *one* point only *(6)*.

At a tiny valley on level ground, clogged with discarded rocks, cross the stream on the R and descend steeply and directly to the loading bays visible below. Take the grassy quarry road which begins at the bays, climbing the boulders across it a little way down to follow the clear rocky quarry road below them to a metalled road, where the route finishes.

The Joey Glover Memorial, Errigal

1   *The Joey Glover Memorial*
     The simple cairn and plaque here are in memory of Joey Glover, a great mountaineering enthusiast, whose special love was for these, his local mountains. He was murdered in 1976 by the Provisional IRA in one of their many 'mistakes'.
2   *Drumlin Country*
     The curious cluster of tiny oval hills seen to the L on the low ground between Errigal and Mackoght appears to be drumlins formed by the passage of moving ice. Most are grassed, but this cluster is of rough stone.
3   *Muckish Gap*
     This is a glacial breach, the most spectacular of several along the line of mountains from Errigal to Muckish. The col was once 400 ft (120 m) higher, but ice moving north from the Derryveagh mountains broke through the low point here to form this impressive gap.

4 *The Disappointments of Caesar Otway*

Caesar Otway, the splendidly named intrepid Victorian traveller, climbed Muckish in the 1820s. After four hours (sic!) exertion he neared the top. 'I ran, covered with perspiration and panting with heat, to mount the topmost ridge; and just as we arrived there . . . and began to feast on the immense vision of the earth and ocean beneath us, a vast murky cloud from the Atlantic, big with sleet and moisture, enveloped us as well as the whole top of the mountain as with a night-cap, and made every thing so dark, indistinct, and dreary, that we could scarcely see one another.'

Some things never change.

5 *The Mine Workings of Muckish*

Fine-quality white quartzite sand (99.5 per cent silica) used in the manufacture of spectacles, was mined here until 1955, when the workings became uneconomic. The path to the upper workings used by the miners was obviously well made, but is now ruined.

6 *The Letterkenny and Burtonport Extension railway*

The grassy embankments marking the route of this disused line can be clearly seen on the descent. The L&BER was a narrow-gauge railway running from Letterkenny in a meandering curve to the town of Burtonport on the west coast of Donegal, and was primarily intended as a means of developing the fishing industry there. The route was a difficult one — mostly unyielding granite rock — or, equally difficult, too-easily yielding soft bogland. Opened in 1903, the line closed in 1940.

The route from Errigal

95

INTRODUCTION

The mountains of the West, that is, of the counties of Galway (pre-eminently), Mayo and Clare, are located in small, distinct groups separated by low passes and long valleys. Access is good, given the scattered nature of habitation which clings to the narrow fringe between ocean, bogland and mountain. From Clifden, the core area to the east is but a short drive away so the roads, though generally poor, do not have to be endured for very great distances.

The most obvious characteristic that all these discrete mountain ranges have in common is that, to use an Irishism, they are all different! Bleak, flat, boggy upland, limestone terraces, fine rocky conical peaks, upland plateaux with cliffy flanks, grassy hills ending in sea-cliffs, are all represented here. This meant that the selection of routes was quite simple. What was required was just one route in each of the best ranges coupled with a firm resolve not to include that almost as good or nearly as satisfying *second* route in each range. The routes therefore almost chose themselves.

The one range where it was most tempting to choose a second route was the Twelve Bens. What a bewitching magical group — a tiny but crowded canvas of conical peaks in bare rocky splendour, soaring skyward so that it is almost impossible to accept that the highest peak is less than 2400 ft (730 m) high. The route chosen is the most spectacular classic.

The Maamturks lie just across the Inagh valley from the Bens. To quote a well-used and observant phrase: they are the Bens straightened out and with the tops sheared off. It is indeed true that the tops barely rise above a rocky quartzite plateau and that the range more or less orients itself in a narrow line. This latter characteristic makes good circuits almost impossible to devise. With this limitation in mind, a route has been chosen to one of the cols that cause such anguish to those hardy souls doing a full traverse of the range, with a return along the Western Way.

There are two routes for potterers, both in very distinct areas just south of the fiord of Killary Harbour, the great divide between Connemara (western Galway) and the mountains of Mayo. A stroll along the fiord, all of it on path or track, is

Doo Lough and Mweelrea

navigationally easy and scenically a delightful juxtaposition of coast and hillside. The other walk is only a few miles away in the Benchoonas, an unfrequented, unpretentious shaggy group of hills with great geological diversity and simply staggering long-distance views — a great area for carefree wandering.

North across Killary Harbour is Mweelrea, at a modest 2688 ft (819 m) the highest mountain in the entire area. The Mweelrea massif, for Mweelrea is one of a group of hills rising from a plateau, is the best of three ranges, sectors of a great circle of mountains split by north-south and centre to east passes. Of the several routes considered onto the summit plateau (including one by boat across Killary!) this one traverses the rim of the corrie cleaving the eastern side of the massif. A memorable excursion that, like some of the others, almost chose itself.

Finally, on the outskirts of the West two greatly contrasting walks: Achill Island provides a comparatively easily accessible cliff walk in an area which has many that are far from accessible — and it also happens to be one of the most memorable; the Burren is unique in Ireland — a strange area of limestone slabs which shelters a bewildering range of rare and varied flora.

Mention should perhaps be made of Croagh Patrick, a notable omission. Croagh Patrick is Ireland's 'holy' mountain, an attribute which has blighted it with an ugly scar of a pilgrimage track and squat chapel on the summit. It is probably better to leave it to the penitential multitudes, and seek spiritual solace on unspoilt and less-frequented hills.

KILLARY HARBOUR

STARTING AND FINISHING
POINT
At Killary Harbour Youth Hostel
(769651) in Rosroe on the
southern shore of the fiord. From
Leenane take the N59 towards
Clifden turning R after 4.4 miles
(7.0 km) (this is the *second* side-
turn within a few hundred yards
on a road which has no side-roads
on this side after Leenane.)
Continue along the length of
Lough Fee and 0.2 miles (350 m)
beyond it fork R uphill. The
Hostel is 1.8 miles (3.0 km)
further on. The approach road is
in poor condition; almost as much
pot-hole and dirt track as it is
tarmac.
MAP
The 1:50 000 Connemara map is
recommended. The OS half-inch
to the mile Sheet 10 suffices.
LENGTH
5 miles (8 km)
ASCENT
400 ft (120 m)

This is an easy walk nearly all of which is on a clear path or track
with little climbing. The route is along the shore of a narrow
fiord, by far Ireland's best (though some would say that it is
Ireland's *only* true fiord). Across the waters the great southern
wall of Mweelrea rises unbroken from shore to summit, 2600 ft
(800 m) of grassy slopes. A good walk for a day of low cloud, but
nonetheless it would be a pity to miss the full glory of the excellent sea and mountain scenery.

ROUTE DESCRIPTION (Map 1.16)

Walk along the road away from the Hostel *(1)* and the tiny harbour beside it, turning L onto a track just before the first house
on the L. Follow this upwards ignoring the gate on the L set in a
stone wall which runs beside the track for a short distance. A
little further on, Killary Harbour *(2)* is fully revealed. Look out
on the opposite shore for the remains of a pre-famine village *(3)*.

Route-finding from here is simple, with one proviso vital for
the return. Watch out for the deserted house (rough definition: a
deserted house is roofed, a ruin is not) half-hidden in rhododendron, and note also the lateral gated wall beyond it. Between
house and wall search carefully for a green track heading back.
Though barely more than a gently sloping stretch of grass amidst
steeply rising ground, it is a stretch of grass that runs surrepti-
tiously slightly uphill and almost parallel to the good track that
you are on. Note this for the return carefully.

For now, continue along the coast, cross a concrete bridge
over a stream which descends briskly as a series of low waterfalls
(a good place for a picnic) and pass the ruin on the L, the first on
the fiord side. Around here the south-east outlier of Mweelrea
descends in a diminuendo of rocky hillocks into Killary and the
end of the Maamturks increasingly dominates the skyline beyond
it. On the near side, old scattered oaks shelter in a slight hollow
ahead.

There is nothing to stop further onward wandering, but the
best of the scenery is behind. For the return take the track L
already noted, and follow it to near a deserted house set at right
angles to the shore. Just before this house the track inexplicably,

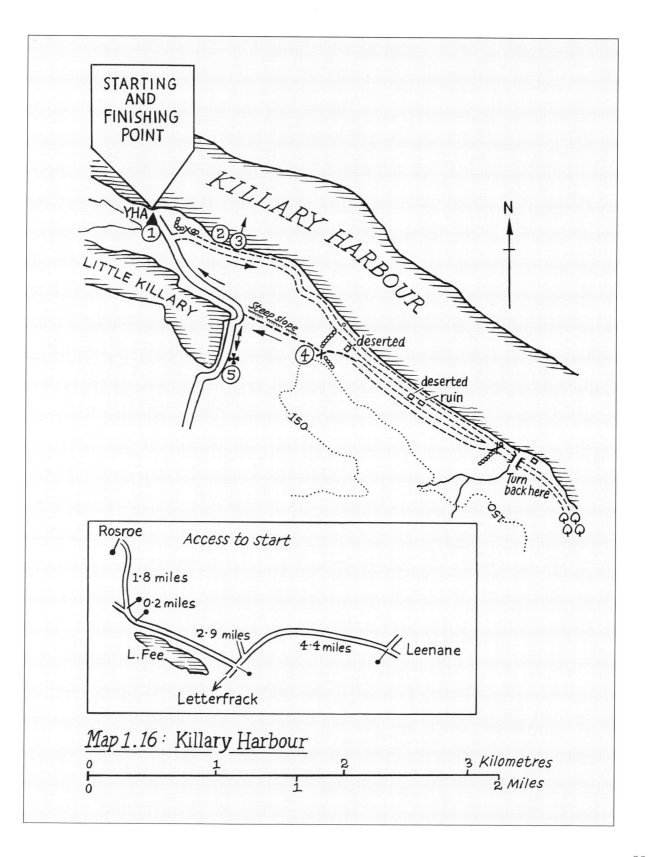

STARTING
AND
FINISHING
POINT

YHA

KILLARY HARBOUR

LITTLE KILLARY

N

Steep slope

deserted

deserted
ruin

150

Turn
back here

Ost

Rosroe

Access to start

1·8 miles

0·2 miles

L. Fee

2·9 miles

4·4 miles

Leenane

Letterfrack

Map 1.16 : Killary Harbour

| 0 | 1 | 2 | 3 Kilometres |
| 0 | | 1 | 2 Miles |

Killary Harbour Youth Hostel

but fortunately only temporarily expires at a wall that must be crossed. Beyond the house it resumes resolutely uphill, no longer meekly paralleling its coastal companion. The path ends at a corner in a stone wall. Take a gate on the L here and follow the fence beyond steeply uphill along a curious rocky escarpment *(4)* running close by on the R. At the crest the delightful Little Killary Harbour comes into view. From here continue steeply downhill to the road.

At the road turn L to visit the tiny Church of Ireland church *(5)* tucked in behind a high wall on the L a few hundred yards away. Afterwards retrace your steps to the starting point.

1   *A Philosopher at Killary*
    The Youth Hostel was the temporary home of the philosopher Ludwig Wittgenstein after World War II (of course it was not a hostel then). Here he wrote his book *Philosophical Investigations*.

2   *Killary Fiord*
    During the Ice Age, a glacier pushed its way out to sea hereabouts along an existing river valley, deepening it from a shallow V to the deep U of the present-day fiord and leaving a bar at the entrance, the equivalent of a moraine. The fiord is deeper at the landward end.

Opposite: *The shoreline at Killary*

The shelter provided by the hills and the unusually deep water in the harbour have made it a centre for mussel farming. The mussels cling to long ropes hanging from the rafts. Apart from being unsightly, questions have recently been asked about the chemical effects of this type of intensive fish-farming.

3   *A Pre-famine Village*

The pre-famine village across the fiord and clearly visible from this side was called Uggool. Tillage beds climb the steep and infertile hill behind the village, indicating how desperate the plight of the land-starved peasants was in the 1830s and 1840s.

4   *The Escarpment*

The curious cliff and trench here was caused by the rubbing of a chain which the devil was pulling to drag away Saint Roc, a local holy man. If that is too difficult to believe, the alternative explanation is that it is a thrust fault caused by the movement of one body of rock relative to a contiguous body. (How dull science is compared to popular theology!)

5   *The Church at Salrock*

The small Church of Ireland church maintained a curious custom in the past. Mourners at funerals smoked clay pipes after the religious service and these were heaped in the graveyard. Two plaques on the inside wall remember two brothers, both born during World War I and killed in World War II. It must have been a heavy sacrifice not only for their parents, but for the tiny Protestant community of the area.

Killary Harbour and Mweelrea

1·17

ACHILL HEAD

STARTING AND FINISHING POINT

Keem Bay (560045) at the western end of Achill Island. Take the N59 to Mulrany and there take the R319/L141 to Dooagh. Continue onwards to the road head at Keem Bay where there are several large car-parks. Leave plenty of time for the drive as the roads are generally poor.

MAPS

The OS half-inch to the mile Sheet 6 is the only contoured map available. A local guide *Achill Island* (published by Bob Kingston) is in the form of a map on a scale of 1.9 in to the mile. Although it has no contours it is quite useful.

LENGTH

5 miles (8 km)

ASCENT

1100 ft (340 m)

Achill (pronounced '*Ack-ill*') is the largest island off the coast, though its insular status is impaired as it is joined to the mainland by a road-bridge. The island is shaped like a right-angled triangle, its most acute angle at Achill Head jutting out defiantly west into the Atlantic. Sea-cliffs dominate the two sides near this angle, low to the west of Keem Bay where the walk starts but rising to nearly 2200 ft (670 m) under the summit of Croaghaun Mountain further north. Between Keem and Achill Head the walk takes in some of the most breath-taking sea-cliff scenery in Ireland. Although the route does not include Croaghaun, the sweep of cliffs under that mountain can be seen clearly from Achill Head — ironically they cannot be seen from Croaghaun itself.

ROUTE DESCRIPTION (Map 1.17)

Before starting it might be of interest to consider the surroundings. Keem Bay is tucked into a bowl of mountains unbroken except for the ocean and the coastal strip whence you drove (*1*). The curious aspect is that nearly the entire sweep of hills around is 'one-sided': the sides hidden from here terminate abruptly either in sea-cliffs or corrie wall. Thus the surroundings uncannily mirror St Kilda, far west of Scotland in the Atlantic.

From the bay (*2*) climb over pathless grass to the top of Moyteoge Head to the south-west, which is crowned by the look-out post clearly visible from the bay. Once there navigation is easy. Turn R and walk north-west towards and over the two great waves of rising ground ahead which fall on the L to the sea in dramatic sea-cliffs. As you advance, the bulky but dull shoulder of Croaghaun (2192 ft/668 m) increasingly dominates the view. A little further on, the high but not sheer cliffs falling from its summit to the sea with the curve of the Belmullet peninsula behind, can be clearly seen. In spite of their height these cliffs are not as impressive as the Achill Head sea-cliffs to the L and further on also to the R.

The cliffs on Achill Head converge gradually to a knife-edge and conditions on the day (for example, wind and the slipperiness of the rocks) combined with the walker's burgeoning fear of an

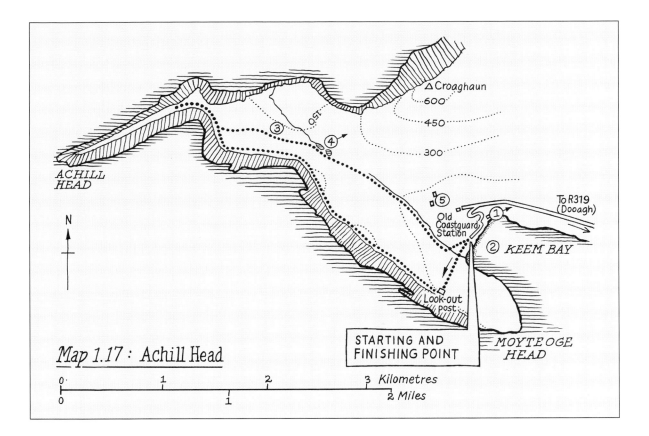

Map 1.17 : Achill Head

unscheduled visit to the slowly pounding sea far below will eventually dictate a retreat. When prudence advises, turn back and initially retrace your steps, with the cliffs now on the R. Where feasible, descend gradually L from the cliffs, walk upstream roughly parallel to a westward-flowing stream *(3)* below on the L and, when they come into view, head to two small lakes at the col between the Achill Head cliffs R and the rising featureless flank of Croaghaun L *(4)*.

From these lakes continue in roughly the same direction (south-east) to pick up a stream, noting at the start of this stretch the distinctive cone of Croagh Patrick ahead neatly framed by Croaghaun and Moyteoge Head. Follow this stream downhill back to the car-park at Keem, passing on the way two imposing ruins *(5)* and an equally imposing deserted house, the latter the old coastguard station.

1   *Amethysts at Keem Bay*
    On the last ridge on the road into Keem, amethysts were discovered in the 1960s in the course of constructing the present road to the bay. The clear purple gemstone can still be found with a little patient searching.

2   *Shark fishing at Keem Bay*
Keem Bay was a centre for the shark-fishing industry for 25 years up to the mid-1970s. Basking sharks up to 35 ft (10 m) long and weighing up to 6 tons (tonnes) were caught in nets attached to the cliffs and were then killed by harpoon from curraghs, the fragile row-boats traditional on the Atlantic coast. It must have been a gory business. Only the sharks' liver oil and fins were used, the latter being exported to the Far East.

Achill coastline with Achill Head in the distance

3   *Booleys*
The oval, stone-wall enclosures along this stream are good
examples of *booleys*, shelters which cattle-minders inhabited
in the summers while their bovine charges grazed on the
summer pastures. Achill is the last place in Ireland where this
practice survived. The context in which this practice occurred is described on p.15.

4   *The Views of Eric Newby*
Eric Newby, the noted English travel-writer, climbed
Croaghaun in his youth. Many years later, as described in his
book, *Round Ireland in Slow Gear*, he climbed it again. He had
exactly the same view on the two occasions — zero visibility
caused by low cloud — so it is unlikely that even the not-
easily-discouraged Newby will ever come to believe in third
time lucky.

5   *Captain Boycott*
These ruins, a substantial house and store, were built around
1857 by Captain Boycott, a local landlord. He later moved
east to the Mayo mainland where he achieved unwanted fame
by becoming the original victim of the effective protest
action named after him.

Keem Bay

2·18

THE BENCHOONAS

STARTING AND FINISHING
POINT
At the car-park of Kylemore
Abbey (748585) on the northern
side of the N59, 2½ miles (4 km)
east of Letterfrack and 9½ miles
(15 km) west of Leenane. The
Abbey is well signposted and its
imposing pile is clearly visible
from the Leenane direction.
MAPS
The Connemara 1:50 000 map is
recommended. The OS half-inch
to the mile Sheet 10 is barely
adequate.
LENGTH
5½ miles (9 km)
ASCENT
2950 ft (900 m)

This modest and little-known range provides one of the most
scenic grandstands in Ireland, a stupendous mix of mountain and
ocean. Mweelrea, the Maamturks, the Bens and the island-
spattered ocean in turn drawing the eye full circle. While it
boasts no 'classic' conical peaks, all its tops being quite mundane
and some even downright shapeless, two are remarkable in other
ways. Duaghruagh/Duchruach is a shaggy little mountain, all
rough rocky hillocks and lochans, which bears a remarkable
resemblance to the much better-known Haystacks in the Lake
District. Altnagaighera/Binn Fhraoigh is simply a narrow spur
but its grassy top is crowned and its western prow guarded by
extraordinary, conglomerate crags. An easy walk of continuously
changing interests.

ROUTE DESCRIPTION (Map 2.18)

Leaving the car-park turn L, walk resolutely L round the back of
the tea-room, whose delights should be reserved for the return,
and continue along the tidy track beyond it to the T-junction.
Turn R here and look out immediately for the sign proclaiming
'The Way to the Statue of the Sacred Heart'. Walk as directed,
zigzagging upward through dense rhododendrons that allow only
brief, tantalizing glimpses of the Abbey. The occasional crosses
along here mark the Stations, a Roman Catholic devotional exercise — not a physical one as you might surmise from the slope.

At the statue abandon the path — it is about to abandon you
— and head diagonally L uphill to the summit of Doughruagh
(1756 ft/529 m) avoiding the occasional easily avoidable crag.
(The only reason for the diagonal rather than the direct approach
is to give a slightly more satisfactory route.) As implied above, it
is well worth allowing time to potter round the hillocks and
lochans of the summit. Incidentally, if a return at this point is
necessary, head straight back to the Sacred Heart to avoid
becoming enmeshed in impenetrable undergrowth if the path
down from the statue is missed.

From the summit, marked by a cairn and a fence post (no
fence), the aim is to descend to the R of the small lake in the

valley between Doughruagh and Altnagaighera. Take an initial swing L of the direct line; the direct descent is steep and rocky, though the recommended route is not all that much better. The lake, Lough na Crapai, is warmed by a thermal spring, which may be an extra inducement if you are contemplating a swim. If you just want a stop for a bite to eat and a rest, the area close to the small waterfalls on the inlet stream is ideal.

The steep wall of grass rising opposite to the top of Altnagaighera is the next goal. First head diagonally L up the slope towards the nose on the west of the summit. Climb through one of several gullies in the conglomerate ramparts to emerge on the long, narrow summit ridge of Altnagaighera (1791 ft/546 m) on which squat the curious 'pudding stone' knolls and a tiny lake.

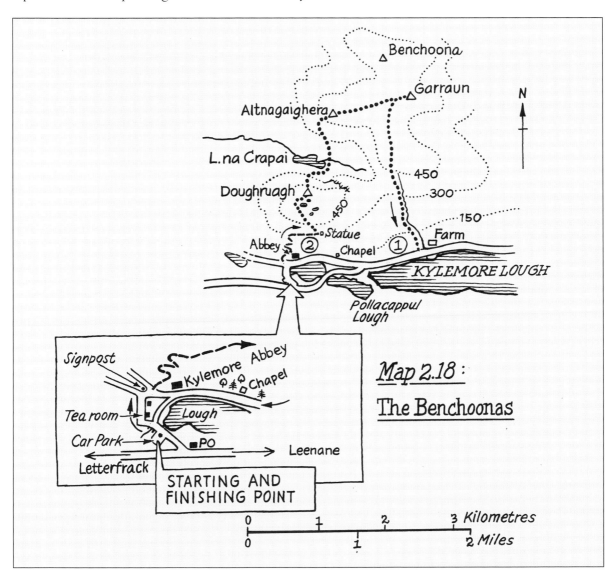

Map 2.18: The Benchoonas

Kylemore Abbey and Doughruagh

From Altnagaighera onward, the underfoot conditions are a trifle anti-climactic, a dull, heaving bogland, though the views remain superb. Climb Garraun/Maolchnoc (1973 ft, 602 m), the highest peak in the Benchoonas. From here retrace your steps a short way along the broad, soggy ridge south-west, and then turn south to point 523 m. Continue south from point 523 m, picking up the R bank of a stream which flows south-east into Kylemore

Lough. When the road (the N59) is first seen, veer a little R of the stream to avoid enclosed fields near a farm. However, do not venture too far R on this descent as thick rhododendron bushes and small but nasty crags fronting the lake form an impenetrable barrier.

The Benchoonas from Letterfrack

Turn R onto the road and walk for $\frac{1}{2}$ mile (1 km) along a lovely stretch of road with Kylemore Lough close on the L, the steeply rising slopes of Doughruagh on the R. Go through the gate on the R where the road veers L, and walk along the track beyond it, which is hemmed in by rhododendron bushes and an oakwood *(1)*. Walk past Kylemore Chapel, the Abbey *(2)* and finally enter the tea-rooms, a visit which will by now have been well merited.

1   *The Rhododendron*
    The rhododendron, which boasts such beautiful flowers every June, is the bane of the oakwoods. A native of Turkey and the Himalayas, it flourished in Ireland before the Ice Age. The cold killed it off here and it remained east of the Black Sea until 1800, when it was introduced. Unfortunately it is now back with a vengeance and thrives in areas with acid soils, where it chokes other plants and is extraordinarily difficult to eradicate.

2   *Kylemore Abbey and Chapel*
    The gothic pile of Kylemore Abbey, set into the oakwoods above Kylemore Lough, was built in the nineteenth century by a wealthy Liverpool merchant and passed into the hands of the Benedictine nuns in 1921. The Chapel to the east of the main house is a replica of Norwich Cathedral. The Abbey is now an international boarding school for girls.

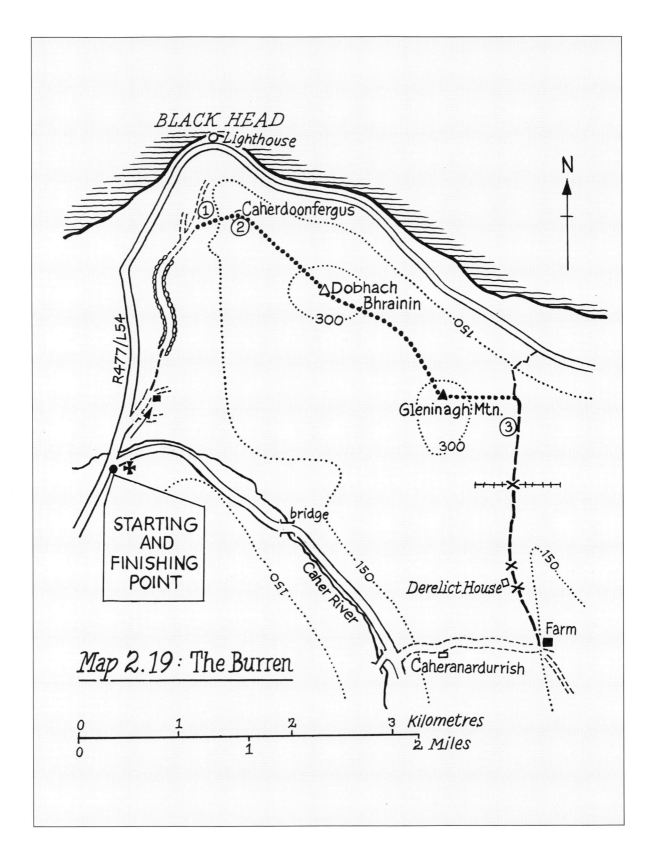

BLACK HEAD

Lighthouse

N

① Caherdoonfergus
②

△Dobhach
Bhrainin

300

OSI

R477/L54

▲Gleninagh Mtn.

③

300

STARTING
AND
FINISHING
POINT

bridge

150

Caher River

OSI

150

Derelict House

150

Farm

Map 2.19 : The Burren

Caheranardurrish

0   1   2   3 *Kilometres*

0   1   *2 Miles*

2·19

THE BURREN

STARTING AND FINISHING
POINT
At or near the side-turn off the
R477/L54 at Fanore (144088).
MAPS
T. D. Robinson's stylish and
artistic map *The Burren*, on a scale
of 1:35 200 (1.8 in to the mile),
while otherwise unsurpassed, is
uncontoured. The alternative is
the OS half-inch to the mile Sheet
14.
LENGTH
$9\frac{1}{2}$ miles (15 km)
ASCENT
1500 ft (460 m)

The Burren of north-west Clare, 60 square miles (160 square km) of karstic country, is quite unlike any other in Ireland. From a distance the hills, which rarely rise over 1000 ft (300 m), look like a pile of stacked grey plates, each smaller than the one below it. Close up, the landscape is almost lunar, a set of platforms composed of flat slabs of limestone broken by long, narrow grooves called grikes. Each platform ends in a short cliff above which is another grey platform.

The botanic and archaeological variety of the Burren matches its scenic weirdness. Plants of widely diverse origins thrive in the lime-rich patches of soil, or shelter in the narrow crevices of the grikes. Sites from many eras from Stone Age to medieval dot the hills.

In such an area the walker might prefer to wander freely rather than be constricted by a formal walk. The walk given here has at least the virtue of providing most of the elements which make the Burren what it is: the limestone terraces and cliffs, the varied flora and archaeology, the excellent coastal views of Galway Bay and beyond, as well as commonplace fields and quiet country roads.

ROUTE DESCRIPTION (Map 2.19)

Walk north, that is, with the coast on the L, along the coast road, the R477/L54 and turn first R up a track. Where the track swings sharply R at a bungalow on the R, turn L off it along a wisp of a path. Continue roughly on the level as it improves to a wide track between stone walls that rises gradually across the hillside. Cross three stone walls (carefully) on this almost imperceptible ascent and after the third, where the track divides, take the R branch. Turn R off it after a short distance *(1)* where it levels off, so heading directly and pathlessly for the great ring-fort of Caherdoonfergus *(2)* across the limestone pavements.

From the ringfort head directly to Dobhach Bhrainin (1045 ft/319 m), climbing several terraces on the way (this is a constant feature until after Gleninagh). The top is marked by a small cairn, a useful edifice in flat terrain. Descend to the pass towards Gleninagh Mountain so avoiding grassy hollows on the

direct route, and ascend directly to Gleninagh, which is exactly the same height as Dobhach Bhrainin, and is marked by a stubby OS obelisk.

Descend to the pass to the east and at it turn R along a track that is difficult to find at the pass itself but is clear a little way down. This track deteriorates to a path through fields in the high grassy Gleninagh South valley *(3)*, scrub and limestone slabs on both sides. Cross a wall and at the gate just beyond, where you may by now have concluded that the path is purely imaginary, head towards a derelict house visible to the R of the valley, picking up the path again closer to it. Take the good track which originates at the house to what appears to be a crossroad (though the L branch terminates at a nearby farm) and turn R uphill here along another track, passing Caheranardurrish, reputedly a sheeben and church, just over the crest.

Descend on a winding course, still on the track, to a metalled road. Turn R onto it and walk steadily downhill all the way to the coast road.

Grikes

1   *Flora of the Limestone Slabs*
     Bloody cranesbill, mountain avens and spring gentians are among the many plants from the Arctic, Alps and Mediterranean which grow here on the calcium-rich soil. Maidenhair and hart's tongue fern thrive in the micro-environment of the sheltering grikes. These plants and many others are best seen in the late spring when the flowers are blooming.

2   *Caherdoonfergus*
     Caherdoonfergus, or as T. D. Robinson's map sternly puts it, 'Cathair Dhuin Irghuis, miscalled Caherdoonfergus', is a fine example of a large ringfort. This formerly lightly wooded area of well-drained land once attracted a large population, as the many ringforts in the Burren testify. Overgrazing and possibly a climatic change led to erosion and the subsequent uncovering of the bare rock.

3   *The Valley of Gleninagh South*
     This area is a fertile contrast to the bare hillside on both sides. The soil is composed of thick glacial deposits which accumulated in the valley. At the end of the walk along the Caher River a cross-section of similar deposits has been exposed by subsidence into the river.

Limestone pavements

The Central Maamturks

STARTING AND FINISHING
POINT
The car-park on the north-east
side of the R344 (Lough Inagh
road) 5 miles (8 km) from
Kylemore and 5½ miles (9 km)
from Recess (847533). The car-
park is signposted 'Mamean Tobar
& Leaba Phadraig' in archaic Irish
lettering. If your knowledge of
this lettering is rusty, look for the
sign for Lough Inagh Fishery
directly opposite.
MAPS
The 1:50 000 Connemara map is
recommended. The OS half-inch
to the mile Sheet 10 is on too
small a scale and is recommended
only if nothing else is available.
LENGTH
9 miles (14.5 km)
ASCENT
2750 ft (840 m)

Like other sections of the Maamturks, the rock-ribbed central section, which is the focus of this walk, runs from one high pass to another in a long, gently curving line. Ascending the rock-strewn plateau above, it takes in two major peaks which, depending on the exact point from which they are viewed, rise above the plateau with varying degrees of success. The panorama from the tops, particularly towards the crowded peaks of the Bens, is excellent. The walk reaches the lowlands along a tiny river valley and ends as it began along the Western Way.

ROUTE DESCRIPTION (Map 3.20)

From the car-park leave the R344 to follow the minor road uphill, thus emulating the route of the pilgrims to Mamean (1). Continue along the part-metalled part-pot-holed road (2) passing through the scattered houses at Illion West/An Uillinn Thair after 1½ miles (2.5 km), and at the dip beyond it where stone walls clamber in a higgledy-piggledy way among rising ground on the L look out beyond them and before the river for a place where there is comparatively dry ground on which to start the walk to Mam Ochoige, a high pass in the Maamturks.

Walk upriver towards the pass keeping to the L bank, and pass through the huge, dark rocky ramparts guarding the pass by taking the only significant gap, that taken by the stream. Beyond is level ground, a miniature Shangri La cut off from the world and an ideal spot for rough camping. From here, continue steeply uphill to the pass (3), where the lake shown on the maps is nowhere to be seen. You have not located the wrong gap however. The mystery will soon be revealed.

The route from the pass to the first peak, Knocknahillion/ Cnoc na hUilleann (1993 ft/607 m) is a straightforward climb through rough vegetation and scattered boulders. Look back on this ascent to see the sought-for lake lying just above the gap. (If the visibility is good and you *still* don't see, you really have a problem.) This climb also affords good views down into the long, grassy-sided Failmore Valley to the R and behind.

From Knocknahillion the route runs north over a bewildering rocky landscape of tiny hillocks and hidden lochans, narrowing at one point to a narrow but flat neck. Beyond this a bulky cairn beckons — the top of Letterbreckaun/Binn Briocain? Alas, no. It marks the edge of the virtual plateau on which Letterbreckaun (2193 ft/669 m) lies. Having gained this plateau note another cairn, and then another. Exactly which one marks the top is difficult to say with certainty. While this is a good reason to avoid indiscriminate cairning, the cairns are so close together that any confusion should not be too serious.

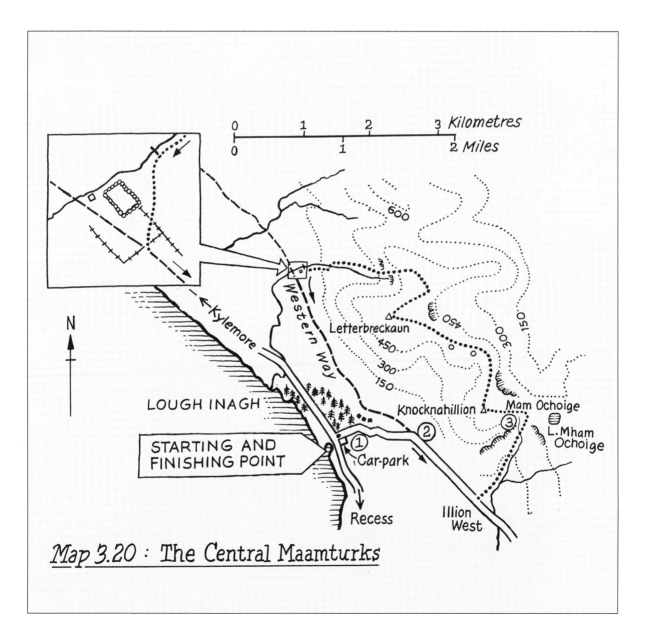

Map 3.20 : The Central Maamturks

The descent route

Careful navigation is required on the descent over irregular broken ground from Letterbreckaun. To keep on the ridge, head first north-east for a few hundred yards and then north-west for a similar distance. When two tiny lochans are seen, one perched directly above the other, look for a point where a direct descent west into a narrow river valley can be made by taking a gully between crags.

That done, the remainder of the walk is easy. Take either bank downstream (but note that you must end up on the L bank), past a delightful little waterfall. Next note the stone walls and ruin ahead. Keep to their L and cross a fence, an extension L of the wall, at an easy point. Turn half-L to reach the Western Way, at this point a wide track but one which blends chameleon-like into the surrounding bogland, so that an act of faith — and a compass — may be needed to follow it along the foot of the Maamturks close on the L. After $1\frac{1}{4}$ miles (2 km) on the Western Way, forest and a few houses heave into sight. Continue on beyond them, following roughly the electricity poles should the Way be unclear. When the Way reaches a metalled road turn R and walk back to the car-park.

1   *The Pilgrimage to Mamean*
    This pilgrimage takes place in early August each year. The ceremonies connected with it take place at Mamean, a mountain pass 5 miles (8 km) from here. Once a place of pagan worship, it was later Christianized, and later still 'enlivened' by the addition of poteen-drinking and faction-fighting. The pilgrimage was revived recently and now has a more decorous format.

2   *The Western Way*
    At present this Long Distance Route runs from Oughterard in County Galway west and north to Westport in Mayo, taking in some of the most spectacular scenery in the two counties. There are plans to extend it northwards from Westport. The route is not waymarked at present.

The start of the climb

3   *The Maamturks Walk*
This marathon walk, which takes place in May each year, is reputed to be the toughest in Ireland. It passes south-east to north-west by Mam Ochoige. Fifteen miles (24 km) long with a climb of 8000 ft (2430 m), it takes in the entire length of the Maamturks from the Maam Cross-Maam Bridge road to Leenane. The descents and re-ascents from the five major passes, of which Mam Ochoige is one, make it particularly arduous. The record for the walk is about 5 hours, nearly half Naismith Rule's reckoning and this does not allow any time for stops.

3·21

MWEELREA

STARTING AND FINISHING
POINT
On the R335/L100 (Glenanane to
Louisburgh road) just north of
Doo Lough (830694), where
there is ample parking on the
roadside. From Leenane turn L off
the N59 or from Westport turn R
off the N59 onto the R335, and
park 8 miles (13 km) beyond this
turn at the far end of Doo Lough.
MAPS
OS half-inch to the mile Sheet 10
covers the area — after a fashion.
See the safety note below.
LENGTH
10 miles (16 km)
ASCENT
3400 ft (1030 m)
SAFETY NOTE
Mweelrea is not a mountain to be
trifled with, and the only map
available is unreliable and on far
too small a scale for detailed
navigation. Therefore, think
carefully before attempting the
climb on a bad day. Under all
conditions leave yourself plenty of
time. Two routes are described to
the massif. If you suffer from
vertigo or wish to avoid some airy
scrambling, take the easier one.

At 2686 ft (819 m) Mweelrea (pronounced '*Mweel-ray*') is the
highest peak in the West. Perhaps peak is not quite the right
word: Mweelrea is, rather, the highest point of a massif, an
undulating grassy area whose eastern side is abruptly terminated
by a gigantic and magnificent corrie — one of several which has
eaten into the massif. It is along the corrie edge that the other
high points of the massif rise, 'half-peaks' with innocent grassy
slopes on one side and the wicked plunging wall of the corrie on
the other. The route's focal point is this corrie, but it also pays its
respects to Mweelrea itself on the far end of the plateau, from
which the views are stunning.

ROUTE DESCRIPTION (Map 3.21)

If there is good visibility it might be helpful to study the route
before starting — most of it can be seen from the road. The
difficult route climbs directly up the northern (R) arm of the huge
corrie on the opposite side of Doo Lough, ascends a small subsidiary peak, from your standpoint well below the skyline, and then
advances directly up to the summit plateau. The *easy* route
climbs the back wall of the corrie on a grassy ramp rising L to R to
a low point on the summit plateau. Here the routes converge for
the final ascent.

The difficult route Cross the stream flowing into Doo Lough
using stepping-stones near the lough, cross the fence beyond and
advance across the bog where, in dry weather, sundews *(1)* are
particularly evident. As you climb along the inner side of the
arm, watch out for a solitary rowan tree and take a narrow gully
20 yards (18 m) or so to its R. If this causes vertigo, retreat
forthwith to the easy variation. A little further up, the summit
plateau appears — bands of gently dipping sandstone strata with
no evident way of breaching the ramparts they form.

Undeterred, climb the small peak mentioned above, and head
for the rocky nose beyond, where the crux of the route awaits.
Keep first to the L of the nose along a faint but reassuring path,
scramble up the airy staircase, and then make a frontal scramble
through rocks which ends in an easily climbed arête. Above this
is the grass of the summit plateau.

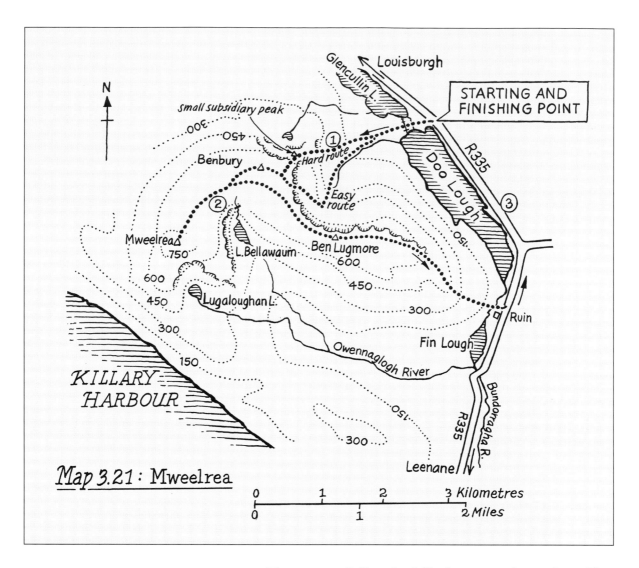

Map 3.21: Mweelrea

The easy route Follow the difficult route to the sundews. Then follow the stream that runs into the north-west corner of Doo Lough. This leads into a valley where you can find your way over, or circumvent, low cliffs. Above the cliffs, ascend the grassy ramp and at its top climb an easy gully L to the lowest point in the corrie rim. Turn R (north-east) to reach the grassy plateau. Here the two routes converge.

From the plateau, walk to Benbury (2610 ft/796 m), which rises none too ostentatiously a few hundred yards further to the north-west, after which head to Mweelrea (2686 ft/819 m) over catastrophically sparse grass *(2)*. The summit area of Mweelrea is undistinguished, but as a viewpoint it is unsurpassed. Killary Harbour winds its sinuous way close at hand, beyond which crowd the Benchoonas, the Twelve Bens and the Maamturks. The Sheffry Hills and Ben Gorm rise to the east. Northwards is

DOOLOUGH TRAGEDY
1849
ERECTED TO THE MEMORY OF
THOSE WHO DIED IN
THE FAMINE OF 1845-49

The Doo Lough Tragedy memorial

bog and fringing the sea the magnificent beach at Killadoon runs far northwards. Beyond it to the west a scattering of islands ride the ocean.

Return along the ascent route, bypassing Benbury, to reach the main corrie edge at its lowest point once more. A dramatic jagged skyline lies ahead. Note here, to the L of the giant 'tooth' rearing skyward, the flat-topped peak Ben Lugmore (2616 ft/797 m). Following the route from this point is child's play. Keep the corrie's rim on the L on a roller-coaster progress, veering R onto grassy slopes where rock formations bar the way.

At Ben Lugmore, take care not to follow the grassy spur south-east; instead swing L to keep close to the corrie rim, here not quite so impressive. Continue steeply downhill, forking L over rocky ground onto the higher branch where the spur divides.

The steep and punishing descent resumes after the rocky ground. As you near the road (it is of course the R335 again) watch out for a ruin between it and the Bundorragha River. Ford the river here (alas, wet feet may be unavoidable) to gain the road, turn L and walk back to the starting point. On this walk, a pleasant one offering varying angles on the day's route, look out on the R for the plaque to the victims of the Doo Lough tragedy in 1849 *(3)*.

1   *The Sundew*
     The sundew is a typical plant of the bogs and is easily recognizable because of the bright red splashes that its leaves impart to the otherwise dull-coloured stretches of bog. It makes up for the lack of minerals in its environment by the simple process of catching mineral-rich insects. This it does by trapping unlucky insects on its sticky tentacles and then dissolving and absorbing them.

2   *Erosion on the Hilltops*
     This area has suffered greatly from over-grazing by sheep, caused by the EC Common Agricultural Policy which gives grants on the basis of the number of ewes run by each farmer, so that it is in each farmer's interest to run the maximum. The result is the erosion evident here (see p. 17).

3   *Tragedy at Doo Lough*
     In 1849, towards the end of the Great Famine, a comparatively small and little-known, yet significant tragedy occurred hereabouts. A group of starving people who were trying to seek refuge in the workhouse at Louisburgh were advised to present themselves in person to the Guardians of the Workhouse at Delphi, 12 miles (19 km) away over rough tracks. The Guardians could — or would — do nothing for them, so the starving people had to return through the cold of an early spring. Some of them died on the way back. While the numbers involved are disputed, the main facts and therefore the poignancy of the incident is not. This event is remembered in a simple plaque on the side of the road here.

Mweelrea: the eastern side

4·22

THE GLENCOAGHAN HORSESHOE

STARTING AND FINISHING
POINT
Ben Lettery Youth Hostel
(777483) on the N59, 6 miles
(9.5 km) west of Recess and 8
miles (13 km) east of Clifden. The
Hostel is on the northern side of
the road and is well signposted.
There is plenty of space for safe
parking. Two miles (3 km) of
tedious walking can be avoided if
two cars are used, the second
leaving the walkers about 1 mile
(1.6 km) along the track
described in the first paragraph of
the route description. Here there
is room for careful parking on the
verge.

MAPS
The 1:50 000 Connemara map is
recommended. The OS half-inch
to the mile Sheet 10 is on too
small a scale and should be used
only if nothing else is available.

LENGTH
10 miles (16 km)

ASCENT
5200 feet (1590 m)

SAFETY NOTE
Although the total distance
walked is modest, there is a lot of
climbing and the descents can be
just as tiring as the ascents. Be
prepared for a long, energetic
day.

This is a classic among Irish hill walks, a demanding circuit taking
in six of the rearing Twelve Bens in a lofty route over steeply
rising and dipping terrain. It is the bare quartzite rock that
distinguishes the walk from nearly all others in Ireland, and
which gives it its unique character. The views all along the route
are excellent: primarily the ever-changing vista of the Bens
themselves into whose deepest recesses this walk penetrates. But
that is not all: the Maamturks lie just across the Inagh Valley, and
between Bens and Maamturks and curving round in a great arc to
the south (thus blocking off the Bens from the watery bogland
further south) runs a long, narrow scenic line of interconnected
lakes. A superb walk in superb country.

ROUTE DESCRIPTION (Map 4.22)

With the Hostel on the L walk along the N59 for 1 mile (1.6 km),
turning first L here onto a track. This track must constitute one
of the most untidy and unprepossessing starts of any walk: 'tem-
porary' caravan dwellings, straggling fences and rough ground
combine to deter the sensitive walker. But persevere; after about
1 mile (1.6 km) of undulating progress, the full view of the
circuit broken only by the curious snout pushing east of
Benbreen/Binn Bhraoin comes fully into view. It is a magnificent
sweep of peaks from Derryclare/Binn Dhoir Chlair nearby on the
R to Ben Lettery/Binn Leitri on the L, vegetation climbing the
lower slopes, glistening quartzite above to the very summits.

Choose any convenient point along here to leave the track and
head half R for Derryclare (2220 ft/677 m) which rises steeply
close at hand. Initially, the ground is rough and boggy, but it
improves if a grassy ramp higher up, not essential for route-
finding, is found. There is a long, unrelenting climb to the
summit of Derryclare, which marks the end of vegetation; from
here on, the route is predominantly over rock all the way to Ben
Lettery. A short drop and rather longer rise *(1)* ends in Bencorr/
Binn Chorr (2336 ft/712 m) where the views to Lough Inagh, and
beyond that to the Maamturks, catch the eye.

Take the ridge of rock slabs heading initially north-west from Bencorr and drop to the pass at Mam na bhFonsai, taking care not to follow the formidable range running north-east that ends overlooking Lough Inagh. From the pass, climb sharply to Bencollaghduff/Binn Dhubh (2260 ft/698 m), a magnificent belvedere in the centre of the Bens, and commanding especially good views of the white cone of Benbaun/Binn Bhan, at 2395 ft (730 m) the highest of all the Bens.

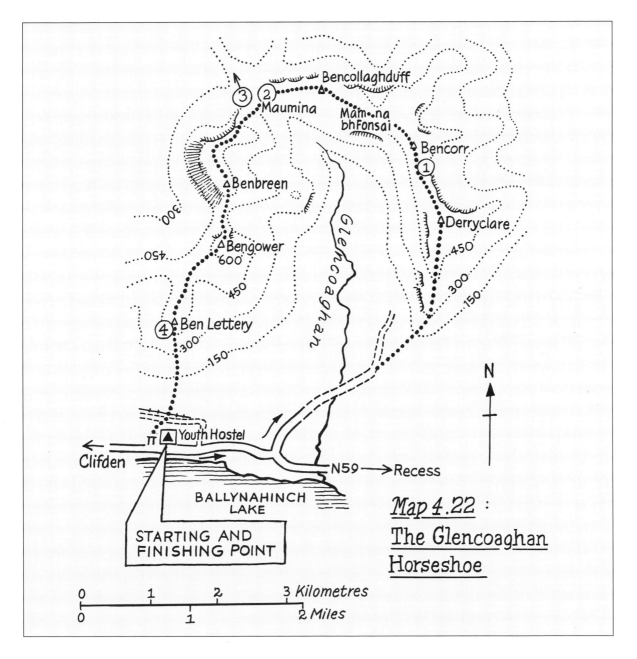

Map 4.22 :
The Glencoaghan Horseshoe

Another steep drop, partly over narrow but safe ground, follows to Maumina/Mam Eidheach, a narrow, comparatively low pass (1476 ft/450 m), which is generally considered to be the centre around which the peaks of the Bens converge *(2)*. Three valleys meet, or rather nearly meet here: the partly wooded valley of the Owenglin river running west, the unwooded part of which is in the Connemara National Park *(3)*; Glencoaghan to the south; and Gleninagh/Gleann Eidhneach, not visible from here but only a little way off to the north-east. Between these three the highest pyramids of the Bens soar skywards, bare and awe-inspiring. Would it be an earthward descent into bathos to mention also that Maumina is an excellent place for a rest and a snack?

There is another steep climb with some avoidable scrambling to Benbreen/Binn Bhraoin (2276 ft/694 m), a difficult peak on which to navigate in bad weather. The initial climb ends in a rock-strewn plateau and a dog-leg L on it brings you to the summit cairn on the far end. If in doubt note that the eastern spur of Benbreen which projects unmistakably into the main valley is directly opposite the summit.

A steep scree descent, partly (but only partly) avoidable ends at another narrow pass. From here Bengower/Binn Gabhar (2184 ft/666 m) is due south. Once again and unsurprisingly, another steep ascent to the summit (you will surely be used to them by now!), this one involving some scrambling, though this is neither difficult nor vertigo-inducing.

South of Bengower, grass once again begins to predominate. Ben Lettery (1904 ft/580 m) *(4)* is but a short stroll away, but take care on this stretch *not* to follow the spur R towards Benglenisky/Binn Ghleann Uisce. Descend south of Ben Lettery towards the Hostel and the road through steep, rough wet vegetation. As you descend, the Hostel, partly obscured by clumps of trees,comes into view, and as is usual on difficult, lengthy descents at the end of a tiring day, seems to get no whit more prominent as you walk.

At length you will see a ruin ahead. Head for this, crossing the fence just before it (look for the place where the wires are bent to facilitate walkers). Cross the track ahead and near the Hostel go to the R side to use the stile at the boundary fence. Take the driveway to the road.

1   *The Patient Surveyor*
The remains of a stone shelter just above the col towards Bencorr was occupied by an OS surveyor in the 1840s when the major triangulation of Ireland was being carried out. He had to wait 7 weeks to get a clear day to see what he called the 'Kerry Man' on Carrauntoohil 90 miles (145 km) away.

Opposite: *The eastern end of the Bens*

2 *Muckanaght, the Green Hill*
From Maumina the peak of Muckanaght/Meacanach to the north-west may be seen. It is more rounded and greener than its neighbours, the reason being that alone among the Bens it is formed of schists, not quartzite. The schist breaks down easier than the quartzite, thus giving a gentler outline and forming better soil, which allows some grass to cling to its sides.

3 *The Connemara National Park*
The Connemara National Park takes in the near sides (only) of the three summits north and west of here as well as the summit of Bencullagh/An Chailleach and the area around it to the west. The Park stretches to the outskirts of Letterfrack, $5\frac{1}{2}$ miles (9 km) away. In all it covers 5000 acres (2000 hectares), mostly mountain but also with some areas of bog, heaths and grassland. The Visitor Centre at Letterfrack, which is open from Easter to the end of September, provides an audio-visual display, a stunning photographic display of Connemara scenery (though not as stunning as the display you should be experiencing here at Maumina), and picnic tables with the free use of electric kettles to brew your own hot drinks (the latter are not free). The Visitor Centre is a good excursion for a wet day.

4 *Caesar Otway on Ben Lettery*
Mr Caesar Otway, whom we last met on Muckish, also climbed Ben Lettery, which he found 'extremely rugged and precipitous'. He had a different type of anguish on Lettery to that which he experienced on Muckish. 'Some of our party', he thundered, 'called for the provision basket. It was little short of treason against the majesty of nature, to fix those eyes on rolls and cold beef, which ought to have been directed to one of the noblest views of Cunnemarra.'

It is more than likely that eating and viewing simultaneously would have compounded the affront.

The view across Glencoaghan

Introduction

The mountains of the South-West, in effect the mountains of County Kerry since the contiguous hill area of west Cork is but a small adjunct, boast nearly all the highest mountains in Ireland, including all but two of its Munros. This paramount but simple fact does not itself make the mountains of Kerry attractive or challenging, but nevertheless they are. Tall (as small) *is* beautiful.

This is an area where the sea, and its numerous inlets, are never far away. The mountains are located on five peninsulas, five rugged fingers reaching westward into the ocean and separated by long, tapering bays — in geological terms drowned valleys. In many mountain areas the sea is ever-present, a deep blue plain stretching to the misty horizon. In others it reveals itself on the climb: sections of what appear first as disjointed lakes coalesce with height to be seen eventually as long inlets of the sea.

The other common feature of the South-West is the relative abundance of vegetation. The area benefits from the warmth of the Gulf Stream and so is characterized by exceptionally mild winters, especially in its southernmost reaches. In particular the area round Glengarriff in the far south is a humid hothouse of vegetation, so that the frequent epithet 'sub-tropical' that is applied to the region is not altogether an exaggeration.

The long inlets and rugged terrain mean that access is not easy in the South-West. Roads hug the coast and cross the peninsulas only by means of tortuous, sinuous passes. Add to that the perennial poor state of the roads so that the rule must be: leave yourself plenty of time for travel; you will probably need it.

In an area of splendid mountains some of the routes were 'musts'. The Coomloughra horseshoe simply had to be included. How could any mountaineering writer omit a circuit which encompasses the *three* highest peaks in Ireland and by far its most spectacular ridge walk? Brandon was in the same category: a great massif on the Dingle Peninsula, a superb juxtaposition of magnificent corrie, rugged hillside and rolling ocean — and a formidable Monro to boot.

Some of the others were not so obvious; two at least were chosen because they are characteristic of their areas. The proud peak of Mullaghanattin is near the centre of Iveragh, the largest by far of the five peninsulas, and provides one fine circuit among

A Paternoster lake on Brandon

many in an area of great mountain country. Several other routes almost as attractive might have been chosen instead of (or preferably in addition to) Mullaghanattin. Further south the Beara Peninsula presented a similarly difficult choice. An area of lush vegetation, highly characteristic sandstone rock formations, but dull uplands, it was no easy matter to pick the best route. Nonetheless the Cummeengeera horseshoe is difficult to better.

133

The two routes which are easily accessible from Killarney are close only in their location. Bennaunmore is a purely serendipitous discovery: on the map an unpromising hilly area first chosen to while away a day of low cloud. However, a pleasant surprise was in store: regions far greater in extent and several times as high cannot boast a terrain as varied and as mountainously rugged, where each few steps reveal fresh delights. The other area near Killarney is quite different, partly open moorland offering wide views, the haunt of the endangered red deer, partly (if you choose the route variation) dramatic rocky defile. This is one of the few routes in comparatively pathless Ireland where a satisfactory circuit can be made purely on path and track. Incidentally, do not be put off by the length of this route. The text also describes shorter alternatives.

The other two routes have connotations other than purely mountaineering ones. Mount Eagle is as much a cultural as a physical journey. At the remote end of the remote Dingle Peninsula it gives not only a highly scenic coastal walk, but also a glimpse into the remnants of Gaelic Ireland, the archaeological and linguistic remains of a once-rich culture now on a life-support system. Lastly, Gougane Barra, which has religious associations as well as cultural ones, is undoubtedly the finest area for walking in West Cork, both because of the dramatic views it gives of the corrie on which the route centres and the wide panorama it allows.

2·23

MOUNT EAGLE

STARTING AND FINISHING
POINT
In the car-park on the seaward
side of the R559 just south of the
village of Coumeenoole (317976).
MAP
OS half-inch to the mile Sheet 20
is barely adequate. (OS 1:50 000
Sheet 70 is scheduled for 1991).
LENGTH
7 miles (10 km)
ASCENT
1700 ft (530 m)

For much of this walk the eye is drawn irresistibly towards the sea, and especially towards the islands which lie scattered over it. Pre-eminent is Great Blasket, a basking whale of a rock just off the pointing finger of Dunmore Head. Beyond it float the other islands of the Blaskets: Inishtooskert, Tearaght, Inishnabro and Inishvickillane — all of them carrying almost mystic significance for the last phase of Gaelic-speaking Ireland. Further away to the south rise the unmistakable Great and Little Skelligs, like the summits of jagged peaks rising sheer out of the ocean. Add to all this splendid views of the mountains of two peninsulas and the result is an easy yet rewarding walk of excellent and varied views.

ROUTE DESCRIPTION (Map 2.23)

With the car-park on the R walk 300 yards (270 m) south along the road and turn L at the 'walking-man' sign to go through a gate. Turn R immediately and follow the wall in which the gate is set, first parallel to the main road and then steeply uphill. Pass another 'walking-man' on your L *(1), (2)*, still following the wall. Where the wall turns sharply R continue straight ahead uphill along an intermittent wall and earth bank which constitutes a boundary line.

This boundary line can be easily followed all the way to the top of Mount Eagle: first fairly steeply uphill, then over rocks and steep ground at Beenacouma (1395 ft/425 m), where it almost disappears, and finally over grass on the nearly level stretch near the summit (1696 ft, 517 m), which is marked by an OS obelisk.

From the summit, head towards the corrie that holds Mt Eagle Lough to pick up the end of a green track. Walk north along it, with the cliff and lough to the R, continuing straight ahead where a branch on the R heads down the northern side of the corrie.

Follow the track all the way to the Dunquin–Kildurrihy road, turn R here and again L at the T-junction, which has three signposts, all pointing to Daingean (Gaelic for Dingle). And you thought all roads led to Rome! Keep on this road, crossing the base of Dunmore Head *(3)*, to reach the car-park.

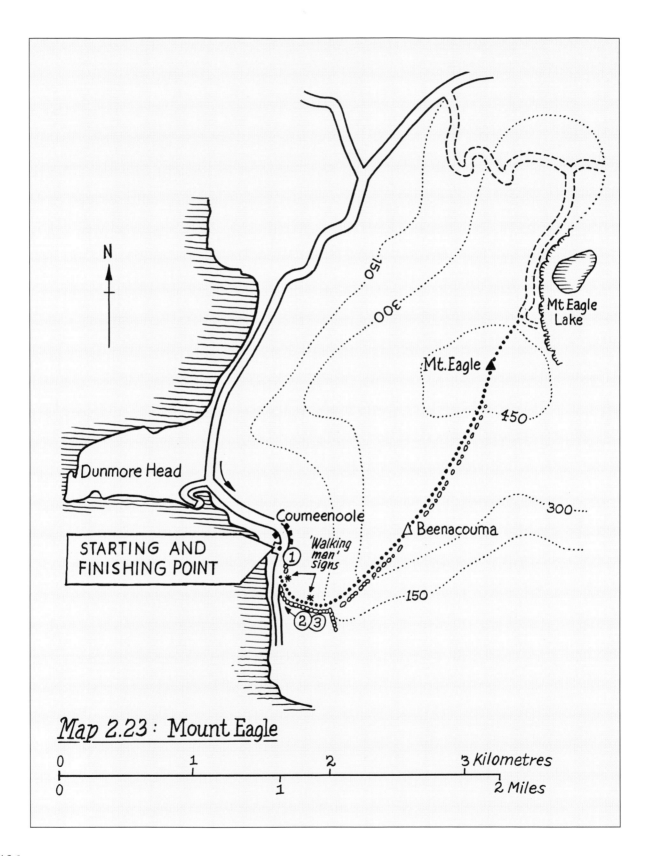

N

Mt Eagle Lake

Mt. Eagle ▲

450

Dunmore Head

150

300

Coumeenoole

'Walking man' signs

△ Beenacouma

STARTING AND FINISHING POINT

①

② ③

150

300

Map 2.23 : Mount Eagle

0		1		2		3 *Kilometres*

0		1		2 *Miles*

Left: *Slea Head from Ventry*

Below: *A shrine on the Slea Head road*

1   *The Slea Head Road*
The road on which this walk starts was built in the second
half of the nineteenth century to relieve unemployment.
This type of civil work, some of it of negligible practical use,
was the usual palliative to relieve a problem which has never
been satisfactorily solved except by the expedient of emigration.

2   *The Blaskets*
The Great Blasket Island was inhabited until 1953, wholly by
Gaelic speakers. In that year the remaining inhabitants were
evacuated. There was a fine tradition of writing among the
islanders, the best known of whom, Peig Sayers, is buried in
the graveyard close to the end of the walk.

The best map of the Blaskets is popular everywhere in
Ireland, among cartographers and non-cartographers alike.
Only a few inches long and not a rarity, it is nonetheless quite
valuable. It is universally known — and valued — as the
Irish £20 note.

3   *Aftermath of the Armada*
A Spanish ship foundered in Blasket Sound between Dunmore Head and Great Blasket in September 1588 after the
disastrous rout of the Armada. Hundreds of Spanish were
drowned and only one, the pilot's son, was saved and he was
captured. A Spanish prince who was among those lost is
buried in the old burial ground at Dunquin.

GOUGANE BARRA

STARTING AND FINISHING POINT

Opposite the church at Gougane Barra (091657), where there is ample parking. Gougane Barra is off the R584/T64 (Macroom–Ballylickey road) on the R travelling from Macroom.
It is well signposted.

MAPS

OS half-inch to the mile Sheet 24 inadequately covers the route. Sheet 21 covers the area just north of the route and is useful for identifying features beyond Sheet 24.

LENGTH

7 miles (11 km)

ASCENT

1750 ft (530 m)

SAFETY NOTE

This is a moderately short walk with what should be a simple navigational objective: to keep the corrie on the R. However, there are few significant landmarks — the 'peaks' barely rise above the plateau so in bad visibility you should use the small landmarks, primarily the lochans, to determine your position. There are only a few places where a direct descent to the valley floor can be attempted.

Gougane Barra (pronounced *Goo-gawn Barra*) is the jewel in the crown of the Shehy mountains of West Cork. The curious name properly refers to the narrow lake whose only major island contains a tiny picturesque church surrounded by trees. West of the lake a long, partly wooded corrie indented by several side valleys is cut into the plateau of the Shehy mountains. The walk circumscribes this corrie in a wide, clockwise sweep. With no real summits to be climbed, the walk's interest centres on the views of the lake and corrie, but more so outwards to the Paps, the great corrie of Lough Nambrackderg and the further-off jagged outline of the Reeks.

ROUTE DESCRIPTION (Map 2.24)

With the car-park on the L *(1)* walk along the road for 80 yards (70 m), turning L here through a gate and up a minor track at a toilet disguised as a circular African straw-hut. Follow the track uphill until it resolutely heads south-east, clearly the wrong direction. Strike diagonally R uphill here, cross a fence, and then aim for a rocky pinnacle high above. Not a peak, this is nonetheless a clear landmark. Its name, Foilastookeen, means 'The cliff of the little pinnacle' and this is a good description.

From here the next target is the unnamed peak close by to the south-west where a fence is visible on the skyline. Around this peak the views open up outwards from Gougane Barra corrie; Bantry Bay and the aptly named voluptuous Paps being conspicuous. Keeping the fence on the L follow it over rough ground past three small lakes on the L. At the last of these lakes (where the fence ends) a grid bearing of 350° will be needed to find Lough Glas high on the plateau to the north-west.

From Lough Glas continue slightly downwards to the head of a gully R *(2)*, crossing a fence close to it to reach a lochan. At this point the immense corrie of Lough Nambrackderg with a long, narrow waterfall plunging into it, can be seen at its finest. Continue across wet bogland to Bealick (1764 ft/538 m), the only 'peak' (a courtesy title) on this route to have a cairn of any sort. Given the number of hillocks hereabouts it is a useful construction.

The walk would appear to be almost over, with only a descent R to the start. Not so. The cliffs overlooking Gougane Barra Lake are low but dangerous, and though they can be circumvented the safe routes are easier to find in retrospect. Keep therefore to the shoulder north-east from Bealick, walking to a small lake set in quaking bog and continue straight ahead beyond it, dropping off the L side of the nose facing the Owenashrone River. Turn R at the river and follow the L bank down through tussocky country to a small copse of conifers where the river swings R. Cross wet bogland here to a narrow metalled road *(3)*, turn R along it and L at the foot of the hill (R leads to the nearby substantial farmhouse). At the main road turn R for the starting point.

1   *The Church at Gougane Barra*
The small church on Holy Island opposite the car-park, which can be reached by a causeway, dates from as recently as 1900 and was inspired by a chapel on the Rock of Cashel. The stone court nearby dates from the end of the seventeenth century. The wooden cross in the centre of the court is

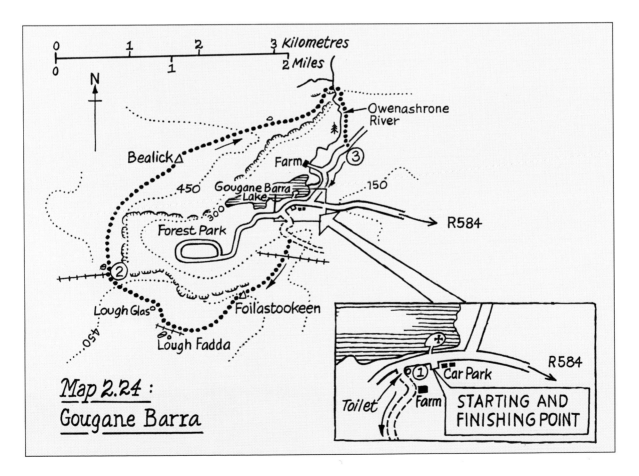

Map 2.24: Gougane Barra

The Church at Gougane Barra

inscribed in Latin, English and Gaelic: 'here stood in the sixth century, the cell of St Finbar, first bishop of Cork'. St Finbar had a monastery here which, being constructed of simple perishable material, has long since disappeared.

2   *The Fortuitous Gully*

This gully played a happy role for Irish insurgents in May 1921 when rebel troops were hemmed in on all sides by superior British forces. Helped by local guides the rebels retreated into Gougane Barra, and at night, led by a local guide, they climbed a long rope up this gully and thus escaped into Kerry.

3   *The Pilgrim's Road*

This road marks the end of the pilgrims' route into Gougane Barra, the start of which is noted in Route 25.

Opposite: *Gougane Barra lake*

2·25

BENNAUNMORE

STARTING AND FINISHING POINT

At the end of the side-road running along the eastern side of the Lough Guitane (034839). From Killarney take the N71 (Kenmare road) turning L at the signpost 'Lough Guitane 2½', which is just after the jarveys' gathering-point about 2½ miles (4 km) from Killarney. Drive straight ahead for 4 miles (6.4 km), turning R onto a gated road here. Drive for a further 1.4 miles (2.2 km) and park on open ground near a bridge which serves a farmhouse.

MAPS

OS half-inch to the mile Sheet 21 covers the route, though very inadequately. Sheet 20 in the same series also covers the route unless you intend to get lost eastwards! (The route is at the very edge of this map.) (OS 1:50 000 Sheet 79 is scheduled for end 1991.)

LENGTH

6½ miles (10.5 km)

ASCENT

1650 ft (500 m)

The area south-east of Killarney close to Lough Guitane is ideal for leisurely free-range exploration. The discriminating walker can enjoy narrow but deep glens, low but soaring peaks flanked by impressive cliffs, ancient oakwoods and tiny hidden lakes, all in a virtually unfrequented area within a couple of miles of Bennaunmore, a peak of volcanic rock. The route given here is a suggestion only, a vehicle to point to the small-scale hidden delights of the area. Take into account the few cautions given below and you can wander around safely as the fancy takes you. Give yourself plenty of time: much of the terrain is difficult — and all of it repays leisurely pottering.

ROUTE DESCRIPTION (Map 2.25)

Follow the track south-east (that is, not over the bridge) past a ruin on the L. Cross two minor streams, and just beyond the second pass through a gate. This gate marks your entry into open country and you should note carefully its position since you will have to find it on the return.

From the gate head south-east (exactly 120° grid) towards a tiny valley visible from here. Walk up the valley (1). ('Walk' is a euphemism for struggle: crossing from one bank to the other and back again, clambering over rocks, climbing through high vegetation, and even stone-hopping up the stream when all else fails.) After at least a half-hour's work with little progress to show for it, you will gain a tiny basin with a hill beyond flanked by two valleys, that to the R sheltering a small copse of oaks. Follow this valley, which gives unexpectedly easy going over long grass, up to a grassy col. Lough Nabroda comes suddenly into view below, and the rocky cliffs on the eastern flank of Bennaunmore (2) come equally suddenly into view ahead. A good spot to rest after your strenuous efforts.

Walk down to the near side of the lake to pick up a path running beside it on its L-hand side. Follow the path to the end of the lake, where it disappears, leaving the walker to face the wet grassy bogland beyond to Lake Crohane alone. Here you have a choice: a difficult route through a mixed wood on the west (i.e. R) side or an easy route through grass and heather on the

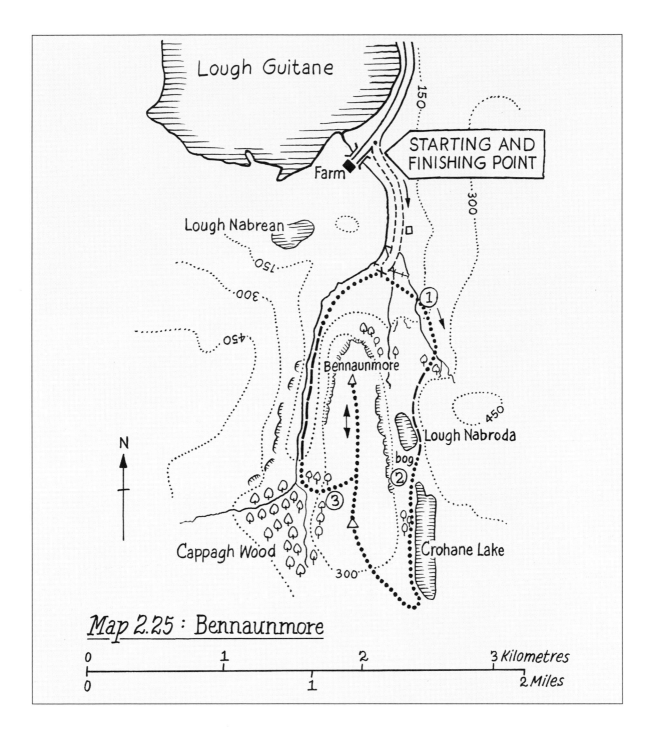

Map 2.25 : Bennaunmore

east (i.e. L). Either way, the view of the Roughty River over the brow of the hill at the southern end is worth a peep.

Next, Bennaunmore (1490 ft/454 m). The south top is easily climbed directly from the far south end of Lake Crohane over rough open country. The north top is a there-and-back to the saddle between it and the south top, but is worth the effort for

Bennaunmore from near the start

the views it gives of Lough Guitane and the high plateau of Mangerton to the west. At the saddle once again descend carefully west into Cappagh Glen *(3)*. This is a steep slope through an ancient 'petrified' wood of oak, holly and birch whose recumbent branches are not for grasping trustingly — they are all too liable to break off in rotten fragments in the hand. Incidentally, the descent directly from Lake Crohane into the south of Cappagh Glen is not recommended: this slope is even more hazardous than the one described.

On the valley floor turn R (north) to walk by a stream on its R-hand bank. This leads to an impressive natural amphitheatre a little way on, the walls especially high on Bennaunmore's flank to the R and a clear indication that a descent anywhere from Bennaunmore's west flank would be suicidal. At this point the amphitheatre looks exitless: luckily the stream has found a narrow but easy passage, so simply follow it along a clear path.

Beyond the exit follow the burgeoning stream into an alluvial plain of short grass and after a distinct bend to the R veer away from it to gain the gate crossed earlier in the day (the fence ahead will halt onward progress anyway). Take the track beyond, the initial track of the day, directly to the car.

1   *The Old Pilgrim Road*
     The stone uprights occasionally seen along here are the remains of an old pilgrim road which led from the plains of Kerry north of here across the mountains to Gougane Barra in west Cork. The pilgrims gathered there for the festival of St Finbar on the last Sunday in September. We have already met the other end of this route in Route 24.

2 *The Giant's Causeway of Kerry* *Lough Nabroda*

The volcanic columnar cliffs of Bennaunmore range for about a $\frac{1}{4}$ mile (0.4 km) and in places are about 200 ft (60 m) high. Only some of the columns exhibit a regular polygonal cross-section. They are not safe for climbing as they come away easily from the cliff face. There is a stream flowing north from Lough Nabroda but it is underground, being blocked by fallen columns and scree from Bennaunmore.

3 *The Petrified Forest of Cappagh*

This forest, because of its remote location and difficult underfoot terrain survived the mass clearing of the native oak to make charcoal for iron-smelting furnaces in the seventeenth century. Many of the trees to the south are leafless, hence the term 'petrified'. 'Cappagh' (ceapach) is the Gaelic for 'decayed', indicating that the forest must have been in decline for many years.

The Cummeengeera Horseshoe

On the road into Cummeengeera
(760559). Drive to Lauragh
village, a strung-out few houses,
church, school and post office
around the junction of the
R571/L62 with the R574 (the
Healy Pass road). Taking the
initial measurement from this
crossroads, drive west, that is,
towards Castletown Berehaven,
for 0.8 miles (1.3 km). Turn L
here, signposted 'Glanmore
Lake'. Turn R after 0.6 miles
(1.0 km) and drive for nearly 1
mile (1.4 km) to a gated track on
the R beyond which is a
bungalow. There is limited
parking here or towards the L
turn a few hundred yards further
on.

MAP
OS Kerry District one-inch to the
mile map.

LENGTH
6½ miles (10.5 km)

ASCENT
2450 ft (750 m)

'Benches' are a notable feature of this walk in the Beara Peninsula. The word 'benches' conjures up a smooth horizontal surface, but used by the locals this is a gross misnomer: the great sandstone slabs called 'benches' lie tilted at high, awkward angles and rise line upon line to form the hills, so that on the skyline they appear like the teeth of a huge circular saw. Along their grain walking is easy; a route crossing them is painfully slow.

The other remarkable feature of this area is the luxuriant vegetation in the lowlands: oakwoods drape themselves over the lower slopes and crowd around lakes; rhododendrons, ferns, mosses and a hundred species of flora thrive in the mild climate and high humidity. All quite memorable when viewed from above, but tortuous when traversed lower down.

ROUTE DESCRIPTION (Map 2.26)

Take the track on the R of the road through two gates, turning L off it before the first farmhouse. A tough climb *(1)*, initially through bracken though along the grain of the benches, ensues to the top of Cumeennahillan (1183 ft/361 m), or rather the tops (there are several), one of which is graced by a few heaped stones masquerading as a cairn.

A short drop through wet, boggy country ends in a climb with the grain of the benches to Knocknaveachal (1685 ft/514 m) which has no cairn, but a jagged pinnacle acts as a satisfactory substitute. From here the convoluted folding of Tooth Mountain ahead can be seen to perfection, one fold uncannily like the imprint of the lower set of a giant's teeth *(2)*.

A distinct, avoidable vertical slab is a reassuring landmark on the route to Tooth Mountain (1945 ft/593 m), the climb to which is short but difficult, through high slabs and along grassy ledges. The top is a tangle of rocky outcrops and puddles with no clear landmark to indicate position.

The terrain changes markedly after Tooth Mountain, slabs yielding to grassy bogland, thus allowing speedier progress. Coomacloghane (1969 ft/600 m) is another indefinite top or rather would be were it not for its OS obelisk. After Coomacloghane, slabs re-appear intermittently as far as the peat-hagged plateau that lies along the Cork-Kerry border. Once on this plateau, swing L to keep to the edge of the steep ground at the head of Cummeengeera. Along here the great rocky bulk of Hungry Hill to the south-east dominates the skyline.

Walk along level ground to Eskatarriff (1973 ft/601 m), an unimpressive set of slabs, after which climb a small but steep pinnacle, unheralded on the maps. This is Bireca, its L flank dropping sheer into the inner recesses of Cummeengeera. The upper end of the valley visible from here is interesting. Separated

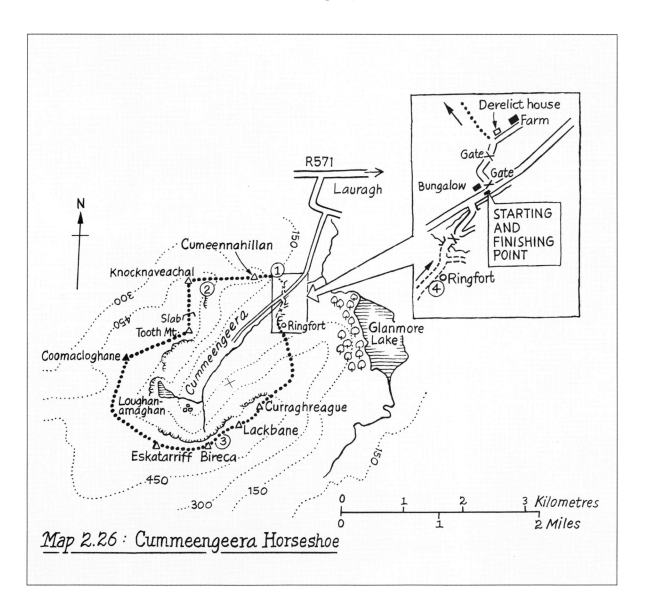

Map 2.26 : Cummeengeera Horseshoe

A 'bench' below Tooth mountain

from the lower end of Cummeengeera by a steep climb along a track, the valley is now deserted though it retains the traces of field boundaries and the remains of a house *(3)*, all of which from this lofty viewpoint appear as though on a map.

The next target is Lackbane (1984 ft/604 m), a stiff climb through rocky terrain. Beyond this, climb Curraghreague (1970 ft/600 m), its sister peak, which has a small cairn and whose north-west side drops far down into the glen in rock formations which look like organ pipes.

From Curraghreague make a steep descent over narrow ground offering excellent views of Lake Glanmore to the R and the lovely wooded lake and inlet country ahead. The drop ends at a narrow pass where the tempting direct descent L should not be attempted; it contains a wicked terrain of bracken and hidden boulder. Instead climb the hill directly ahead (it is only 100 ft/ 30 m or so) and descend north heading for the grassy circular mound below *(4)*. Take the path to its L, cross the area where it appears as if rhododendrons have been deliberately planted (surely not!) and carry on north to pick up a track.

Follow this across a bridge of rock slabs and through a gate. Beyond this turn L onto a better track at a hairpin bend (on the better track). Follow this track over a bridge to a metalled road and turn R for the starting point.

1   *Sub-tropical Gardens at Dereen*
    The woods of the Dereen Tropical Gardens just beyond Lauragh should be visible on the ascent. Built up over 130 years, the gardens flourish in the warm, damp climate. They include New Zealand ferns which although rare in the British Isles, thrive here; and giant conifers of north-west America, some of which are over 100 ft (30 m) tall.

2   *A Dental Mix-up at the Ordnance Survey*
    Knocknaveachal means 'the hill of the teeth' and the next mountain is called 'Tooth Mountain'. It seems that the English sappers got their nomenclature a little garbled when they were surveying in the nineteenth century. Considering this imprint the latter mountain seems the better candidate for the dental title.

3   *The Rabach*
    The ruined village in the upper reaches of Cummeengeera, which never had a road into it, illustrates the lengths to which people had to go to find a modicum of cultivatable land in pre-famine Ireland.

    There is a macabre story of a double murderer, Sean an Rabach, who dwelt here. He killed an Englishman, probably a deserter from a ship in Berehaven, and strangled a woman

The ruined village in Cummeengeera

who found out about this crime. Many years later he was caught and hanged, the last person in the province to be executed, it is said.

4   *The Earth Ringfort*
This earth ringfort is one of the tens of thousands scattered all over Ireland and dating from about 2000 BC to AD 500, though some date from much later and a few were inhabited until 1700. Homesteads were built within them and the fort acted as a shelter from the wind, and a protection at night for cattle against wolves, etc. They seldom had any direct military significance (see p. 15).

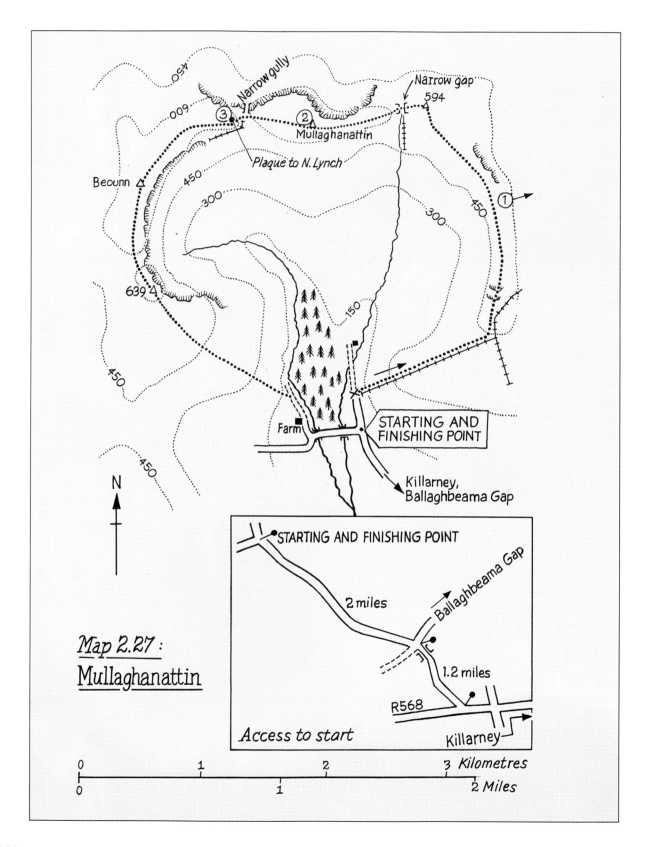

Narrow gully

Narrow gap

594

③

②
Mullaghanattin

Plaque to N. Lynch

Beounn △

600

450

450

300

①

300

639 △

450

150

Farm

STARTING AND
FINISHING POINT

Killarney,
Ballaghbeama Gap

N

Map 2.27 :
Mullaghanattin

STARTING AND FINISHING POINT

2 miles

Ballaghbeama Gap

1.2 miles

R568

Killarney

Access to start

0   1   2   3 Kilometres

0   1   2 Miles

2·27

MULLAGHANATTIN

STARTING AND FINISHING POINT

On a side-road south of Mullaghanattin (747747). Take the N71 from Killarney to Molls Gap, then the R568 for 6.1 miles (9.8 km) to a crossroads. Continue straight ahead for 0.3 miles (0.5 km), then turn R signposted 'Glencar'. Continue straight ahead after 1.2 miles (1.9 km) onto a side road marked 'cul de sac', where the main road swings R. Drive onward for 2 miles (3.2 km) to a side road L. There is room for considerate parking hereabouts.

The start may also be approached from the Ballaghbeama Gap. In this case the 'cul de sac' road is a R turn 3.3 miles (5.3 km) south of the Gap.

MAPS

The OS 1:50 000 Sheet 78 is recommended. The OS 1 inch to the mile Killarney District map is also satisfactory. The OS 1:25 000 map 'The MacGillycuddy's Reeks' covers all but the first and last few hundred yards of the walk but does not adequately cover the approach to the starting point by road.

LENGTH

6 miles (10 km)

ASCENT

3300 ft (1010 m)

Mullaghanattin is sometimes called the Matterhorn of Kerry; from many angles this peak, in the centre of the mountainous Iveragh Peninsula, displays in miniature the same proud triangular profile of the famed Swiss Alp. This route, with Mullaghanattin as its centrepiece, is a high-level circuit round a secluded basin appropriately called the Pocket. There is therefore little possibility of navigational error, these errors being more probable in finding the start! Nonetheless, as you gaze initially around at the horseshoe looming above, you might be forgiven for doubting if you are in the right place. Mullaghanattin is straight ahead along the line of the incoming road but it scarcely appears to rise above the horizon line. Patience! The pyramid emerges into full view as you traverse the circuit, along with an unexpected bonus: the first sight of the tangle of mountains west of Cloon Lough — bare, grotesquely distorted rock strata and tiny lochans one above the other — is a spectacle to remember.

ROUTE DESCRIPTION (Map 2.27)

Walk onwards for 300 yards (270 m) to a gate, and beyond it turn R beside a fence. Follow the fence steeply uphill through crags. Mercifully the steepness soon relents, yielding to a more gentle slope of short grass. At the fence junction near the crest of the hill swing L with the line of fencing that you have followed thus far, and where it eventually veers R downhill continue along the bumpy ridge taking in some steep but avoidable crags among the first of the bumps (they are hard to enumerate exactly).

Walk along the high broad ridge to enjoy easy terrain and good views of the nearby Reeks to the north-east and the even nearer Lough Brin *(1)*. At a small, circular, flat and grassy mound — an unexpected feature hereabouts — turn west, i.e. to the L, to face the increasingly impressive cone of Mullaghanattin. First drop to a very narrow gap and then climb steeply with cliffs R all the way to the OS obelisk marking the summit *(2)* (2539 ft/773 m).

Continue west steeply downhill from the summit to a fearsome gully on the R (do not take it!). Just beyond this on higher ground look out for the simple plaque to Noel Lynch *(3)*. Ascend

Mullaghanattin from Lough Brin

further along the ridge to Beounn (2468 ft/752 m), which is not named on the maps. It is the highest point on a very narrow grassy ridge giving truly spectacular views to the west of Cloon Lough, an amazing tangle of bare rock and lonely lochans.

From Beounn descend south to a pass and climb from there to a broad, rounded peak simply labelled 639 m on the 1:50 000 map. Continue south-east from point 639 m, so dropping towards the corner of the Pocket and crossing diagonally a series of sandstone slabs which further slow down already slow progress. At the valley floor pick up a rough track, turn R and follow it to an impressive group of farm buildings. Ask permission to go through the farmyard (it will be readily given) and continue along the track to a metalled road. Turn L here, cross two bridges and you will reach the parking area at the (relatively) main road.

The Pocket

1 *Monster at Lough Brin*
This lake is reputed to harbour a Loch Ness type monster; it is only one of a number of Kerry lakes to make such a claim. However, the evidence is a lot more slight than for the Scottish monster.

2 *Rainfall in Kerry*
A few miles north-east of here at Ballaghbeama Gap the greatest annual total rainfall (156 inches/3965 mm) was recorded. A few miles north-west (Coomacarrea) is the area that had the greatest monthly total (27 inches/686 mm) — a rather unenviable propiniquity!

3 *Plaque to Noel Lynch*
This plaque commemorates a Dublin man, an international climber who was killed in a simple walking accident in 1973. The sentence translates as 'The Blessings of God on his soul'.

153

Trails Around Killarney

STARTING AND FINISHING POINTS

Start at the car-park of Muckross House (970861) which is well signposted. From Killarney take the N71 (Kenmare road) for about $3\frac{1}{2}$ miles (5.5 km) turning R here for the House. The short route also finishes here. The long route ends at Kate Kearney's Cottage (881887), which is also well signposted. Take the R562/T67 (Killorglin road) from Killarney turning L after $5\frac{1}{2}$ miles (9 km) and follow the signs for the cottage.

MAPS

This walk is covered by a variety of OS and other maps at 1:50 000 and one-inch to the mile scales. The recommended map is the OS 1:25 000 Killarney National Park (scheduled for 1992).

LENGTH

The short route is $14\frac{1}{2}$ miles (23 km) long but this can be shortened to 7 miles (11 km) if a car is available at Derrycunihy church (914803). The long route is also $14\frac{1}{2}$ miles (23 km) long.

ASCENT

1050 ft (320 m) for the short route; 1750 ft (530 m) for the long.

Killarney is sickly-sweet famous, the subject of scores of maudlin songs and tasteless ballads. This type of tourist shrine is usually best avoided as the reality all too often fails to live up to expectation. Nevertheless, Killarney, or rather the area around, does not disappoint: it is a spectacular interplay of woods, lakes and mountains.

Two routes are described here, both following the Old Kenmare Road. They start at Muckross House and climb by Torc Waterfall before settling down to paths over moorland and through oakwood in an area that is one of the last fastnesses of the Irish red deer. One route returns towards Killarney along the Kerry Way, and gives good views of Muckross Lake and its wooded shores. This we call the 'short route' in the following text, though it actually only involves less climbing.

Alternatively, one can continue away from Killarney on the Kerry Way, descend to the shores of the Upper Lake and from there climb the awesome cleft of the Gap of Dunloe with towering cliffs to right and left to end at Kate Kearney's Cottage near Killarney. This we call the 'long route'.

ROUTE DESCRIPTION (Map 3.28)

From the car-park walk round the R of the House (1), to meet the Kerry Way (2), which should be followed until otherwise indicated. Take the driveway west (3) and then south with the shore of Muckross Lake on the R and the heavily wooded Torc Mountain ahead. Continue along the driveway through woodlands and take the tunnel at a clearing on the R under the N71.

On the other side of the road a steep climb ensues alongside the cascade below Torc Waterfall, the climb's severity only partly disguised by dense vegetation. At the T-junction towards the top, turn L to gain a car-park, this evidence of motorized ascent being a rather annoying revelation in the light of recent efforts. Here is the start of the tracked section of the Old Kenmare Road (4).

The Upper Lake, Killarney

Take the forest road south-west passing the forest bar, cross a bridge and turn L immediately afterwards to walk through a pleasant oakwood. Less than a $\frac{1}{2}$ mile (0.8 km) further on pass a gate which has a notice explaining that one is entering the terrain of the red deer *(5)*, and listing certain misdeeds that one is emphatically not to perpetrate. No need to specify: responsible walkers would not dream of committing them.

The forest road continues steadily upwards to the south-west, shrinking to a narrow path at the Crinnagh River, where planks form several rudimentary bridges. If in doubt a little further on, keep between the low Cores Cascade on the L and a quaking bog on the R and head for a few oak trees sheltered by massive slabs.

The path resumes faintly beyond the oaks, passing to the L of further slabs *(6)*. Ascend gradually to the crest of the hill, beyond

NOTE
Dogs are strictly forbidden in the deer country through which these routes run.

155

which pass to the R of a ruin (the first prominent ruin). From here on, old sessile oaks dominate with green moss growing luxuriantly on tree trunk, ground and rocks alike in profusion, stimulated by warmth and high humidity. At the clear track beyond this wood, turn R and walk down to the N71 at Derrycunihy church. At this point there is a choice of route.

Short route Assuming no car pick-up here, one can take the short route back to Muckross. Leaving the Kerry Way turn R along the N71 and walk down the road for $4\frac{1}{2}$ miles (7 km) to the sign for Dinis, a road giving enchanting views of Muckross Lake and the mountains beyond. Turn L here to follow a narrow, metalled road over peninsulas between Muckross Lake and Lough Leane all the way back to Muckross House.

Long route Alternatively, one can tackle the long route. Turn L on the N71, walk 100 yards (90 m) along the road, then go R at the walking-man signpost to follow a path down through woods. This stretch of path is marked by indicators — posts or paint spots — every few yards, and all are needed given the errant path's perverse tendency to shake off walkers. The path ends at a signpost near a ruin. Turn L here to follow a well-mannered path which runs round the end of the Upper Lake and leads eventually to Gearhameen, where the tower of a lime kiln and a lovely old stone bridge herald a road.

Turn L at the T-junction beyond the bridge (a waymark would be useful here) and continue on the road through pastoral land past Black Valley Youth Hostel and thence to the hamlet of Black Valley beyond.

The next task is to penetrate the great wall of mountains to the north (R): easily described, less easily done. Turn R steeply uphill in the hamlet onto a rough but motorable track (thus leaving the Kerry Way) and climb to the Gap of Dunloe, whose high point is at the near end, 450 ft (140 m) above and only $1\frac{1}{4}$ miles (2 km) away by road. Once there, the full magnitude of the Gap *(7)* becomes apparent, a deep defile cut between the Purple Mountain group to the east (R) and the Reeks to the west (L).

From the high point of the pass take the road on a slow but steady descent past four lakes and into a gradually widening valley all the way to Kate Kearney's Cottage. The slow physical descent is matched by a slow descent into mundaneness; jaunting cars *(8)* and day-trippers become more frequent and all sense of isolation eventually disappears. However, as you await your lift at the cottage, sipping a beverage in comfort, you may conclude that the mundane aspects of life bring some small but welcome comforts in their train.

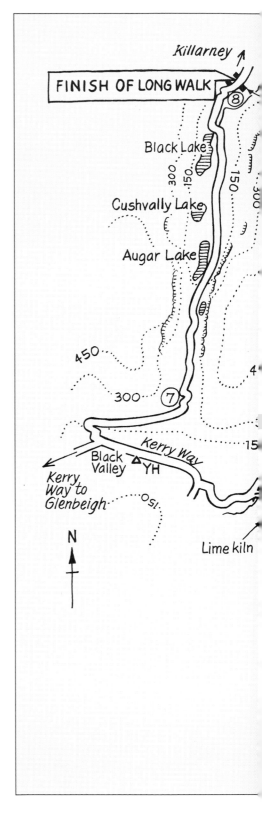

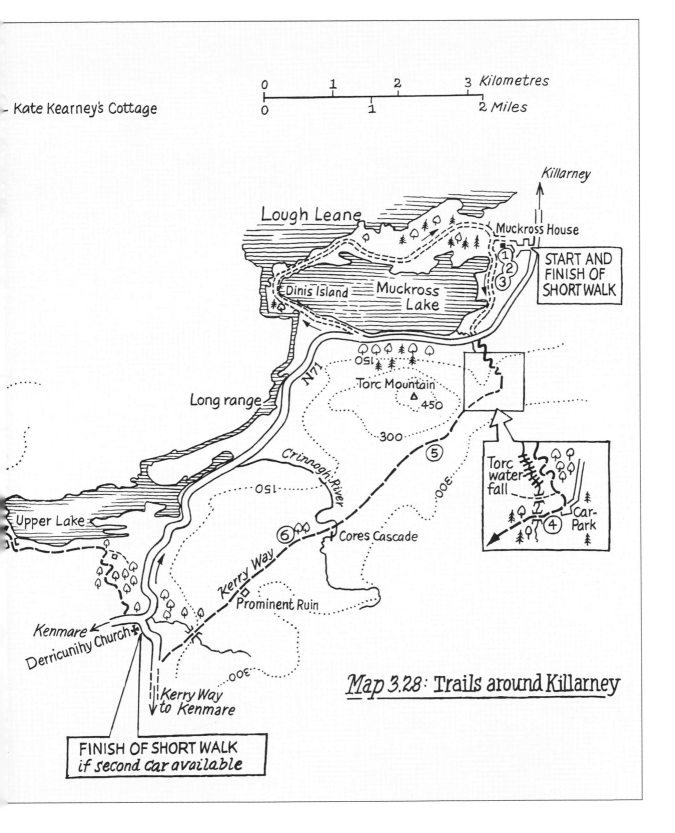

Kate Kearney's Cottage

0   1   2   3   Kilometres

0   1   2   Miles

Killarney

Muckross House

Lough Leane

START AND
FINISH OF
SHORT WALK

Dinis Island   Muckross Lake

150

Torc Mountain
△ 450

300

Long range

N71

Crinnagh River

150

Upper Lake

300

Kerry Way

Cores Cascade

Torc
water
fall

Car-
Park

5

6

Prominent Ruin

Kenmare

Derricunihy Church

300

Kerry Way
to Kenmare

FINISH OF SHORT WALK
if second car available

Map 3.28: Trails around Killarney

1   *Muckross House and Killarney National Park*
The House was completed in 1843 in the Elizabethan style. It lay vacant for a number of years prior to 1964, when it was opened to the public as a museum of Kerry folk life. This museum still flourishes and there is now an audio-visual display illustrating the environment of the National Park. The gardens are informal with large expanses of lawn fronting magnificent vistas of lake and mountain.

Killarney National Park covers 25,000 acres (10,000 hectares) and is the largest designated park in Ireland. It takes in the area west and south of Killarney, encompassing a wide variety of mountain and lake habitats. On its south-western edge it includes the summit of Mangerton Mountain; its western edge runs parallel and close to the Gap of Dunloe (see note 7 below).

2   *The Kerry Way*
The Kerry Way is shaped like the frame of a tennis racket. The 'handle' runs from Killarney south-west to near Derrycunihy church, where it forms a loop which runs right round the Iveragh Peninsula. The total distance is 135 miles (215 km), thus making it the longest of the Republic's Long Distance Routes. Wherever possible, it follows paths and unsurfaced roads with only a few linking stretches of metalled road. Since it runs generally higher than the motor roads, the views, already excellent from these, are even further enhanced.

3   *Kerry Cattle*
The grazing area here is for a pedigree herd of Kerry cattle. At one time the dominant breed of cattle in Ireland, these sturdy cattle have been largely confined to Kerry for the last 200 years.

4   *The Old Kenmare Road*
This was the main road between Killarney and Kenmare until the 1840s when it was closed by the local landowners who wanted the land for deer-hunting rather than farming. There are still remains of tillage, ruins and field boundaries along the route, testimony to the unfortunates who were so summarily driven from their homes.

5   *Red Deer*
The red deer of Killarney, numbering about 350–400, are the only deer of any kind in Ireland of native stock, all others being introduced. The main herd roams the moorlands and mountain slopes around here and towards Mangerton to the east. The smaller but more numerous sika deer live mainly in the woodlands. The deer are particularly impressive during the rutting season in October.

6   *The Napoleonic Peace in Ireland*

The Reeks from the Kerry Way

Nineteenth-century graffiti adorns the sandstone slabs here, the most prominent of which reads in a neat script: 'James Neill Tippy Regt 1815' ('Tippy' is short for 'Tipperary'). Exactly why James Neill had time to pursue such peaceful pastimes in rural Ireland while Europe was at war is not known.

7   *The Gap of Dunloe*

This great U-shaped gash 1500 ft (460 m) deep is a glacial breach formed from a major regional ice-sheet centred around Kenmare to the south. The glacier emanating from it pushed northwards, gouging out the Gap to reach the plains around Killarney.

8   *Jaunting Cars and Jarveys*

The jarveys of Killarney, the drivers of the jaunting cars, have been habitually described in Victorian guide books as a band of cut-throat, ruthless mercenaries who would sell their grannies for a quick profit. You will have to judge for yourself whether the Victorians underestimated their black-guardism!

159

3·29

The Coomloughra Horseshoe

STARTING AND FINISHING POINT

At the junction of the unclassified road running along the north-west side of Lough Acoose with that running along the eastern side (759859). Assuming that one is facing uphill on the main street in Killorglin take the road signposted Cappanalea on the L of this street. After 0.8 miles (1.3 km) fork R, also signposted Cappanalea, and continue ahead for another 6.8 miles (10.9 km). The exact parking place is not critical and you may wish to drive the car a few hundred yards up the road along the eastern side of the lake, thus shortening the walk at both ends.

MAPS
This walk is well covered by a variety of OS and other maps at 1:50 000 and one-inch to the mile scales. The recommended map is the OS 1:25 000 'The Macgillycuddy's Reeks'.

LENGTH
6½ miles (10.5 km)

ASCENT
4050 ft (1240 m)

The sharp arête of the Beenkeragh Ridge is the finest in Ireland, falling in stretches sheer to the east and almost as steeply to the west. At its south stands Carrauntoohil (pronounced *Carawn-too-hill*) at 3414 ft (1039 m) the highest peak in Ireland; to its north is Beenkeragh, only 100 ft (29 m) lower and the second highest mountain. Beyond these proud and stately peaks the ridge sweeps in one direction to Skegmore and in the other to twin-peaked Caher (pronounced *Care*), the third highest. All these peaks and the fine ridges between them surround the hour-glass shaped lakes of Coomloughra and Eagher. This is by far the finest ridge walk in Ireland and many would say the most exhilarating and rewarding circuit.

ROUTE DESCRIPTION (Map 3.29)

Walk a ½ mile (800 m) down the minor road along the eastern side of Lough Acoose, turning L off it opposite a prominent headland of Lough Acoose to cross rough, pathless ground and meet a fence and path parallel to it running along the north-west spur of Caher. Turn R here and follow the path and fence over good ground. Where the fence ends continue upwards still on a clear path through a boulder field to attain the first of the two peaks on Caher, which inexplicably has two adjacent cairns. The main top, which has to make do with one cairn, is a little farther on. At 3200 ft (975 m) it predictably commands marvellous views. Cliffs fall steeply L into Coomloughra, Carrauntoohil rises ahead and to its L the jagged Beenkeragh Ridge terminates in the great rocky mound of Beenkeragh. Among the many peaks to the west the pyramid of Mullaghanattin is the most prominent.

Still on a clear path follow the narrow ridge east of Caher. From the col towards Carrauntoohil take the broad boulder-strewn ridge to the summit itself by-passing, near the summit, the Beenkeragh Ridge on the L. On this ascent, note the long ridge running east. This is the eastern section of the Reeks *(1)*, a fine arc of mountains which boasts no fewer than three or five

SAFETY NOTE

The route, mostly a narrow ridge, is easy to negotiate navigationally, as the many cliffs in the area do not allow much latitude for error. If you suffer from *severe* vertigo do not attempt the ridge from Carrauntoohil to Beenkeragh (the 'Beenkeragh Ridge'), especially if the rocks are likely to be wet or if winds are high. The walk is in an anti-clockwise direction: this allows the highest peak in Ireland, Carrauntoohil, to be climbed *before* the Beenkeragh Ridge, so that one will at least have had the satisfaction of achieving this if one has to retreat. An anti-clockwise circuit also means that the difficult stretch of the Beenkeragh Ridge (it is near Carrauntoohil) is tackled early on thus facilitating a return if necessary.

Monros (it depends what is considered a Munro as there is not much of a drop between some of them).

Carrauntoohil (3414 ft/1039 m) is crowned by an ugly cross, a cairn and an OS obelisk *(2)*. Its summit stands as a promontory squarely facing north, looking over the plains of Kerry beyond the Hag's Glen. The views encompass much of what has already been described on the ascent and so need not be repeated. Among the many mountain features visible the formidable, steeper side of the Beenkeragh Ridge undulating jaggedly near at hand must attract what is hoped is a not too nervous eye.

So to the Ridge. Retrace your steps to the south-west for 100 yards (90 m), and then descend directly and steeply to the Ridge, which runs initially north-west (*Important: it is suicidal to attempt to walk directly to the Ridge from the summit of Carrauntoohil*). Once on the Ridge the crux, a rocky gendarme, comes early. The vertigo-free will clamber over the airy summit, the rest will scramble ignominiously lower down on the L. After this, the rest of the Ridge can be enjoyed as there is nothing half so scaring ahead. Now that *some* relaxation is possible (but not too much, carelessness can still easily result in disaster), watch out particularly for the Hag's Teeth far down on the R, great prongs of rock in the glen of the same name.

Beenkeragh is reached after a short, steep, rocky ascent. At 3314 ft (1010 m) it is the only mountain in Ireland besides

The Beenkeragh Ridge from Caher

Carrauntoohil to attain 1000 m. The views are magnificent, especially back towards Carrauntoohil. After Beenkeragh take the ridge heading north-west (not the one north-east) towards Skregmore (2790 ft/850 m) and if this is done correctly, navigation thereafter is simple; the ground, steep on both sides, is ample warning against carelessness and the only possible error is the gross one of wandering down the subsidiary ridge towards Skregbeg.

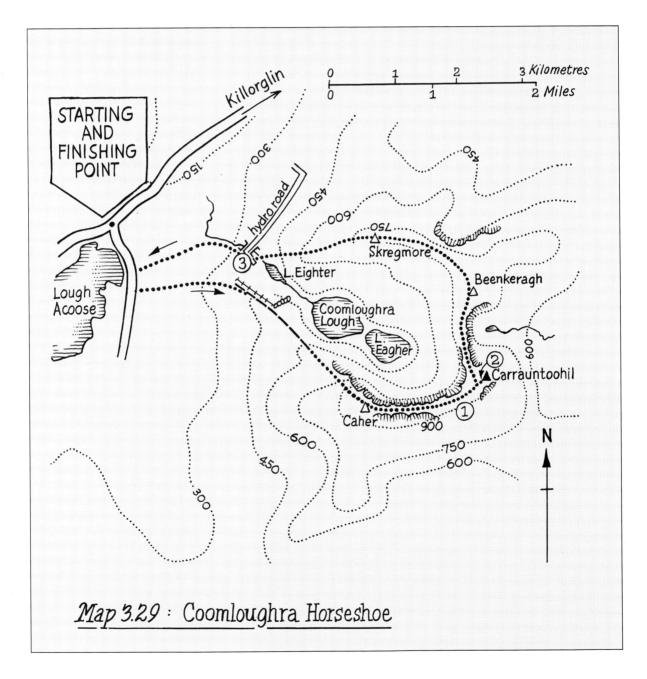

Map 3.29 : Coomloughra Horseshoe

Skregmore is, for the theoretically minded anyway, a problem. The five tops are difficult to distinguish, having only three
cairns between them. For the record, the third of these tops, the
one from which a ridge heads to Skregbeg, is the highest. Skregbeg is useful to the academics for determining exact positions —
while the rest of us get on with the job of climbing all the tops.

There is likely to be no mistake about the descent from the
'fifth' Skregmore: its steepness has an air of finality. From its
foot, head for the mouth of the long narrow Lough Eighter (not
to be confused with Lough Eagher to the east). Take the rough
road *(3)* at the mouth for the short distance to the bridge, and
leave it here to follow the L bank of the river downstream. After
500 yards (450 m) where the river bends sharply R, veer south-
west over a boggy saddle between rocky outcrops. Beyond these,
head to the R side of the prominent headland mentioned in the
first paragraph of the route description to reach the road. Turn R
for the starting point.

1   The Reeks

The Reeks (properly the Macgillicuddy's Reeks — so
named after a former local landlord) stretches from the Gap
of Dunloe and runs all the way to and including Skregmore.
The Munros and Tops (doubtful Munros), starting at the Gap
of Dunloe and working west, are: Cruach Mhor (3062 ft/
933 m), an unnamed top, Knocknapeasta (3190 ft/973 m), an
unnamed top, Cnoc an Chuillin (3141 ft/958 m), Carrauntoohil and Beenkeragh (3314 ft/1010 m). The Reeks Walk,
an annual long distance walk starting at the northern end of
the Gap of Dunloe, took in all the peaks to Carrauntoohil and
ended at Lough Acoose. It was discontinued in recent years
partly because of the erosion caused by too many walkers.

2   Carrauntoohil

At 3414 ft (1039 m) this is the highest mountain in Ireland,
though only the third of the four highest mountains in each of
the countries in the British Isles. The bicycle which unaccountably used to be suspended on a bar at the summit has
equally unaccountably disappeared.

Isaac Weld, an early mountaineer writing in 1807, used
only barometric observations estimated the height of the
mountain at 3418 ft, a remarkably accurate figure. He gives a
vivid account of a direct descent from the summit of
'Gheraun-tuel' (as he spells it), one which cannot be recommended:

We were conducted to a precipice, at least sixty feet deep,
down which we were told it was necessary to take our
course. The proposal startled us, nor did we consider how it

Lough Acoose and the Reeks

was practicable; but the guide seating himself at the brink of it, on a rock which presented an even surface nearly to the bottom of the precipice, slid down it, taking the precaution, however, to impede the velocity of the descent, by catching hold of the tufts of long grass which grew from the crevices at either side. His example was followed without hesitation.

3   *Hydro Scheme at Lough Eighter*
This scheme is funded as a Valorean EC project. It generates a minute amount of electricity in a country which already has an ample supply. The approach road, which is all too evident, is a brutal intrusion in an area of great beauty. Two pipes run from here: a 6-inch one for Killorglin water supply and an 18-inch one for the generation at Cottoner's River.

164

4·30

BRANDON

STARTING AND FINISHING
POINT
The church (on the L) in the
village of Cloghnane (511114).
From Tralee take the R559/T68
and then the R560 following signs
for Brandon or Brandon Point.
The village itself is rather
indifferently signposted, and to
make it worse the Gaelic form
'Cloghan' is used in places along
the road.
MAP
OS half-inch to the mile Sheet 20
covers the area, but very
inadequately. (OS 1:50 000 Sheet
70 is scheduled for 1991.)
LENGTH
$11\frac{1}{2}$ miles (18.5 km)
ASCENT
4000 ft (1210 m)

At least one Scotsman has declared Brandon to be the finest
mountain in the British Isles. While the not-so-canny Hamish
Brown may now regret what might have been a hasty, off-the-
cuff-remark (let's be charitable to the disloyal Scot), Brandon is
undoubtedly a superb mountain. Far out towards the western end
of the Dingle Peninsula, its eastern side plunges in a series of
corries and cliffs to Brandon Bay, to inert boglands and to the
high Conor Pass. West and north it confronts the Atlantic in a
sweep of sea-cliff broken by isolated coves. A unique delight is
the chain of paternoster lakes, a dozen or so (it depends on what
you count as a lake) perched one over the next. These are set into
the long corrie which truncates the summits of both Brandon and
Brandon Peak, its high southern extension. The route described
is probably the finest traverse of the mountain, offering marvellous scenic views on a safe, not-too-long circuit with, unusually
for this part of the world, a clear path at least as far as the
summit.

ROUTE DESCRIPTION (Map 4.30)

With the church on the L, walk past a plaque to airmen lost in
World War II *(1)*, on the R of the village street. Turn L onto a side
road after $\frac{1}{2}$ mile (0.8 km) from the start (it is signposted 'Hill-
crest'), walk uphill to the T-junction, turn L and at the upper end
of a severe S-bend where the road ends at a farmhouse, follow
two signposts encouragingly labelled 'Mt Brandon'. This is the
start of the Pilgrims' Route.

The second signpost leads to a grotto near at hand from where
a path, needlessly adorned with obtrusive red and white poles,
leads gradually uphill with higher ground on the R. At a large
cairn (the first) the views, up to this point dominated by Brandon
Peak and only slowly varying, open up dramatically. The paternoster lakes *(2)* are revealed one by one, and as the path swings R
it faces directly into the head of the corrie, cliffs rising jaggedly
and menacingly in nearly all directions.

Keeping to the path *(3)*, pass a lochan (four close together will
be visible from higher up) and ascend the corrie wall on a steep
but safe path. At the corrie top, turn L and with the sheer drop

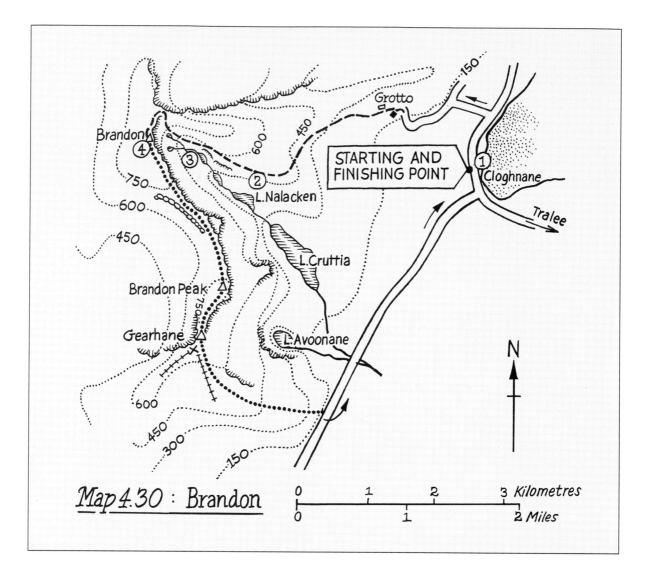

Map 4.30 : Brandon

into the corrie L, walk 350 yards (320 m) to Brandon (3127 ft/953 m) *(4)*. The views from the summit are varied: dominated by the ocean to the north and west, and by plain and mountain in other directions. It is a wonderful panorama — when it can be seen — for Brandon is often cloud-topped, or as they say in the neighbourhood — 'it mostly wears its cap'.

South of Brandon the path disappears, but no matter since all that is needed is to keep the corrie cliffs on the L and walk downhill (except for one short rise) all the way to the col towards Brandon Peak. In bad weather, the col may be recognized by a wall which meanders in from the R across the slope near the col, and abdicates to a line of stones at the col itself. South of the col climb steadily, cliffs still on the L, to cairned Brandon Peak (2764 ft/842 m).

The Paternoster Lakes

From the Peak continue south on a gently undulating slope to Gearhane, a short narrow ridge about 2250 ft (685 m) high with steep grassy slopes on both sides. Walk down the gentle slope south of Gearhane on what is now a spur to an upland gate, flanked by fences at an unusually acute angle. Keep to the L of the fences and the gate so keeping close to the steep ground on the L.

Follow the spur as it swings L and gently descends, a descent which postpones and exacerbates the inevitable — a short but tough, steep descent through high heather. On this descent veer L to a sheep dip on the road to avoid new forestry directly below the nose. Gain the road at the dip and walk $2\frac{1}{2}$ miles (4 km) back to the village, turning L at the outskirts of the village to reach the church.

167

The Blaskets from Brandon

1   *The Plaque in Cloghnane*

The plaque commemorates the Polish, British and German airmen who died in four separate plane crashes, all of which occurred in the area in the years 1940–43. One of the crashes occurred on the hill to the R of the Pilgrims' Route. Another crash in those years was that of a German fighter plane which landed with little damage. The crew set it on fire before it could be impounded.

2   *Paternoster Lakes*

The paternoster lakes are so called because the chain resembles the beads on a rosary, one of whose prayers is the 'Our Father' (*Pater Noster*). Some authorities claim that there are 16 lakes in the chain.

3   *St Patrick's Cabbage*

St Patrick's Cabbage (*Saxifraga spathularis*) grows freely in the rock crevices here. The flowers, which are open from May to July, are pink and white with crimson spots; the leaves grow in a basal rosette and are narrow towards the base. It is prolific among the mainly acid rocks of Cork and Kerry. London Pride is a hybrid of it.

4   *Brendan the Navigator*

The mountain is named after St Brendan the Navigator, who set sail from Brandon Creek near here in about the year 550 with a band of fellow monks, and who (apocryphally) discovered Greenland and even America. It is accepted that Iceland and probably Greenland were colonized from Ireland before the arrival of the Vikings, so the hagiography has some basis. The unimpressive mounds of stones on the summit are termed St Brendan's Well and Oratory.

In 1868 an amazing 20,000 people attended a mass here.

APPENDICES
Access and Rights-of-Way for the Walker

Particularly in the Republic, but also in Northern Ireland, there is a great discrepancy between the strictly legal situation on rights-of-way and public access and the practical situation. *Legally*, in both jurisdictions hillwalkers have right of passage only in National Parks, on Long Distance Routes and in some state forests. In addition, in Northern Ireland there is a modest system of rights-of-way along the lines of those in England and Wales. In practice, however, in both jurisdictions the situation is much more favourable than this.

If a walker is in open (i.e., unenclosed) country he has little to fear and is much more likely to be exchanging greetings rather than trading insults with the farmers he encounters. In enclosed fields and near farmhouses it would be prudent to seek permission to cross land or walk through farm-yards, and it is unlikely that a polite request will be refused. In this context the closing off of common-age (see p. 16) at present a minor but growing threat, makes access considerably harder.

Of course, the walker can expect a less than civil reception if he is not following the Country Code. To the farming community, the two most important items of this Code (but not the only ones) relate to dogs and fences.

Dogs must be under proper control, particularly in sheep country — and most of the uplands are sheep country. Walkers should never stand on fence wires; they may look the same afterwards but they are in fact irretrievably weakened. In a few places on these walks fences are to be crossed. However, there are gaps in most fences, and where there are not, there are always convenient rocks to facilitate a crossing.

Walkers enjoy this live-and-let-live attitude everywhere in the uplands. The only possible exception is Wicklow, which is so near a large city and its hordes of vandals that some farmers' tempers have understandably become somewhat frayed. The routes given in this book for Wicklow should not result in clashes. Elsewhere in Wick-low and, of course, in the contiguous mountains of County Dublin, one should be circumspect and heed notices.

It has to be admitted that, especially for visitors, this situation is not completely satisfactory. A visitor used to cast-iron rights-of-ways may, at least initially, feel uneasy in a country of goodwill but no guarantees. A few forays should improve their confidence; after all, it is supposed to be Ireland of the welcomes!

Safety

Safety is a dull topic — until an emergency when the effects of not taking safety measures will be suddenly and powerfully evident. Do not postpone sensible precautions until it is too late.

Of all the factors influencing safety, weather is the most important by far. The easiest route in bad weather can be far more hazardous than the hardest one in good weather. Cloud, wind and rain disorientate, weaken and chill, as well as drastically reducing your enjoyment. In cloud it is easy to veer by 180° in a few minutes when you think that you are walking straight ahead.

Other variables are the area and how well you know it, the number of people on the walk and their abilities, the quality of available maps (a severe handicap in the Republic), the time to darkness and the severity of the route. For instance, in good weather with a small, strong party, in an area you know well you can try a far more strenuous route than you would try if all these factors were unfavourable. In any event, an experienced party in bad or changeable weather should always consist of at least four people.

The route you walk and the precautions you take will depend on the variables listed above, always remembering that in Ireland the hills are likely to be unfrequented and a mountain rescue service may take a long time to reach the scene of an accident.

Before you set out, therefore, in a spirit of fine, careless rapture you should refer to the following checklist, all items of which should be carefully considered.

Before you go
Listen to the weather forecast.
Choose a route appropriate to your experience and the weather.
Leave a note of your intended route.

Take with you
A basic first aid kit, sufficient food and drink, proper clothing (especially boots) with some as spare, a small torch in winter, map and compass (the latter is particularly important in Ireland). Leave a change of clothing in your car.

On the walk
Keep an eye on deteriorating conditions and turn back if these warrant it — if you think you can just about make it, don't try.
Keep clear of cliffs, especially in high winds.

If an accident occurs
Keep calm. Keep the patient as warm and comfortable as possible and then go for help with a note of the injuries and the patient's exact position. Mountain rescue may be alerted, north or south, by ringing 999 and asking for mountain rescue.

Lastly, at all times take with you a few cells of commonsensical grey matter between your ears. They are your best guarantee against disaster.

Giving a Grid Reference

A grid reference is an excellent way of 'pinpointing' a feature, such as a church or mountain summit, and can be determined from all Ordnance Survey and most other maps mentioned in this book.

Grid lines, which are used for this purpose, are shown on these maps. They are the thin lines one kilometre apart drawn vertically and horizontally on the map thus producing a network of small squares. Each line, whether vertical or horizontal, is given a number from 00 to 99, with the sequence repeating itself every 100 lines. The 00 lines are slightly thicker than the others thus producing large squares each side representing 100 km and made up of 100 small squares. Each of these large squares is identified by a letter. The entire network of lines covering the island of Ireland is called the National Grid.

The left-hand diagram shows a corner of a map which contains a Youth Hostel. Using this map, the method of determining a grid reference is as follows:

Step 1

Holding the map in the normal upright position, note the number of the 'vertical' grid line to the left of the hostel. This is 72.

Step 2

Now imagine that the space between this grid line and the adjacent one to the right of the hostel is divided into ten equal divisions (the right-hand diagram does this for you). Estimate the number of these 'tenths' that the hostel lies to the right of the left-hand grid line. This is 8. Add this to the number found in Step 1 to make 728.

Step 3

Note the number of the grid line below the hostel and add it on to the number obtained above. This is 21, so that the number becomes 72821.

Step 4

Repeat Step 2 for the space containing the hostel, but now in a vertical direction. The final number to be added is 5, making 728215. This is called a six-figure grid reference. This will enable the Youth Hostel to be found on *any* map on which the National Grid is drawn.

A full grid reference will also include the identification of the appropriate 100 kilometre square of the National Grid; for example, R728215. This information is given on each map.

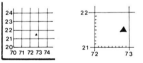

Maps for the Walker

The present position on maps for walkers is quite complicated. Because the recommended map or maps is given for each walk within the text, it is more appropriate here to concentrate on the advantages and disadvantages of the various series and to give the coverage, which is patchy and in any case changing rapidly, only in very general terms.

Northern Ireland

A good 1:50 000 layer-tinted series with 10 m contour intervals covers the entire area and a few neighbouring parts of the Republic. It shows paths, forests and cliffs accurately, and although the colouring is in places laid on with a heavy hand so that it can be difficult to read contours on the hills, these maps are generally excellent.

A 1:25 000 map covers the Mournes; it is in the same series as the excellent British series. One disadvantage of this map is that its large size makes it hardly suitable for refolding in high winds on a mountainside, which its large scale makes necessary frequently.

The other relevant Northern Ireland series is the half-inch to the mile (1:126 720), which is useful not because of its coverage of Northern Ireland, but because it covers large areas of the north of the Republic not covered so well by the Republic's maps.

The Republic
Here the situation might be described as an uncertain dawn after a long dark night.

The whole state is covered by a half-inch to the mile (1:126 720) series with 100 ft contour intervals. The series is none too accurate: forests are vaguely indicated; roads and paths tend to be out of date; and cliffs are indicated, but are so patchy and inaccurate that the symbols are of limited value. Where there is a choice, the half-inch Northern series should be used as it is much superior, not least in presentation. It is hardly necessary to add that the scale is far too small. For instance, to represent the 48 sq miles (12,500 hectares) of the complex tangle of peaks, ridges and valleys of the Twelve Bens on a baggage-label-sized 12 sq in (80 sq cm) is clearly grossly inadequate.

Four areas, three of which are of interest to walkers, are covered by the 'District' one-inch to the mile (1:63 360) series. The maps in this series are layer-tinted and have a 100 ft contour interval to 1000 ft and 250 ft above 1000 ft — hence they give the impression that Irish mountains are gently sloped in their higher reaches. Paths are shown except for the very significant omission of the Long Distance Routes. Perhaps it might be more accurate to say that they are shown as they were 100 years ago. Cliffs are badly and inaccurately depicted. Forests are clearly depicted but are not always up to date; inexplicably, forest tracks are usually highly inaccurate. In general this series is barely adequate, and the contouring in particular is poor. It should also be noted that only a small proportion of the mountain area is covered.

The latest series to appear is by far the best, but only a few sheets are at present available and even these are labelled 'preliminary'. This series, on a scale of 1:50 000, is not layer-tinted, but is accurately contoured with 10 m intervals, the latter a huge attraction to the mountaineer. Cliffs are not explicitly depicted and have to be judged solely by the convergence of contour lines, which are never omitted no matter how close they are. Paths are not adequately shown (except some Long Distance Routes) and the depiction of forests may be out of date, but these are comparatively minor matters. This series is recommended for the areas — at present small areas — which it covers. The Ordnance Survey hope to cover the entire state at 1:50 000 and to cover some mountain areas at 1:25 000 by 1998–99. They expect that two at the latter scale covering some of the mountains of the south-west will be available in 1992.

Finally, one special-purpose series and one privately produced map should be mentioned; other maps of specific areas are covered as they occur in the walk descriptions. The special-purpose series is that published by the Office of Public Works and is available at National Park centres. The series covers the small National Parks and surrounding areas on a scale of one-inch to the mile (1:63 360) with 100 ft contour intervals, and with cliffs roughly indicated (one of the series, Glendalough is at 1:25 000 with a 15 m contour interval). The series is quite reliable and up to date. The paper is flimsy, but since the maps cost only a few pence each this does not matter too much, unless the map disintegrates in pouring rain on an unknown mountainside — as tends to happen.

A private firm, Folding Landscapes, Roundstone, Co. Galway, has published a map (and guide) to Connemara on a scale of 1:50 000 with a 30 m contour interval and cliffs accurately depicted. Unfortunately, the paper is very flimsy. However, the map shows paths, forests and place-names accurately and comprehensively. Place-names are shown in the original Gaelic form, not the anglicized versions recorded by English surveyors in the nineteenth century (see p. 20).

For the walks covered by the Connemara map this has led to a problem: whether to use the mangled but well-known anglicized versions or the 'correct' but little-known Gaelic ones. Both versions are given at the first mention and thereafter the anglicized. The OS has not yet finalized which version it will adopt for the new 1:50 000 series.

At the moment the Connemara map is the best available in the south and almost as good as those in the north.

Addresses of Useful Organizations

Republic of Ireland

An Oige — Youth Hostel Association of Ireland,
39 Mountjoy Square,
Dublin 1
Dublin (01) 363111

An Taisce — National Trust for Ireland,
Tailors Hall,
Back Lane,
Dublin 8
Dublin (01) 544794

Association for Adventure Sports,
House of Sport,
Longmile Road,
Dublin 12
Dublin (01) 509845

Bord Failte Eireann — Irish Tourist
 Board,
Baggot Street Bridge,
Dublin 2
Dublin (01) 765871

Coillte Teoranta — Irish Forestry Board,
Leeson Lane,
Dublin 2
Dublin (01) 615666

Conservation Volunteers Ireland,
Royal Dublin Society,
Dublin 4
Dublin (01) 681228

Cospoir — The National Sports Council
Hawkins House,
Hawkins Street,
Dublin 2,
Dublin (01) 734700
(responsible for Long Distance Routes)

Irish Peatland Conservation Council,
3 Lower Mount Street,
Dublin 2
Dublin (01) 616645

Irish Wildbird Conservancy,
Ruttledge House,
8 Longford Place,
Monkstown,
Co Dublin
Dublin (01) 2804322

Irish Wildlife Federation,
132a East Wall Road,
Dublin 3
Dublin (01) 366821

Mountaineering Council of Ireland,
House of Sport,
Longmile Road,
Dublin 12
Dublin (01) 509845

Office of Public Works,
51 St Stephens Green,
Dublin 2
Dublin (01) 613111
(OPW is responsible for National Parks)

Ordnance Survey of Ireland,
Phoenix Park,
Dublin 8
Dublin (01) 213171

Northern Ireland

Conservation Volunteers (Northern
 Ireland),
The Pavilion,
Cherryfield Playing Fields,
Ravenhill Road,
Belfast BT6 0BZ
Belfast (0232) 645169

Department of the Environment,
Conservation Service,
Calvert House,
23 Castle Place,
Belfast BT1 1FY
Belfast (0232) 230560

National Trust,
Regional Office,
Rowallane House,
Saintfield BT24 7LH
Belfast (0238) 510721

Northern Ireland Tourist Board,
River House,
48 High Street,
Belfast BT1 2DS
Belfast (4) 246609

Ordnance Survey of Northern Ireland,
Colby House,
Stranmillis,
Belfast BT9 5BJ
Belfast (4) 661244

Royal Society for the Protection of Birds,
Belvoir Forest,
Belvoir Park,
Belfast BT8 4QT
Belfast (4) 491547

Sports Council for Northern Ireland,
House of Sport,
Upper Malone Road,
Belfast BT9 5LA
Belfast (4) 381222
(Responsible for Long Distance Routes)

Youth Hostel Association of Northern
 Ireland,
56 Bradbury Place,
Belfast BT7 1RU
Belfast (4) 324733

INDEX